Advanced Praise

"Katherine Cottle has delivered a wonderful realization of her strikingly original idea: to get at *The Hidden Heart of Baltimore* via analysis of the correspondence of its significant citizens—ranging from Frederick Douglas and Harriet Tubman to F. Scott Fitzgerald and H.L. Mencken—and capturing along the way a good many people I had not known had anything to do with Baltimore: including Mark Twain, W. E. B. Dubois, Eleanor Roosevelt and more. Baltimore has always been a crazy quilt kind of city, in Cottle's phrase, 'messy, intersectional, layered, and incomplete.' An accessible compendium of small and tasty surprises, this book adds and organizes layers to our knowledge of the place."

> — Madison Smartt Bell, critically acclaimed author of more than twenty novels, short fiction collections, and nonfiction texts, including *All Souls' Rising*, *Toussaint Louverture: A Biography*, *Devil's Dream*, and *Charm City*.

"Did you think that the cartographers had already completed the map of Baltimore? Think again. With *The Hidden Heart of Charm City: Baltimore Letters and Lives*, Katherine Cottle sheds new light on the city through the examination of intimate letters by some of the city's most prominent residents and visitors. From John Adams to Eleanor Roosevelt, Frederick Douglass to Harriet Tubman, Mark Twain to Ralph Waldo Emerson, F. Scott Fitzgerald to Edgar Allan Poe, Cottle shows us Baltimore as it was to those who experienced it—in a way that only personal letters between friends and loved ones can."

> — Eric D. Goodman, author of *Setting the Family Free*, *Womb: a novel in utero*, and *Tracks: A Novel in Stories*

"*The Hidden Heart of Charm City* makes a bold claim for intimate letters written by renowned Baltimoreans. Yes, we can read these candid individual expressions as gateways into the hearts of Baltimore residents like Frederick Douglass, Edgar Allen Poe, and H. L. Mencken. But we can also read them as portals into the multiple desires, hopes, and frustrations that give Baltimore its singular identity. The heart of Baltimore pulses both slavery and freedom, groundbreaking medical treatment and incurable illnesses, opportunity and stagnation. In lively engaging prose, Cottle teases out the multiplicity of feelings privately expressed in letters by public figures, showing that intimate letters are not antiquated documents, but vital signposts for understanding our current times."

> — Dr. Michelle Tokarczyk, author of *Working-Class Women in the Academy, Critical Approaches to American Working-Class Literature,* and *Bronx Migrations.*

"*The Hidden Heart of Charm City* brings Baltimore history to life for contemporary readers. By drawing connections between the city's past and present history, by linking the streets, historical buildings, and tributary markers of Baltimore to individual people (both famous and obscure), Cottle highlights the human desires that transcend any given era. The writers of then and the Baltimoreans of now share desires for similar things: love, respect, equality, health, companionship, home. The project thus humanizes history by allowing historical figures to become individual people whose stories remain with us because we have entered into their private, intimate worlds."

> — Dr. Julie Cary Conger, editor of *Passing Interest* (SUNY Series in Multiethnic Literature)

"*The Hidden Heart of Charm City* produces an altogether new theoretical framework that promotes and innovates recently scholarly trends to expand the boundaries of what constitutes primary texts in literary and socio-historical scholarship."

> — Dr. Joy Myree-Mainor, author of *Re-reading the Social Protest Tradition: Progressive Race, Gender, and Class Politics in the Fiction of Ann Petry and Dorothy West* (University of Kentucky)

The Hidden Heart of Charm City

A BIRDS-EYE VIEW OF THE HEART OF BALTIMORE

The Hidden Heart of Charm City

Baltimore Letters and Lives

Katherine Cottle

Apprentice House Press
Loyola University Maryland

First Edition

Paperback ISBN: 978-1-62720-247-3
Ebook ISBN: 978-1-62720-248-0

Printed in the United States of America

Designer: Peter Goodman
Development editor: Rodlyn-Mae Banting
Promotions editor: Rachael Miller

Published by Apprentice House Press

Apprentice House Press
Loyola University Maryland
4501 N. Charles Street
Baltimore, MD 21210
410.617.5265 • 410.617.2198 (fax)
www.ApprenticeHouse.com
info@ApprenticeHouse.com

Contents

Other Apprentice House Books

by Katherine Cottle

I Remain Yours: Secret Mission Love Letters

of My Mormon Great-Grandparents, 1900-1903

(Creative Nonfiction, 2014)

Halfway: A Journal through Pregnancy

(Memoir, 2010)

My Father's Speech: Poems

(Poetry, 2008)

Dear Baltimore,

Heart: a hollow muscular organ of vertebrate animals that by its rhythmic contraction acts as a force pump maintaining the circulation of the blood.

- Merriam Webster

Sometimes I'm terrified of my heart; of its constant hunger for whatever it wants. The way it stops and starts.

- Edgar Allan Poe

Foreword

Dear Reader,

I hope this finds you well and in good spirits as you embark on the adventure of reading an innovative new book. You'll find this one to be of special interest as you explore the intimate letters of many prominent figures who have passed through the streets and history of Charm City. Exploring the intimate letters of notables we already know from the history books casts both the city and the people in a new and more personal light.

That's the magic of private, handwritten letters: they offer an unfiltered and uniquely intimate perspective on the people and the place. Today, letter writing seems a dying art form, kept alive only by the few who still appreciate giving and receiving these warm gifts that arrive in mailboxes and provide so much more than an email, text, or social media post. Perhaps appreciating letters from the past will spark a renewed interest in letter writing in the present.

My own personal interest in this book is threefold: as a long-term Baltimore resident and author, as an admirer of Katherine Cottle's work, and as someone who fondly remembers the days when the giving and receiving of letters was a daily way of life.

Growing up in a navy family, my father was out to sea for months at a time. During these stretches of season that seemed an eternity to a young child, we remained in contact through a steady stream of letters. I remember the excitement of receiving a letter from Dad. I wrote to him about my new toys and bicycle, adventures with friends, school, and even about the birth of my brother during his extended deployments.

Moving around every couple of years provided another opportunity for regular letter writing. Each new place we lived would provide a new set of friends, many of whom became pen pals when we moved away. I'm still in touch with friends that I met in middle school some 35 years ago, thanks to the power and perseverance of letters.

After studying abroad in Japan and Russia, I remember the years following my returns back home to the United States when letters to and from my international friends (and my Russian fiancé) would often take a month or more to make the journey from door to door. Today's instant emails, posts, and texts do have their advantages. But in an age when the only way to avoid thousand-dollar phone bills was to write international letters, there was a joy in the slowly building anticipation you felt when you knew that letters were crossing the sea; an excitement in the receipt of such a letter; a pleasure in putting pen to paper and drafting a return letter to take to the post office the next day.

As Cottle points out, a letter is more than a communication, more than a phone call, text, or email. The time between writing and delivery gives it an element of time-travel: the letter you write, destined for the future; the letter you receive, a visit from the past.

Cottle explores these letters to and from Baltimore addresses with experience, having previously written the book *I Remain Yours: Secret Mission Letters of my Mormon Great Grandparents, 1900 – 1903*. She expertly excerpts and examines the intimate lines between people, their relationships, and their connections with and within the city of Baltimore.

Exchanges between F. Scott and Zelda Fitzgerald are enlightening; between Edgar Allan Poe and Virginia and Maria Clemm somewhat disturbing; the letter from Frederick Douglass to Anna Murray inspiring. And it is amusingly reassuring to note that John Adams, even back in 1777, was complaining about the (horse) parking situation in Baltimore.

Some things never change.

Like, for example, the intimacy in letters between friends, family, and loved ones. The times change, the city changes, but the effect of personal letters endures. It may seem somewhat voyeuristic to read these Baltimore letters in which many personal details are revealed and discussed—illnesses, infidelities, immoralities, as well as fondness, feelings, and affections. But, as

Cottle points out, the heart we're spying on, in many ways, is our own—as individuals, as citizens, and as humankind.

Once you've read this book and explored the letters of Baltimore's past, getting to better know the people who have passed through the city's veins and touched Charm City's heart, you may find yourself afflicted with the yearning to pick up your own pen and paper and open your own heart to the enchantment of letter writing.

Eric D. Goodman, 2019
Baltimore resident and author of
Setting the Family Free,
Womb: a novel in utero, and
Tracks: A Novel in Stories

Introduction

Anatomy of an Epistolary Heart

Now, more than ever, Baltimore needs a new mapping. This depiction can skip existing roads and chronological timelines—the usual methods for viewing places, people, and words. This design doesn't include literary or GPS tours of the city (those can be found with the click of a button) or, to suit the more nostalgic sensibility, another tale of Poe's mysterious death upon the city's streets. A more intimate lens is needed for viewing Baltimore and the people who have passed through its veins, a lens which goes beyond standard routes and names and uncovers the hidden blueprint of the city's long-beating heart. This lens should highlight what is missing from our current maps, websites, and public histories: the private words and desires that brought life and love to past and present-day Baltimore.

Every morning, cars flow through Baltimore streets, many which are named for important historical figures in the city's and the country's history. Every evening, residents and visitors walk by statues, memorials, buildings, and schools which have been built in tribute to these figures. However, these individual "salutes" to history and people are viewed in isolation, as separate pieces of separate decades, often detached from and seemingly unrelated to contemporary life. Most days, residents and visitors are too overwhelmed with their own longings (for work and/or income, for someone, for support, for knowledge, or for simple understanding) to take the time to actually connect their own hearts to the Baltimore landscape.

While Baltimore has long been recognized as a key setting in America's literary and political history, the city is generally unrecognized in regard to the intimate communication which has passed through its borders and helped to create that history. By unveiling the range of needs and desires found in some of the intimate letters of Baltimore's most historical figures, we reveal the societal inequities that have both fueled and clotted the city since its birth. In turn, we also view the city through the lens of its heart, seeing how the personal connections and communication within the city met and challenged those inequities. Baltimore's historical and ongoing contradictions, noted by F. Scott Fitzgerald as "civilized and gay, rotted and polite," and reinforced by contemporary writers, such as Laura Lippman, who is often re-quoted as saying "Anyone can love a perfect place. Loving Baltimore takes some resilience," are part of the city's anatomy. That anatomy stems from a human and urban heart which contracts and releases in flawed, continually aging, and bittersweet rhythms.

With the ease of electronic exchange deletions, coupled with the ethical and logical complexities of archiving digital communication, the study of print letters of an intimate nature is paramount in mapping the heart of any city, especially for a current generation who has never experienced a non-digital life. The intimate letter is surely considered an "endangered species" today, as print letters slide toward extinction and the need for postal services declines by the hour. Yet, new and old intimate letters continue to be discovered and processed through both personal and professional settings, letters which ache for an appropriate archive within our digital age.

Therefore, this project is presented as a moment of critical capture within an endless process of intimacy-discovery, establishing the significance of intimate letters in conjunction with local landscape and holding to the perspective that unfiltered, private material is vital to understanding the lineage of current conditions. This project follows its own author's personal longing to create an intimate map of Baltimore with desires that traveled not by road or by foot, but by words—reflecting the "Baltimore" she knew was beating behind the maps tacked to the walls of her childhood classrooms— the map of people and places only those who looked past public surfaces could see, read, and feel.

Like all collections, this project has the potential to grow to include new figures, addresses, communities, and histories. Perhaps one day someone else will map the desires that drove the intimate exchanges circulating through

Baltimore during the beginning decades of the twenty-first century, discovering desire's role within an even larger historical circulatory system than the one drafted here. Hopefully, more intimacy maps and locative hearts (both urban and rural) will be constructed in the future, documenting the interlocking paths of private words and public needs that are so often separated, instead of embraced. As our present-day society perpetually debates the blurry line between public and private discourse, the next longing that may very well dominate the intimate communication of Baltimore, as well as many other cities, may be—ironically—the desire to keep private words *private* within an ultra-public world.

Macroscopic Anatomy

-The examination of relatively large structures and features usually visible with the unaided eye, including surface, regional, systemic, and developmental anatomies.

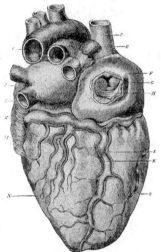

Anatomy of the arteries of the human body
1881/John Hatch Power

The recent replacement of electronic communication—for what is now referred to as "snail mail"—reinforces the contemporary world's need for instant and compact communication which is available for delivery 24/7. While communication has gained speed, accessibility, and storage capabilities in this electronic transition, *intimate literacy* has lost its former sensory

7

characteristics. In "The Fading Art of Letter Writing," Catherine Field explains how "[a] good handwritten letter is a creative act, and not just because it is a visual and tactile pleasure. It is a deliberate act of exposure, a form of vulnerability, because handwriting opens a window on the soul in a way that cyber-communication can never do." The vulnerability of the physical intimate letter stems from its status as a tangible, personalized, and individual expression—a presentation that cannot be replicated in key strokes or multiple winking faces. The multi-sensory experience of opening an envelope containing an intimate letter (utilizing increased sight, touch, smell, sound, and sometimes even taste faculties) is not comparable with the experience of clicking the mouse or touching the screen of an electronic device, even if both communicative vehicles contain identical content.

"It is too simple," Francine Prose suggests in *Illustrated Letters: Artists and Writers Correspond*, to view "letters merely as relics of a bygone era—of a time that existed before the telephone, before e-mail—and to lament the fact that communications as eloquent and glorious as these may never be created again." Additionally, it is too simple to view intimate letters in a past versus present lens. The transition from paper to electronic form as the standard means of communication has shifted not only the medium of epistolary expression, but also the general realities and expected patterns of time with regard to intimate correspondence. In the same fashion that the optometrist must use and layer a variety of measuring lenses to find the most accurate, if perhaps never perfect focus, we must combine interdisciplinary efforts, including temporal ones, to create new visions of intimate letters and communication, especially in regard to history and place.

Thomas Mallon theorizes in *Yours Ever: People and Their Letters* that "[l]etters have always defeated distance, but with the coming of email, time seem[s] to be vanquished as well." Mallon explains that today's "'[r]eal time' . . . isn't time at all, but rather . . . our goal in communicating between one place and another," and asks, "was the old passage of days, and weeks, as letters traveled, 'false' time?" Mallon's question unveils the well-founded fear that electronic communication has caused a devaluation of delayed and long-distance exchanges, categorizing *wait* time in a negative and polarizing manner against *instant* time.

Mallon presents an astronomical metaphor to help in explaining the letter's power to transcend traditional time frameworks and to heighten universality:

> A telephone call or instant message actually conveys one place to another, whereas letters always conveyed not only a place, but a time as well, one that had already passed. If written vividly enough, they made the recipient forget that what he was reading about had actually taken place weeks before—the way an astronomer looking at the explosion of a star has to remember that he is in fact looking into the past, at something that happened ages ago and whose light is only now being delivered.

By viewing the intimate letter as an entity that enables us to simultaneously experience both *past* and *present* time, "place" becomes not only a setting but also a delivery of a more thoughtful, holistic, and textual understanding of our society. As Anaïs Nin famously noted, "We write to taste life twice: in the moment and in retrospect," and as readers of words in the twenty-first century, we continue to read to experience our human desires "in retrospect," as well as "in the moment."

John Willis divides epistolary study into four parts in *More than Words: Readings in Transport, Communication and the History of Postal Communication*: the post, epistolary practice and culture, people and their letters, and communication and transport—to emphasize the complicated layers of examining postal communication within one unified framework. He presents postal communication as a particular, and perhaps ornery, type of communication when compared to other traditional forms, explaining that "[h]istorically, the post has facilitated communication. As such, it belongs to the universe of communication that operates on many levels at once. It cannot be subsumed in some category of political economy, much less in one separate department of government." Consequently, the role of the postal system in transporting intimate letters is as much about the unwitting force of the delivery and movement of the letters within their temporary homes, as it is about the content within the envelopes. "Readings

9

in transport," as Willis refers to the study of postal mail, validate the physical travel and transitional existence that print letters experience, which is unlike most other forms of communication, especially today's electronic communication.

"Communication, by post and any other media," Willis reinforces, "is rooted in historical context, but owing to the relative autonomy or unpredictability of its human practitioners it may have a means and a mind of its own." In fact, autonomy and unpredictability are often the primary driving factors behind the power of intimate letters, especially when viewing them from interdisciplinary and cross-generational lenses. The inability for intimate letters to consistently follow public standards is precisely the reason they are treated differently from other preserved communications.

Part of the allure of studying the intimate letter is in the opportunity to see the private sphere through a public perspective, yet this lens includes much more than peeping pleasure. In *Other People's Love Letters: 150 Letters You Were Never Meant to See*, Bill Shapiro explains that the "fascination [with intimate letters] is more complex than a simple case of voyeurism. Because, on a deeper level, the heart you're looking into is your own." The transference of the self, from writer to recipient, also extends to future unknown readers of the letter. The view and discovery of the common self is ultimately what bridges the private and public spheres of the intimate letter; by studying and valuing these letters, that bridge extends past correspondents, place, and conventional time, enabling readers to become, literally, part of others' lives and hearts.

Therefore, viewing the heart of Baltimore requires the deliberate pull of material from the private sphere into the public realm. "Many scholars contend that letters serve as the best source for researching literary history," Jeffrey B. Berlin asserts in "On the nature of letters," "since epistolary documents usually provide authentic and substantive reflections, thereby revealing the impact of the events that individuals experienced." The intimate letter mimics a time machine that bypasses the public filter of established histories and lands directly in the private homes, minds, and hearts of histories' inhabitants.

By seeing and feeling the first-hand effects of desire on Baltimore's past residents and visitors, we can better understand our own contemporary longings within a larger map of intimacy. The intimate letter is, according to Dorothy A. Lander in "Love Letters to the Dead: Resurrecting an Epistolary Art," "a momentary experience which incorporates but stands outside orthodox conceptions of material and immaterial existence." Consequently, capturing the crossroads of intimacy and geography must take non-linear forms, as Isabel Roboredo Seara states in "Epistolary: from hidden dialogue to an obsession to dialogue," due to the "hybrid, nomadic, intricate, and oxymoronic nature" of the intimate letter. Instead of viewing intimate letters narrowly as inherently "private," unimportant to public vision, problematic, or contradictory, we can see letters as desire-driven catalysts for societal shifts within their locales.

The intimate letter's inability to be categorized under singular theoretical frameworks and its innate contradictory nature has caused it to suffer the scholarly life of a difficult child; yet, the intimate letter's complex and unable-to-be-captured status enables it to transcend traditional frameworks and static perspectives. In *Epistolary: Approaches to a Form*, Janet Gurkin Altman explains how the letter becomes both "the distance [and] the bridge," allowing "[t]he lover who takes up his pen to write his loved one [to become] conscious of the interrelation of presence and absence and the way in which his very medium of communication reflects both the absence and presence of his addressee." Both there, and not there, the unmet needs of the intimate letter writer are the driving forces of the communication, and the letter becomes a mediator that enables the needs to be met, if only temporarily and on a metaphorical bridge across neighborhoods, streets, states, and countries.

Simultaneously giving and receiving, the intimate letter is in constant flux, and its presence as both a read and unread entity is crucial to its function in viewing its historical routes through cities, such as Baltimore. Passing unread and unopened through the public world, the intimate letter is able to straddle both the public sphere (in its form and physical entity) and the private sphere (in its contents and exchange). Accepting the framework and content contradictions of the intimate letter not as signs of tension but as fuller and more open views of the human condition allows for a perspective where individual writers and recipients can be *both* private and public beings—and maps can represent multiple representations of human history and experience.

New maps and archives, though, are needed to chart and validate this intimacy. Michael L. Carrafiello confesses in "Archives of Passion: Using Love Letters to Teach the Methods of History Inquiry" that "love" is often perceived as a non-scholarly and irrelevant theme within the academic community, which is unfortunate since it is precisely "[b]y understanding how those who lived before us loved, [that] we may grasp how our love affects us and those around us today. In the process, we may also gain insight as to how the love we and millions of others seek and hopefully will find is likely to shape the course of events in the future." The layered, interdisciplinary, and non-categorical nature of love reinforces intimacy's hidden penetration within all areas of life, including academic and career fields.

Love's ability to resist traditional "studiable" elements is also what gives it its raw strength, direction, and unapologetic charge. Carrafiello explains:

> The letters of Einstein and Maric, for instance, suggest strongly that passion can and does move science to greater effort and more spectacular results. For psychology, the readiness of those in times of conflict—especially soldiers and the people they leave behind—is affected by love or the lack of it. In terms of politics and political theory, the efficacy of government and leadership depends on the emotional pitch and stability of those who would presume to exercise power . . . Similarly, engineers and computer programmers are undoubtedly affected in their work by what they bring and take with them emotionally each day.

Love remains the persisting and core force behind the majority of humanity's movements and decisions, whether we want to admit it or not, surpassing individual hosts in its influential power and societal traces. Thus, viewing a city's heart through the vehicle of the intimate letter helps to create a new type of archive which is actually quite old, as for many centuries the primary source material held most dear to historians, as Kasper Risbjerg

Eskildsen reminds in "Inventing the Archive: Testimony and Virtue in Modern Historiography," "were not held in archives or governmental or educational-supported storage facilities, but in homes."

Fittingly, it is only "[w]ith the disappearance of the original correspondents," Caroline Bland and Marie Cross assert in *Gender and Politics in the Age of Letter Writing, 1750–2000,* that "we can be more objectively concerned with [letters'] impact as historical documents and with an overview of their political context." This reality, of the loss of authorial ownership of personal correspondence over time and death, acknowledges the intimate letter as an entity which transfers from the private sphere into the public sphere with its maturity, both in its creation and in its long-term status as a historical artifact.

To accommodate the personal/public transformative status of intimate materials, "[t]he archivist has been transformed" in recent years, Terry Cook explains in "Evidence, Memory, Identity, and Community: Four Shifting Archival Paradigms," as "archival thinking has moved from evidence to memory to identity and community, as the broader intellectual currents have changed from pre-modern to modern to postmodern to contemporary." This shift grants space for richer explorations of people and place, as the archivist has moved, Cook clarifies, "from passive curator to active appraiser to societal mediator to community facilitator." Like all other humanistic forms, the archive (especially one containing intimate letters) builds and transforms, changing as its internal composition and external influences age, just as the human heart does.

The letters examined in this project include private correspondence between married partners, fiancés, lovers, and intimate friends. Most of the included letters have been anthologized in print and/or are available for public viewing through online archival databases; however, some letters are still being processed, and some letters remain inaccessible to the public due to various reasons which will be explored in this project.

Most often, intimate letters are found in repositories belonging to the more famous correspondent, yet letters can also be combined into larger family or thematic archival collections, and there are exceptions to all archival standards. There is not a common research method for gathering intimate letters of a particular geographical area; one must follow one's own heart and scholarly faith in searching, linking, and believing in the city's heart—in order to find traces of love scattered in pieces among its different chambers.

Here, the early epistolary scans of Baltimore begin in Fell's Point—the entryway for not just ships, goods, and soldiers since 1763, but also for the delivery and escape of free and enslaved African Americans, some transported with the help of Harriet Tubman. This particular port and its fluid mixture of free and enslaved people produced an unusual community and intimate communication system which operated due to the most human desire: a desire for freedom. Fell's Point marks the unpreserved grounding of Frederick Douglass's pivotal and unpreserved letter, written and sent to his fiancée, Anna Murray, in Baltimore after he successfully escaped to New York. The fact that Douglass had to send his communication *back* to Baltimore in order to alert his fiancée of his escape *from* Baltimore reinforces the city's history as a perpetual contradiction of public and private desires. As well, the unpreserved letter, noted by Douglass's granddaughter in her memoirs, signals the need for the purposeful hiding and destruction of intimate letters by early African Americans in Baltimore for the sake of their safety.

Baltimore's waterfront community also housed the "lost" writing of Frances Ellen Watkins Harper, including her recently "discovered" first poetry collection, *Forest Leaves*, originally published in Baltimore in 1845 (though "lost" in the public archives until 2015). Harper's prolific writing and correspondence, like Douglass's, is only preserved after her move from Baltimore. The arteries and veins of Baltimore's heart, therefore, are the unpreserved and lost intimate communications which created and sustained the city, yet still remain devoid of public knowledge or traditional recognition. Included in the flow of these private routes are the traces of Harriet Tubman's personal communication through alternative channels and roads, as well as the lost words of countless early African Americans and other marginalized people.

Past the port of entry, within the growing downtown district, Baltimore's nineteenth-century history is revealed from the lenses of prominent visitors. Lorena Hickok, Mark Twain, Ralph Waldo Emerson, and John Adams describe the city in unfiltered format during their visits, allowing their significant others to also view the urban landscape and its residents through unique outsider perspectives. Untranslatable letters by Eleanor Roosevelt meet translatable accounts by her journalist, Lorena Hickok, as Hickok documents the toll of the Depression on Baltimore City. Mark Twain's lecture stops in Baltimore provide published and unpublished narratives of a railroad tycoon's former estate, as well as sarcastic jabs at the city's elite. Ralph Waldo Emerson's tour stop presents his view of a city lacking in philosophical and literary enlightenment, compared to his New England standards. The correspondence between John and Abigail Adams, written while an early Congress-in-the-making gathered in Baltimore, reveals the daily details of a new and unfolding country, government, city, and family for the man who would become the 2nd President of the United States.

The influence of Johns Hopkins Hospital and other medical facilities in Baltimore guides the opening and closing valves of letters between H. L. Mencken and Sara Haardt, F. Scott Fitzgerald and Zelda Fitzgerald, and Dr. Esther Loring Richards and Dr. Abby Howe Turner. Unable to physically reside with each other, the intimate letters of these literary couples and early American female medical figures function as alternative homes in providing sanctuaries of health, literary inspiration, and career support.

Haardt's chronic tuberculosis and accompanying ailments, requiring long-term residencies in Baltimore area hospitals, prompt Mencken to accompany her in finding a literary meeting place where they can be together—united in their ideas, if not with their physical bodies. Zelda Fitzgerald's mental illness necessitates the physical walls that separate her and F. Scott Fitzgerald while she resides at Sheppard Pratt Psychiatric Hospital and Johns Hopkins Hospital during the 1930's, facilities which prove unable to help her successfully reenter mainstream society. Like Mencken and Haardt, Scott and Zelda utilize letters to locate a literary sanctuary for the health and creativity that was unattainable through their physical lives.

Johns Hopkins Hospital Psychiatrist Esther Richards's intimate letters to Mount Holyoke College Professor Abby Turner expose the desire for female support and epistolary sanctuary within the male-dominated world of science during the early twentieth century.

The largest geographical sections of Baltimore's heart, the Eastside and Westside chambers, provide limited material and research findings, even though intimate correspondence was vital for love, career advancement, and civil and human rights in these ventricles. The Westside displays minimal traces of Edgar Allan Poe's intimate markers in Baltimore, especially concerning his desire for unrequited love and language. The missing intimate letters between Supreme Court Justice Thurgood Marshall and his first wife, Vivian Burey Marshall, emphasize the complexity of publishing private materials by civil rights figures who reached prominent social platforms after leaving Baltimore and the public desire for pioneering individuals to remain uncompromised in their popular reputations. Published excerpts of Clarence Mitchell, Jr.'s letters to his fiancée, Juanita Jackson, highlight the selectivity and censorship of contemporary archives in providing different levels of accessibility for public and private audiences. W. E. B. Du Bois's letters to his first wife, Nina Gomer Du Bois, written during the last decade of her life in Baltimore, map the intimate communication of a civil rights leader and spouse who sacrificed a traditional familial home for the sake of long-distance socio-political aims. The Du Boises' letters uncover "Du Bois Cottage" in Morgan Park to be a place of societal compromise, versus an anchoring geographical location.

Exploring the intimate chambers of Baltimore's history may open and aggravate flawed and raw veins and tissue; however, these internal words also contain the discoveries of expression, support, substitution, longing, and hope needed to sustain life and progress. The view of Baltimore's heart opens and widens when intimacy is understood as both a tool for personal connection and a weapon for public growth.

Microscopic Anatomy

-the examination of structures involving the use of optical instruments, including histology (the study of tissues), and embryology (the study of an organism in its immature condition).

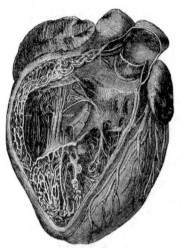

The Heart, Showing the Interior
1890/Charles Henry May

In addition to the challenges involved in locating and accessing intimate letters within a particular city are the intricacies involved in the critical and creative reading of letters as multi-field texts. Emilija Dimitrijevic views the practice of critiquing private letters in the public sphere as a displacement in "Poets' Love Letters: Private Affairs or Cultural Objects?" reinforcing "what is written for a particular person, what is meant to be read and hopefully answered by that person, becomes a matter of cultural significance, destined to be read by a large public—a public, however, that is not required to reply or partake in the specific emotional involvement typical of lovers' correspondence." How, then, do we come to terms with the intimate letter's contradictory status as both a temporary emotionally-driven private mode and a permanent and critically-driven public formation? Using macroscopic *and* microscopic lenses to view and analyze intimate letters provides wider and deeper views of our relationships to people and places, and this understanding helps to uncover the human condition which both creates and sustains this history.

Dimitrijevic claims "that we are dealing not only with the question of interpreting and understanding a writer but, more importantly, with a problem of ownership" while examining intimate letters. When multiple fields, institutions, and cities can claim ownership of a singular written work (in addition to the author's ownership), as is often the case in preserved intimate letters by prominent figures, there will be automatic tensions between internal (content and correspondents) and external (form and readers) intentions. That clash, however, need not cause resistance between public and private spheres; rather, we can adjust our lenses and expectations to see correspondence as "readings in transport" on multiple levels.

Two ways to acknowledge and tackle the authorial challenges in bringing private work into the public sphere are by widening the view of connections and parallels between correspondents and recipients and by reevaluating the conventional definitions and critical perspectives of letters and their movements across space and time. Dimitrijevic suggests revising the standard meaning of *possession* when examining letters, as the intimate text is "something that one cannot possess in the common sense of the word any more than one can possess a language or a meaning." As intimacy is, by its nature—transitory—its possession is also transitory and based on both fluctuating and temporal societal influences and personal emotionality.

Presence, additionally, must be viewed from a transitory standpoint to fully understand the geographical influence behind the intimate letter. In *Letters, Postcards, Email: Technologies of Presence*, Esther Milne argues that "[p]resence is a term that need not refer always to *material, corporeal* presence. Rather, presence is an effect achieved in communication (whether by letters, postcards, or email, for example) when interlocutors imagine the psychological or, sometimes, physical presence of the other." When we understand *presence* to be both literal (in terms of the letter *body* and the correspondent self) and non-literal (in terms of emotionality), it allows us to see intimate exchanges by others beyond the boundaries of the correspondents and their physical bodies. When *presence* is acknowledged as an emotional interaction, in addition to a static state, readers' and critics' entrances into the exchanges of others' intimate letters are suddenly welcomed, rather than discouraged. Indeed, the intimate letter then becomes the basis upon which many *presences* and *bodies* are charted and viewed within our human histories and geographical anatomies.

By bridging contemporary and historical *presences*, the intimate letter becomes "the social history of private life and intimacy," as Eva L. Wyss suggests in "From the Bridal Letter to Online Flirting: Changes in Text Type from the Nineteenth Century to the Internet Era." Highlighting the platforms which created the geographical environments that perpetuated the separations between the included correspondents, the letters referenced in this project are, in their *presence* and *body*, much more than letters. They are the tactile negotiations of an intimate search for identity and validity, both as individually crafted communications, as well as hidden veins between partners and their societies. The intimate letter, unbeknownst to most of its writers as they craft its literary entrance into the world, is mediated not just within itself and its correspondents, but also through the larger societal connective tissues of its creation, even if functioning inside its own countercultural rules.

Redefining *desire* is also necessary when viewing the intimacy and longings of any geographical location. In "The Poverty of Desire: Spivak, Coetzee, Lacan, and Postcolonial Eros," Eugene de Klerk illustrates how "[d]esire often presents itself first and foremost as a problem, a potential obstacle to the rationality, piety, modesty or humility thought to be appropriate to an intellectual, social, political or historical context" and, as such, "[b]rute attempts to eradicate it entirely only seem to prompt it to adapt, attaching its characteristic excess of feeling to new objects." In the same manner that water, when finding itself restricted, will erode resistance and establish new channels (often using the very materials obstructing it in order to do so), *desires* also create their own fluid and uncompromising routes in order to survive. The intimate letter's ability to carry unmet *desires* within the oppositional forces often contributing to its creation (in some cases, by utilizing its own societies' standardized communication systems) attest to its existence as a leading-primary source of historical and geographical relevance. By finding alternative and publicly hidden routes, *desire* sustains life, even when forbidden or denied.

In order to thoroughly showcase the letter's role in revealing the hidden heart of Baltimore, an epistolary exploration must plot tangible locations within the intangible movements of desire and note the temporal momentum that enables intimacy to travel back and forth between its correspondents. Peter Turchi breaks down the charting of text into two steps in *Maps of the Imagination: The Writer as Cartographer*. First, *exploration* must be performed, which is "assertive action in the face of uncertain assumptions, often involving false starts, missteps, and surprises." Only after exploration is executed and experienced can *presentation* happen, which "[a]ppl[ies] knowledge, skill, and talent . . . [to] create a document meant to communicate with, and have an effect on, others." While professing *presentation* in its initial creation for an intended recipient, the intimate letter is, at its core, an *exploration*—which explains its contradictions, flaws, and unfiltered content—or "false starts, missteps, and surprises." As well, we can view the intimate letter as the *exploration* that must be completed in order for the *presentation* of societal changes to emerge. Instead of seeing the private exploratory qualities of the intimate letter as being subsequent to publicly presented material (as is customary in most historical and academic venues), an equitable standing should be validated between *exploration* and *presentation* for writers, recipients, and readers at every stage of *possession*.

The visual markers of the Baltimore locations where the intimate letters under study here originated and/or were received are documented in order to tangibly represent the heart of the city and the connective geography of its history, neighborhoods, and people. However, the intimacy *explored* in this project is also *presented* as an internal organ, with routes and emotions that often defied physics for its correspondents, allowing places and people who could not logistically, appropriately, or literally touch one another . . . to do just that. This project also charts alternative houses, rooms, and geographies that do not exist on any historical or contemporary maps, but did exist (and continue to exist) within Baltimore's intimacy narrative. This anatomy depicts the non-linear routes of language, love, and imagination within Baltimore, and the pathways held tight within the folded seams of once-sealed envelopes containing those human expressions.

The following project is not an absolute depiction of all desires, histories, prominent figures, and/or societal quests within the history of Baltimore, but rather an asymmetrical and temporal scan which captures a few locative points of precursory societal shifts through an intimate marking system. Hopefully, contemporary readers will be able to navigate through Baltimore with a new appreciation of the desires that drove its past and continue to influence its present, recognizing that anatomical mapping does not have right or wrong turns; rather, it offers *exploratory* travel—by its contributors, its readers, and its creators—to highlight alternative *presentation* routes and passages currently not found in any travel site, library archive, or academic department.

"What elements of the literary space can be mapped and what might prove to be unmappable (and should consequently be accepted as such)?" Barbara Piatti and Lorenz Hurni ask contemporary readers and writers. The unmappable element of intimacy, this project proves, *is* mappable when linked to its originating desires within particular geographical frameworks. "Envisioning maps as a compelling form of storytelling," Sebastien Caquard furthers, allows multiple aims and field intersections to function not in opposition, but in collaboration with one another. Combining traditional cartography with literary and metaphorical mapping allows for the opening of an experience-based realm that enables readers to enter into the heart of intimacy and to understand history as a series of both public and private desires that continue to build up to, and include, the current moment.

In many ways, private material and intimate letters have been treated as "dangerous elements . . . forced into the blank spaces, ocean, or the margins of the maps" for years, Karen Piper asserts in *Cartographic Fictions: Maps, Race, and Identity*, having been regularly forbidden, hidden, neglected, or destroyed—as opposed to encouraged, shared, published, and preserved like their public and revised literary counterparts. Remaining unpredictable, unfiltered, and routinely contradictory, intimate letters have housed the internal "monsters and brutes" of many prominent figures in American history. Yet, intimate letters have also housed the fears and vulnerabilities of those same figures, as viewed through their desires. By providing an anatomical lens in which to view Baltimore, we can understand private communication as "the blank spaces, ocean[s], [and] the margins" that actually compose the heart of the city.

With a new view of an old heart, we will be better able to appreciate Baltimore not only as a tourist attraction, a historical port, a point of tension, or a literary clubhouse. The city is revealed to be an integral organ of generations of intimate desires. Those private desires, consequently, often prompted major public shifts which permanently affected the rest of the state and country. The following letters uncover the heart of a city whose people loved each other enough to risk their lives, careers, health, reputations, and rights to express their desires for others and for societal change. Recognizing this anatomy allows us to see our own desires as vital elements within a much larger circulatory system that extends past the included correspondents, geographical chambers, and centuries. It is this author's hope that this approach will be adopted in other cities and that forthcoming and existing archives will welcome new maps that negotiate humanity and geography—through the vehicle of the hidden heart.

Part One
Veins and Arteries

Port of Entry—*Hidden, Lost, and Unwritten Letters*

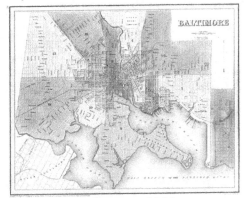

Baltimore, 1838
T.G. Bradford

Countless generations of letters have passed through Baltimore, though most will remain unknown or undiscovered. Thus, to validate the majority of composed intimate correspondence included in this collection, the letters explored in this chapter are non-existent or unpreserved, though unarguably as pivotal as preserved sources in their historical and literary impact.

Baltimore's African American community and historical figures, in particular, lack literary and epistolary proof in the traditional sense of the "word." Therefore, the first letters and writers examined in this collection are not traditional in their representation of "proof"; rather, "word" is viewed through receipt, discovery, and action. The "proof" of these letters is actually found in the witnesses of future generations and our ability to view the consequences of intimate communication which risked lives, relationships, and reputations to improve an unjust world.

While the city's waterways fed the needs of a slavery-based economy in the first century of its establishment, the port of Baltimore provided the fluid cover necessary to hide and enable intimate communication of many of the country's earliest writers . . .

Chapter One

Hidden Correspondence

by Frederick Douglass to Anna Murray (Douglass)

Frederick Douglass, 1855

Anna Murray Douglass, circa 1860

Anna Murray

Fell's Point, Baltimore

X

Frederick Douglass's escape from slavery in Baltimore in 1838, told through his narratives, is surely one of America's key literary and historical events. William Lloyd Garrison's Introduction to the *Narrative of the Life of Frederick Douglass* proclaims "the most thrilling . . . [moment in the narrative] is the description Douglass gives of his feelings, as he stood soliloquizing respecting his fate, and the chances of his one day being a freeman, on the banks of the Chesapeake Bay—viewing the receding vessels as they flew with their white wings before the breeze, and apostrophizing them as animated by the living spirit of freedom." Contemporary readers are hard pressed not to be inspired by the story of the once-enslaved child from the Eastern Shore of Maryland who eventually became the man many consider "the greatest African American of the 19th century," Tom Chalkley asserts in "Native Son: On the Trail of Frederick Douglass in Baltimore, "and arguably the greatest American ever to rise from the streets of Baltimore."

While millions of students have read Douglass's narratives about his life, and Baltimoreans are quick to connect local setting—particularly the port of Fell's Point—to Douglass, few know about the letter Douglass wrote to his fiancée, Anna Murray, after successfully escaping from Baltimore. Few recognize that Frederick Douglass's and Anna Murray's ability to begin new and free lives for themselves as a married couple in New York hinged on one piece of unpreserved communication which declared Douglass's freedom through its intentionally hidden words and delivery.

Douglass's published narratives provide extensive background about his life in Maryland, and many people know his stories. Frederick Augustus Washington Bailey, who would change his name to Frederick Douglass after arriving in New York in 1838, was born as an enslaved child in Talbot County on Maryland's Eastern Shore in 1817 or 1818. When Douglass was eight years old, he was sent to work as a house servant for the Hugh Auld family in Fell's Point and lived intermittently in the city for the next twelve years.

It was during Douglass's pre-teen years in Baltimore that he first learned to read through the help of Hugh Auld's wife, until her husband forbade the practice. Douglass's second full-length narrative, *My Bondage and My*

Freedom, describes how he continued to learn to write "[w]ith playmates for my teachers, fences and pavements for my copy books, and chalk for my pen and ink," expanding his literacy training through his observations of the language in the shipyards and with the help of the children at the nearby Bethel church. The impact of the waterfront city was pivotal for Douglass, and the following words from his first account, *The Narrative of Frederick Douglass*, often accompany contemporary Baltimore public landmarks and tributes to him:

> It is possible, and even quite probable, that but for the mere circumstance of being removed from that plantation to Baltimore, I should have to-day, instead of being here seated by my own table, in the enjoyment of freedom and the happiness of home, writing this Narrative, been confined in the galling chains of slavery. Going to live at Baltimore laid the foundation, and opened the gateway, to all my subsequent prosperity. I have ever regarded it as the first plain manifestation of that kind providence which has ever since attended me, and marked my life with so many favors.

Yet, Baltimore presented constant contradictions in terms of its acceptance of slavery and its paradoxical attempts to both advance and block African American rights, including literacy. The ports symbolized the freedom and oppression of a landscape straddling man-made laws and oppositional forces in regard to those artificial regulations. Douglass could assert that "a city slave is almost a free man compared with a slave on a plantation" and simultaneously acknowledge that while in Baltimore "I often found myself regretting my own existence and wishing myself dead." Baltimore did provide more physical freedom for Douglass than the Eastern Shore, as he was often allowed to travel about the city on his own; however, in many ways, the injustices and impact of slavery were even more pronounced and visibly evident in Baltimore than on the Eastern Shore.

After the death of Douglass's suspected father—Captain Aaron Anthony—in 1833, Douglass was sent back to the Eastern Shore under the rule of Anthony's son-in-law, Thomas Auld. In order to attempt to temper Douglass's defiance, Auld rented 16-year-old Douglass as a field hand under the brutal watch of "slave breaker" Edward Covey. Douglass's rebellion continued to grow, eventually manifesting into a physical fight with Covey, after which Douglass was rented for two years to the Freelands, another Eastern Shore family related to the Aulds. Douglass returned to Hugh Auld in Baltimore in 1836, after which time he learned the trade of ship caulking in Fell's Point. Two years later, Douglass disguised himself as a free black sailor, used money earned by his fiancée, Anna Murray, a free woman living in Fell's Point, and boarded a train at Canton for New York via Havre de Grace, Wilmington, and Philadelphia.

"My Escape from Slavery," chapter twenty-one from *My Bondage and My Freedom*, still rings with suspense as Douglass notes how he narrowly convinces the conductor of his free status while leaving Baltimore: "Minutes were hours, and hours were days during this part of my flight . . . The heart of no fox or deer, with hungry hounds on his trail in full chase, could have beaten more anxiously or noisily than did mine from the time I left Baltimore till I reached Philadelphia." However, as Douglass admits, even after the conductor "left with the assurance that I was all right, though much relieved I realized that I was still in great danger; I was still in Maryland, and subject to arrest at any moment."

Douglass's first published narrative recounting the day he narrowly escaped—including his recollection that, "[i]f life is more than breath and the 'quick round of blood,' I lived more in that one day than a year of my slave life"—published in 1845, leaves out a major factor in the planning and successful execution of his escape. *My Bondage and My Freedom*, however, published ten years later in 1855, documents that one of Douglass's first acts as a free man was to write to Murray in Baltimore in order to let her know he had arrived safely in New York:

> Once in the hands of Mr. Ruggles [secretary of the New York Vigilance Committee], I was comparatively safe. I was hidden with Mr. Ruggles several days. In the meantime, my intended wife, Anna, came on from Baltimore—to whom I had written, informing her of my safe arrival at New York—and, in the presence of Mrs. Mitchell and Mr. Ruggles, we were married, by Rev. James W. C. Pennington.

Douglass's pivotal private communication sent to Baltimore, expressed not only because of his declaration of freedom, but also due to his desire to legally marry Murray, was the proof that his "free life began on the third of September 1838."

Douglass's and Murray's daughter, Rosetta Douglass Sprague, mentions the hidden correspondence in her short biographical essay, "Anna Murray Douglass: My Mother as I Recall Her": "When the escaped slave and future husband of Murray had reached New York in safety, his first act was to write her of his arrival and as they had previously arranged she was to come on immediately." There is no further research available about Douglass's underground letter sent to Baltimore, which is not surprising, due to the dangerous nature of the letter's creation and its intended temporary existence. Douglass's letter to Murray in Baltimore remains silent and invisible within conventional and preserved histories, even though the letter marshaled the first intimate and communicative entry of the free "Frederick Douglass" so repeatedly celebrated in Baltimore's preserved public histories.

It was, in fact, Douglass's "sense of [his] newfound love's vulnerability to the whims of the domestic slave trade [that] convinced [Douglass] to break for freedom," notes Douglass scholar David Taft Terry. Equally concerned for the life and freedom of his fiancée, Anna Murray, Douglass realized any actions, including escape, would impact his "circle of honest and warm hearted friends." Douglass describes the personal void that he would be required to inhabit if he left Baltimore, one where correspondence and future reunions would be prohibited for the sake of his and others' safety and lives: "The thought of such a separation, where the hope of ever meeting again is excluded, and where there can be no correspondence, is very painful."

Douglass's narrative admits that the link between correspondence and community is one of both body and words—a vital bridge necessary for physical health, as much as for social and familial connections. Douglass confirms the reality "that thousands would escape from slavery who now remain there, but for the strong cords of affection that bind them to their families, relatives and friends." Douglass's faith in utilizing personal communication as the means of stretching that "cord of affection" from New York back to the port of Baltimore, was ultimately what enabled him to move forward with his plans to escape, to legally marry Murray, and to devote his entire life to ending slavery and social injustices.

The likelihood that the letter declaring Douglass's safe arrival in New York was immediately destroyed for the sake of Murray's and Douglass's safety is further complicated by the fact that historians believe Murray was illiterate, so it is probable that Douglass may have sent word via another recipient or through alternative correspondence means. Or, Douglass's letter might have been disguised as something very different from a typical letter and/or written in predetermined code.

As well, the letter would likely not have been sent to the Auld's home on Aliceanna Street, but rather to an address connected to Murray, so that the letter's content could be safely revealed—rerouting the historical map and traditionally-viewed direction of Douglass's pivotal prints within the port's streets. One possible address of receipt could have been Caroline Street, as Murray was working as a domestic worker on Caroline for a man named Wells, who also happened to be a postmaster at the time of Douglass's escape.

We will most surely never know the demise of Douglass's letter sent to Murray in Baltimore. Was it destroyed purposefully upon its receipt? Was it lost? Or, was it secretly kept, only to be destroyed in the 1872 fire that burned down Douglass's house, along with the bulk of his early writings?

Sprague's "My Mother as I Recall Her" examines the publicly neglected relationship of Douglass and Murray and acknowledges Murray's role in enabling Douglass to escape from Baltimore. Sprague's essay, published in 1923, was one of the first sources to credit Murray in Douglass's legacy. Sprague admits that "[t]he story of Frederick Douglass' hopes and aspirations and longing desire for freedom has been told—you all know it. It was a story made possible by the unswerving loyalty of Anna Murray."

Murray was born around 1813 in Caroline County, Maryland. She was the first free-born child (out of four free-born children following seven enslaved children) of Bambarra and Mary Murray. Murray and her three free-born siblings left Caroline County in 1832 to find work in Baltimore, where Murray obtained domestic employment in the home of the Montells, a French family. Two years later, Murray went to work for the Wells family on South Caroline Street. Sprague explains that soon thereafter Murray met Douglass within the African American social circles of Baltimore—circles which often excluded enslaved persons but which made an exception for an already notable young man named Frederick Bailey.

Until very recently, Murray has been overlooked in her role as both Douglass's wife and as an integral part of his public legacy. Some of this neglect may be due to Murray's illiteracy, as a lack of textual documentation inevitably challenges historical preservation of any person. Unfortunately, Murray was not alone in her level of illiteracy within Baltimore, as many other free and enslaved African Americans (especially women) were prohibited or limited from the resources which were vital for long-term life literacy.

Indeed, within Baltimore's port landscape, Murray's and many other African American women's stories disappeared among the docks and narrow row homes. Sprague explains how "[Murray] had lived with the Wells family . . . so long and having been able to save the greater part of her earnings was willing to share with the man she loved that he might gain the freedom he yearned to possess. Her courage, her sympathy at the start was the mainspring that supported the career of Frederick Douglass." Later in Murray's life, "as [was] the condition of most wives," Sprague reminds, "[Murray's] identity became so merged with that of her husband, that few of their earlier friends in the North really knew and appreciated the full value of the woman who presided over the Douglass home for forty-four years." Only in the past few years have scholars showcased the women who stood in the shadow of Douglass and strived to present Murray as someone more than the illiterate first wife of Frederick Douglass.

The Library of Congress currently holds the majority of the personal and public papers (including letters) of Frederick Douglass. However, the earliest dated document in *The Frederick Douglass Papers* is from 1841, written three years after Douglass escaped from Baltimore. Douglass's intimate letters to and from his second wife, Helen Pitts Douglass, are indexed and available online. The letters that have gained the most attention in regard to

Douglass's intimate communication, though, are actually not those written to Murray or Pitts, but those written to Ottilie Assing, a white abolitionist Douglass is suspected of having an affair with for many years, as documented in *Love Across Color Lines: Ottilie Assing and Frederick Douglass* by Maria Diedrich and *Radical Passion: Ottilie Assing's Reports from America and Letters to Frederick Douglass* by Christoph Lohman.

Lohman admits the lack of preserved letters, too, between Assing and Douglass is the invisible "port" of his research: Assing ordered all of her letters destroyed after her death (by suicide after Douglass married his second wife), and there is currently no trace of any of the letters (except one fragment) by Assing held by Douglass. "It is possible," Lohman suggests, "that Douglass never archived her letters as conscientiously as [Assing] did his; it is possible that he destroyed them after Assings' suicide; it is possible that they were discarded by heirs anxious that posterity apotheosize the icon rather than understand the man." It is possible, Lohman's options present, that the Douglass/Assing letters' formal lack of preservation—and the multiple possibilities for that status—are just as important as their missing content preservation in validating the "man," Frederick Douglass.

Preserved letters Douglass mailed to Baltimore, even if not written to Murray, do help in highlighting the impact of Douglass's personal words within the city's heart. Douglass's 1848 letter to Thomas Auld, mailed a decade after his escape, discusses Maryland's resources, which benefitted only those who could experience the state as free citizens:

> You may perhaps want to know how I like my present condition. I am free to say, I greatly prefer it to that which I occupied in Maryland. I am, however, by no means prejudiced against the State as such. Its geography, climate, fertility and products, are such as to make it a very desirable abode for any man; and but for the existence of slavery there, it is not impossible that I might again take up my abode in that State. It is not that I love Maryland less, but freedom more.

Douglass's letter to Auld captures Maryland's contradictory role, as both a "desirable" and an "undesirable" state for men, depending on their race. The letter, too, reinforces the separation of men from women within ownership hierarchies at this time, as Douglass emphasizes the many traits that make Maryland a compelling home "for any man."

Even close to twenty years after his escape, Douglass finds he cannot completely cut ties with his former "home" of Baltimore, and he writes to Hugh Auld in 1857, asking: *Will you favor me by dropping me a line, telling me in what year I came to live with you in Aliceanna St . . . The information is not for publication – and shall not be published.* Douglass's desire for accurate biographical data is also a desire for accurate self-preservation—private, versus public, validation. The irony resonates well into the twenty-first century in the recognition that Douglass had to escape from Baltimore in order to enter it, decades later, as a free man.

Douglass's physical return to his Baltimore "home" actually did not occur until 1864, when he attended an emancipation celebration at the former Strawberry Alley Church in Fell's Point. The event was held two weeks after Maryland officially abolished slavery through its state constitution. This was the historical day in which Douglass declared, "Maryland is now a glorious free state . . . the revolution is genuine, full and complete." The revolution turned out to be insincere, empty, and incomplete, however, as the Auld family refused to accept Douglass back onto their property—more than twenty-five years after his escape.

In fact, it was not until 1892 that Douglass officially left his residential mark on the geographical landscape of Baltimore. Douglass purchased the land and financed construction for a row of 5 modest rental homes on Strawberry Alley (now known as Dallas Street) for local African American residents. While there is some speculation as to the exact reason for the location, most historians believe the project was inspired by Douglass's memories of his former church (and some of its influential members), which was located on or near the site.

524 South Dallas Street
Douglass Place homes

However romantic it may seem to both locals and tourists to accept Baltimore as the home of Frederick Douglass, the city was never "home" to Douglass in any conventional sense of the word. Perhaps further revision needs to be added to Douglass's Baltimore history, as Chalkley declares: "[Douglass's] words still ring, his story is still relevant. It's time for Frederick Douglass to come home." Increasing the understanding of Douglass's unpreserved private communication to Murray as a catalyst for his life-long struggle for freedom enables Douglass to simultaneously "come home" and "escape" from the port of Baltimore. Douglass's [preserved and unpreserved] letters, then, become "letters . . . of the [societal] battlefield": the private force of a public legacy.

Douglass's unpreserved "word" to Murray symbolizes Garrison's reaction after hearing Douglass speak publicly in Nantucket in 1841: "There is in him that union of head and heart, which is indispensable to an enlightenment of the heads and a winning of the hearts of others." That narrative, carried in the hidden news of Douglass's successful escape from Baltimore, was initially born from Douglass's desire for Murray to join him in marriage in New York; in addition, that intimate communication held the future freedoms for an immeasurable amount of people, miles beyond Baltimore's port of entry.

Chapter Two

Lost Writing

of Frances Ellen Watkins (Harper)

Frances Ellen Watkins Harper

Frances Ellen Watkins
Baltimore, Maryland

PAID
5

Unlike Frederick Douglass, whose name is known by most Americans— in and outside of Baltimore—Frances Ellen Watkins Harper, one of America's early leading African American women writers, remains relatively unknown—in and outside of Baltimore—though many scholars consider Harper to be "the best known and best loved African-American poet prior to Paul Laurence Dunbar." Harper's name is also consistently listed in Baltimore writers' anthologies and maps, yet her personal geographical markers are noticeably missing from most websites or blogs other than through generalized references. Like her early writing, Harper's young life in Baltimore remains undocumented—noted, but not fully realized.

Frances Smith Foster admits in *A Brighter Coming Day: A Frances Ellen Watkins Harper Reader* that "[f]ew sources offer additional information about Harper's life, and most directly reference [William Still's *The Underground Rail Road* (1871)] as their source." William Still was a prominent abolitionist and friend to Harper. He "devoted thirty pages of his history of the Underground Railroad to Harper's biography," noting that "'[t]here is not to be found in any written work portraying the Anti-slavery struggle, (except in the form of narratives) as we are aware of, a sketch of the labors of any eminent colored woman.'" Harper remains both a known and unknown Baltimore figure; she is a woman whose preserved contributions have found contemporary public tribute, but whose unpreserved works, early writing, and private life are just beginning to be rediscovered.

The Baltimore Literary Heritage Project provides a short summary of Harper's childhood in Baltimore:

> Frances Ellen Watkins Harper [was] born in 1825 in Baltimore to free blacks. An aunt and uncle saw to it that she received good care and a quality education. That uncle, William Watkins . . . taught in a school for black children at Sharp Street Memorial Methodist Church. He started his own school, known as the Academy for Negro Youth . . . and there Harper received a classical education.

Camden Street Station
Former site of William Watkins's school

Harper's life was heavily influenced by her uncle, William Watkins, who was "a fervent abolitionist, a community leader, and a highly regarded teacher." Harper's work and her "intense commitment to abolitionist and other social welfare crusades," along with "her familiarity with classical and Christian mythology, and her reputation for oratory and general deportment were obviously influenced by her education at the academy," in addition to her extended family.

Harper's childhood and young adulthood in Baltimore are primarily mapped through her male authority figures, rather than herself: one who was her caregiver (her uncle) and one who was her domestic employer (a Baltimore bookseller). The Archives of Maryland notes that "differing sources suggest [the family who employed Harper and owned the bookstore in which she apprenticed] may have been Quakers by the name of Armstrong." Harper is also defined by her marriage name, "Harper," which she did not take until 1860, when she married Fenton Harper at age 35.

The *Archives of Maryland* attempts to fill in a few gaps in Harper's life through a geographical and theoretical lens, proposing that Harper's "free" status and her early years in Baltimore "directly shaped the rest of Harper's life opportunities and choices, where she was able to relate to people from both an insider and outsider point of view in many of her conversations, lectures, and literature."

"As an insider," the *Archives of Maryland* suggests, "[Harper] was a black woman who felt spiritually connected to her race and their hardships. But, she was also an outsider because she was an educated, free woman with access to a variety of white societies where the majority of African Americans were not accepted." Harper's ability to juggle roles as both an insider and an outsider likely nurtured her post-Baltimore writing and speaking success, yet it is these contradictory roles which continue to make categorizing her problematic for contemporary scholars and public tributes.

For many decades, biographers chose to simply skip over Harper's childhood in Baltimore and to assume all of Harper's early Baltimore-based writing was lost. However, that assumption was abruptly revised in 2015 when doctoral student Johanna Ortner discovered *Forest Leaves* (published in 1845, when Harper was only twenty years old, which was five years before Harper left Baltimore). Harper's "lost" poetry manuscript, "found" 170 years after its original publication, was actually preserved and archived. Ortner discovered the manuscript after performing a simple catalogue search at the Maryland Historical Society. What makes this literary disappearance and rediscovery extra problematic, especially regarding Baltimore's contemporary tributes to Harper, are the assumptions made in scholarship circles regarding unpreserved materials (even when those materials are preserved and often archived, though unknown to the public). Foster and many other contemporary Harper biographers have reinforced this perspective with the repeated published assumption that "no known copies [of *Forest Leaves*] exist."

If Harper was able to professionally publish a book of poems while in Baltimore in 1845, it is only logical to believe she also wrote many other literary pieces during the first two-and-a-half decades of her life spent residing in the city, including personal communication that also remains "lost." The disconnect between Harper's unpreserved early literary life in Baltimore and her later success and preserved literary career post-Baltimore is due to more than her geographical exit from Maryland after the passing of the Fugitive Slave Act of 1850 (a law which forbade free blacks from entering the state or otherwise face the penalty of forced slavery). Dissemblance must also be taken into account in addressing Harper's lost and unpreserved writing, as Darlene Clark Hine reinforces in *Hine Sight: Black Women and the Re-Construction of American History*. The reality of purposefully destroyed or hidden material, including personal communication or desired privacy for intimate feelings, by early African American women such as Harper, heightens the layers of silencing.

Intentional invisibility regarding personal communication adds yet another challenge in the complex effort of reimagining and remapping letter routes of early African American women in Baltimore. Personal words that could be later found, traced, and used against early African American women were usually muffled, if not completely silenced for the sake of the women's safety. Intimacy, including that expressed in personal letters, was equated with dangerous public ramifications—a powerful disincentive for its tangible creation. Resurrecting Harper and her unpreserved communication, therefore, grants validity to a much larger history and range of early African American women in Baltimore who also expressed their desires for equality through private and often less politicized and/or popular venues than their male counterparts.

Harper's preserved work (excluding the recently discovered *Forest Leaves*) only dates back to 1853, and, like Douglass's preserved works, surfaces years after her flight from Baltimore. We may never know if Harper had a personal relationship during her Baltimore years which prompted personal correspondence. Yet, the plausibility of the existence of such artifacts is strong, due to the vast amount of Harper's preserved post-Baltimore letters. Melba Joyce Boyd admits the challenges of scholarship pertaining to such unpreserved correspondence in *Discarded Legacy: Politics in the Life of Frances E. W. Harper, 1825–1911*: "[I]t is impossible to retrieve that which has been materially discarded"; therefore, research must adapt in the endeavor to construct "a contribution to the reconstruction of the fragmented and obscured legacy of Frances Harper."

Boyd's desire to rediscover Harper and advance her within the American canon is poignant, yet its recognition of Baltimore's role in silencing Harper's writing and living history is lacking. Boyd announces and reviews the recent publication of comprehensive Harper scholarship: "[*A Brighter Coming Day*] provides Harper's full range and reflects ten years of arduous research . . . With the exception of *Forest Leaves* (1846), which remains unrecovered, Harper's writings have now been substantially retrieved from obscurity."

Now and *obscurity*, however, take on new meaning when positioned within a framework which acknowledges unpreserved *and* undiscovered writing. The statement, "Harper's writings have now been substantially retrieved from obscurity," automatically propels Harper's other missing "works" out of obscurity, even if some of those "works" are not currently "found" in the conventional sense of the word. Boyd indirectly admits the validation of unpreserved materials in her disclaimer at the end of her introduction to *Discarded Legacy*, stating that "[s]ince the writing of this book no buried diaries of Harper's have been uncovered in some attic." The defining word in Boyd's sentence is "since," as it exposes the possibility of future discovery of additional items—preserved and previously unpreserved—in Harper's literary repertoire, which did happen after the publication of Boyd's biography.

Harper is a prime example of current rediscovery and the reality that historically and socially transformative writing is still waiting to be uncovered and viewed—both in private homes and in public facilities. In addition to Ortner's discovery of *Forest Leaves* in the Maryland Historical Society Archives in 2015, a letter written by Harper to William Still, published in the *Philadelphia Press* on July 31, 1867, was re-released and analyzed in the spring of 2017 by Jana Koehler in *American Literary Realism*. Other recent examples of rediscoveries by African American writers include Henry Louis Gates's catalogue auction purchase of a cloth manuscript from the 1850's which he later published and introduced as *The Bondswoman's Narrative by Hannah Craft* in 2002. The manuscript is "possibly the first novel written by a black woman and definitely the first novel written by a woman who had been a slave." An unpublished poem by Jupiter Hammon, an enslaved man born on Long Island in 1711, was also re-discovered in 2013 by doctoral student Julie McCown, after being "buried" in the documents in the Yale University Library.

Harper is part of both Baltimore's "lost" and "found" writers—an early African American woman who continues to blur the boundaries of public/private realms, preserved/unpreserved works, and lost/discovered texts, yet easily finds a mapping within the entrance and exit veins of Baltimore's heart. What makes Harper's "lost" writing and potential Baltimore letters contrast even more among other "lost" African American material and authorship is the reality that she was not a "lost" writer during her lifetime (with the first twenty-five years of it spent living in Baltimore). She was, in fact, known as the "Bronze Muse," due to her clear, resonating, and inspiring voice and works.

Harper's case demands a redefinition of "lost" that includes new geographical and temporal considerations. Foster explains that "[s]trictly speaking, Frances Ellen Watkins Harper is not one of the many writers restored to us by recent literary archeological projects;" unlike many African American writers, Harper has "long been included in the discussion of early African American literature." Foster reinforces that "Harper was neither lost nor ignored for many reasons . . . [c]ritics and scholars embraced Harper . . . For over sixty years, Harper earned her living by and devoted her life to composing poetry and prose that spoke to and about the moral, social, and political conditions of African Americans." Yet, Harper's published Baltimore work *was* "lost" for decades, even while preserved. Harper's "lost" Baltimore correspondence may one day surface; however, for now, it—like Harper—waits to be fully documented and validated.

Chapter Three

Unwritten Words

Harriet Tubman

Harriet Tubman, circa 1880

THREE HUNDRED DOLLARS REWARD.

RANAWAY from the subscriber on Monday the 17th ult., three negroes, named as follows: HARRY, aged about 19 years, has on one side of his neck a wen, just under the ear, he is of a dark chestnut color, about 5 feet 8 or 9 inches hight; BEN, aged aged about 25 years, is very quick to speak when spoken to, he is of a chestnut color, about six feet high; MINTY, aged about 27 years, is of a chestnut color, fine looking, and about 5 feet high. One hundred dollars reward will be given for each of the above named negroes, if taken out of the State, and $50 each if taken in the State. They must be lodged in Baltimore, Easton or Cambridge Jail, in Maryland.

ELIZA ANN BRODESS.

Near Bucktown, Dorchester county, Md.
Oct. 3d, 1849.

☞The Delaware Gazette will please copy the above three weeks, and charge this office.

46

Even within the dangerous parameters of a slavery-based society, the desire for both intimate and public freedom prompted countless, untraceable acts of communication by African American women that will never be known, many which will remain lost in the depths and layers of Baltimore's port. The traces that do remain must often be uncovered through secondary documents and the male companions and authority figures of the women.

Frederick Douglass's August 29, 1868 letter to Harriet Tubman is such an example. Tubman, like Douglass's first wife, Anna Murray, was illiterate and secretly left Baltimore with the intention of *not* leaving her mark. In fact, it was Tubman's ability to see pathways beyond those on existing maps that ultimately enabled her to find the uncharted routes on land and along the Chesapeake that would allow for successful escapes from the city.

Douglass's letter to Tubman gives "witness" to these untraceable letters: *Most that I have done and suffered in the service of our cause has been in public, and I have received much encouragement at every step of the way. You on the other hand have labored in a private way. I have wrought in the day—you in the night . . . only . . . [t]he midnight sky and the silent stars have been the witnesses of your devotion to freedom and your heroism.* When only "the midnight sky and the silent stars" are "witness" to hidden voices and actions, it is up to future scholars to find human "witness," as Douglass does, in validating early desires and routes, especially of those who do not seek—intentionally or unintentionally—public recognition or platforms. In *Bound for the Promised Land*, Kate Clifford Larson gives examples of the Underground Railroad "letters" utilized by Tubman and other early African Americans, which used body parts and movement instead of pen and paper:

> [I]n a world of suspicious whites, a letter could elicit unwanted attention. Like the heavily coded spirituals Tubman would later use to guide fugitive slaves north, a look, a glance, a movement, a shift of the foot, or a wave of a hand could be invisible to the white master, yet speak louder than words to fellow blacks, passing messages in times of need, when the stakes were life or death.

The artifact most closely resembling written communication by Tubman found to date (and included in the Harriet Tubman Exhibit at the

Smithsonian National Museum of African American History and Culture) is a hymnal, published in 1876, which has several Xs penciled on its songs. However, it must be noted that even the curators at the National Museum of African American History and Culture, where the hymnal is housed, cannot determine that Tubman was the person who wrote the Xs in her hymnal.

The lack of first account record by Tubman, as well as by many early African Americans, has led to the repeated question: How *does* a city adequately honor a historic figure whose personal deeds were purposefully concealed from public view and whose words were only saved through second party recollections and scribing? Baltimore, as well as the rest of the country, has battled with this dilemma for years.

Additionally, Tubman's illiteracy represents much more than a lack of reading and writing. Her unwritten "words" symbolize the language and freedoms withheld from generations of African Americans, as well as the non-conventional language substitutions needed for safety and survival. The challenge of proper tribute, then, is reliant on future generations who must find the appropriate words and communicative avenues to document a private woman whose societal aims intentionally avoided traditional public prints and preservation.

A range of scholars have attempted to "write" their own representations and life accounts of Tubman, born Araminta "Minty" Ross in 1822, on the plantation of Anthony Thompson in Dorchester County on Maryland's Eastern Shore. In *Harriet Tubman: Imagining a Life*, Beverly Lowry explains how "Tubman's illiteracy certainly presents a problem for scholars looking for primary material. Beyond government records, court documents, property assessments, and census figures, everything we have has been interpreted or—as historians say—mediated, even when the writer interviewed Tubman directly or took down a dictated letter."

Lowry's project, to write a book-length biography about Tubman by piecing together known documentation and publications, is a possible version of "what life might have been like for the American hero Harriet Tubman," including her actions and communication in Baltimore. Lowry admits that "[t]his book does not pretend to be a work of intense scholarship

. . . [but] the story of a life as I have studied and reimagined it." The intersection of research and imagination remains a crossroads which must be admitted and addressed when negotiating lives and words lacking primary record. As Lowry's project demonstrates, the personal aims and stakes of the researcher inherently become a part of the historical retelling.

Milton C. Sernett takes a slightly different approach than Lowry in *Harriet Tubman: Myth, Memory, and History* in his desire to remove the "lady" from the "legend" of Harriet Tubman and to locate "the remembered Tubman—that is . . . the myth that draws on the factual core but is often in tension with it." Sernett argues that "Tubman may be America's most malleable icon[;]" however, she holds unmalleable "significance for . . . how we are to remember the nation's struggle with the issue of slavery." Tubman's malleability, while complex in its traditional historical context, actually welcomes a widening of her universality and creates a larger setting for the framework of personalized public histories. "By learning of Harriet Tubman and her place in the American memory," Sernett asserts, "we learn about ourselves as the American people." Thus, "[b]y learning about Harriet Tubman and her place in [Baltimore] memory . . . we learn about ourselves as [Baltimoreans]."

Additionally, Sernett admits the constantly shifting public perception and its influence on historical figures, explaining that "[t]he intersubjective process by which certain personalities from the past gain and lose stature in the American memory is convoluted and often clouded by the interjection of myth." Tubman's "unwritten" status, therefore, encourages historically pro-slavery cities, such as Baltimore, to gather myth and history into a blurry map, which Sernett calls a "distilled" and "inherited" American memory of Tubman. Sernett solves the dilemma of having to locate a singular Tubman within this distillation by presenting two separate Tubmans and "chronicles the life history of the commemorated Tubman (the symbol) in relation to the historical Tubman (the life)."

Similarly, Tubman's hidden routes *and* hidden communication are in need of validation in order to fully appreciate today's geographical and societal landscapes. Part of Baltimore's dilemma regarding its tribute to Tubman, and other African Americans with unwritten words and records, is its own pressure to find a public representation of a private life which does not produce artificial results in that translation. Often, Tubman is seen as more-than-human and capable of super-hero actions beyond those of ordinary people. By presenting Tubman as a brave, unique, and embodied woman whose unwritten words played a vital role beyond her own history, Tubman's life can better resonate with young people today who may feel unable to or discouraged from writing their own personal narratives and communication. Baltimore, too, can be unwritten in its capacity to be more than a geographical footnote within Tubman's legacy.

Tubman learned the cost and importance of personal communication in achieving freedom early in her life, as Larson describes: "On the cusp of adulthood, the disabled Tubman went to work on a timber gang, exhibiting great skills laboring in the logging camps and in the fields. There she was exposed to the secret communication networks that were the province of black watermen and other free and enslaved blacks." Hidden communication was created out of necessity, when public and/or direct discourse was not an option, as unwritten words delivered the thoughts, support, and instructions needed for survival. Tubman's success in navigating the Underground Railroad hinged on her ability to see and read beyond traditional legal, literacy, and geographical limits.

Tubman's temporary status in Baltimore as a fugitive, as well as her illiteracy, make her unable to be completely and/or accurately portrayed, yet her actions and unwritten personal communication altered the city's and country's history. How then to find the proper "word(s)" to address Tubman and other literacy voids in mapping pivotal historical figures' personal communication routes?

Enough research does exist to summarize details from Tubman's first rescue to and from Fell's Point—the first of multiple successful rescues which would bring over 70 family members and friends to freedom:

> [After the passage of the Fugitive Slave Act of 1850, Tubman's] niece, Kessiah Jolley Bowley and her two children were set to be auctioned to the highest bidder at the [Cambridge] County Courthouse. Kessiah's free husband, John Bowley, devised a plan with Tubman to bring Kessiah and the children away before they could be sold. On the day of the auction, John bid on his wife and children, even though he did not have the money to pay for them. Before the auctioneer could

call for payment, John quickly and safely hid his family in a nearby home. That night, he secretly sailed them to the Fell's Point waterfront in Baltimore where Tubman hid them until she was able to safely bring them to Philadelphia.

Tubman's brother-in-law, Tom Tubman, lived in Fell's Point, and, as Kate Clifford Larson suggests, "Tom was possibly working as a stevedore on Baltimore's docks; in fact, there were many former Dorchester County free blacks [and possibly some runaways and a few slaves, who had been hired out to Baltimore, much as Frederick Douglass had been] living and working in Baltimore."

The setting of Fell's Point, as a crowded working and residential dock, "made Baltimore's waterfront an ideal location from which Tubman could operate," as [in Fell's Point, Bowley and his family] "[c]ould circulate among the city's 36,000 blacks—29,000 of them free—and become indistinguishable to slave catchers and federal marshals alike." There were many other extended relatives and friends of Tubman from the Eastern Shore black community in Fell's Point, who "were also perfectly positioned to receive news about any threats to Harriet's family."

The waterfront area provided adequate cover and camouflage for Tubman's movements both on and off of the docks, driven by the communication of a vast network of people and a geographical community that had forty years earlier been called "a nest of pirates" by former British merchant ship captains blocked by aggressive Baltimore Schooners.

Fell's Point: *The "home" of Frederick Douglass, nearby neighborhood of Frances Ellen Watkins Harper, and an entry/exit for Harriet Tubman and the Underground Railroad*

Larson, like many other biographers, acknowledges the inability to thoroughly document Tubman's life story, as well as many other early African Americans' histories. Thus, Tubman's biography is also an account of "perhaps," "possibly," and "likely," as much as it is a definite narrative. While admitting the uncertainty of Tubman's personal actions and words, Larson is certain in describing the alternative communication that Tubman was required to use, in place of written words and letters, in her pursuit of safety and freedom for herself and others: "a look, a glance, a movement, a shift of the foot, or a wave of a hand."

Tubman's unrecorded words belong to a genre that will never receive its due credit or full validation—unwritten communication—even though this unpreserved genre is often more impactful than its preserved counterparts in influencing historical and societal shifts. It is up to current and future generations to find new routes to validate unpreserved personal communication, especially in cases where the only witnesses of "word(s)" are "[t]he midnight sky and silent stars."

Part Two
Atriums

Inside Views of Prominent Outsiders—
Untranslated, Unpublished, Unfiltered and Unfolding Letters

Baltimore Circa 1846/Photographer: John Plumbe

Baltimore's status as a host of hidden histories quickly reveals the communication that guided the city's residents and visitors as they navigated through, beneath, above, and around the geographical and societal boundaries of their times. Hidden relationships, loyalties, outsider perspectives, and societal expectations highlight the need for indirect subversion in communicating the opinions, observations, predictions, and concerns necessary to address tensions, inequities, and discoveries of the landscape throughout Baltimore's history. The range of correspondents included in this section magnifies the wide array of intimate communication that both separated and connected Baltimore's past visitors. While the genders, decades, philosophies, and anxieties of the following correspondents may initially seem disconnected, a closer look reveals parallels in their reach for intimacy through words and vision.

Chapter Four

Untranslated and Destroyed Words

Letters between Eleanor Roosevelt and her Journalist,
Lorena Hickok

Eleanor Roosevelt and Lorena Hickok, *March 1934*

Lorena Hickok
The Lord Baltimore Hotel
20 W. Baltimore Street
Baltimore, Maryland 21201

Eleanor Roosevelt
The White House
1600 Pennsylvania Ave. NW
Washington, DC 20500

Lord Baltimore Hotel
Baltimore, MD

Darling—in a blue velvet dinner gown or out of it—I love you

--Lorena Hickok, November 2, 1934

Hick my darling . . . for I love you and you've made of me so much more of a person just to be worthy of you

--Eleanor Roosevelt, 1934

Eighty-four years after Tubman's first rescue mission to and from Baltimore, another one of America's most recognized female figures also sent her own secret messages through the city. Unlike Tubman, however, this woman's written words were housed inside paper envelopes and the safety of a federal postal system which prohibited interception. This woman was also functioning under a completely different set of American standards, due to her race, class, education, and—in particular—the position of her marriage to the President. Additionally, unlike Tubman's unwritten words, produced for the desire for freedom, this woman's written words took cover due to their content, which expressed a desire for female intimacy. These words were mailed to the Lord Baltimore Hotel, located at 20 West Baltimore Street, one of the many temporary communication hubs of Eleanor Roosevelt's and Lorena Hickok's intimate correspondence.

The Lord Baltimore Hotel
Temporary Residence of Eleanor Roosevelt's Journalist, Lorena Hickok

Eleanor Roosevelt and Lorena Hickok initially met in 1928, when Hickok, who was reporting for the Associated Press, landed the "first formal interview with Eleanor Roosevelt on November 7, the day after FDR won election as governor of New York." Both women had experienced betrayal in their personal relationships during the previous decades. As Rodger Streitmatter notes in *Empty Without You: The Intimate Letters of Eleanor*

Roosevelt and Lorena Hickok, "Eleanor had discovered [in her mid-thirties] that her husband, FDR, was having an affair and had agreed to continue the marriage—but not sexual relations with [him]." Ironically, ER discovered FDR's infidelity by "stumbl[ing] upon a packet of lightly scented [hidden] letters that documented [FDR's] affair with the very young and very beautiful Lucy Page Mercer," who was ER's social secretary. Hickok's betrayal came from the abandonment of her live-in companion of eight years, Ellie Morse, a woman from a very wealthy family who had dropped out of Wellesley College to work at the *Minneapolis Tribune,* where she met Hickok.

In the summer of 1932, Hickok was assigned to FDR's Presidential Campaign, though, as Michael Golay describes in *America 1933: The Great Depression, Lorena Hickok, Eleanor Roosevelt, and the Shaping of the New Deal,* Hickok "found herself drawn more to the candidate's wife than to the candidate himself." As the women grew closer, the pressure of juggling public journalistic duties with growing intimacy began to take its toll, and Hickok decided to leave the Associated Press in 1933. ER arranged for Harry Hopkins, friend of the presidency and head of the Federal Emergency Relief Administration, "to offer [Hickok] a job as chief investigator for the agency."

Hickok was hired to travel around "the country to gauge the effectiveness of the nation's relief programs and then write detailed reports on her findings for [Harry] Hopkins, identifying which programs were working and which were not." Hickok's Relief Program reports and public communication were sent to ER, "who often showed them to Franklin . . . [who often] read them out loud at Cabinet meetings." The reports offered a very different perspective and tone than the second set of pages that Hickok regularly composed during those years "at the end of the day and often while lying in bed" to ER.

Golay credits the early partnership of ER and Hickok in "mak[ing] it possible, in eighteen months spanning 1933 and 1934, for Hickok to assemble as powerful a documentary record as we have of the hardest of American times (The Great Depression)." Many of Hickok's letters to Harry L. Hopkins are included in *One Third of a Nation: Lorena Hickok Reports on the Great Depression*, edited by Richard Lowitt and Maurine Beasley, as well as one letter Hickok wrote to ER.

Hickok was stationed in Baltimore in the late fall of 1934, where she and ER continued and sustained their long-term relationship through postal correspondence. Their preserved letters were made public in 1978, when "the Franklin D. Roosevelt Library opened eighteen cardboard boxes filled with Eleanor Roosevelt's and Lorena Hickok's personal correspondence to each other." At that time, ER had been deceased for sixteen years; Hickok, for ten. Hickok had donated the letters to the FDR Library in 1958, along with the proviso that the material not be opened until ten years after her death. In the collection "3,500 letters that [ER] and 'Hick' had written during their thirty-year friendship—the first lady sometimes writing two letters in a single day—documented that the women had shared a relationship that was not only intense and intimate, but also passionate and physical."

The first historian to read through ER's and Hickok's letters, Doris Faber, expressed her discomfort with what she found within the sealed boxes at the FDR Library and Museum National Archives in *The Life of Lorena Hickok: Eleanor Roosevelt's Friend*, released in 1980. The preface and ending note describe Faber's elation, and then anxiety, over being chosen to be the first historian to read through the letters and to present them to the public. Faber admits her discomfort with the female intimacy found in ER's and Hickok's letters, and in the disclosure of that information writes, "Because of Eleanor Roosevelt's renown, their story belongs to history. I wish this were not so. In my Personal Notes starting on page 329, I have described my own unavailing effort to postpone the inevitable disclosure." This disclosure is that of an intimate female/female relationship—one which Faber foresaw as being problematic for public reception, even close to twenty years after ER's passing.

Like Faber, one of Streitmatter's main goals in collecting and publishing some of the intimate letters between ER and Hickok was to uncover "glimpses . . . of an Eleanor Roosevelt who is strikingly different from the icon she has become"—a complex woman, not just a political and historical "figure." Streitmatter defends his collection's intentions, stating that the public exposure of ER's letters to/from Hickok "should not diminish [ER's] stature, but rather should serve to reassure us that she was, like all of us, *human.*"

ER's and Hickok's preserved communication begins in March 1933, not long after FDR's inauguration and ER's move into the White House, and continues until September 1962, only two months before ER's death in November 1962. Only a few of ER's and Hickok's preserved letters are published in print or digital format.

There is little mention of the letters written while Hickok was stationed in Baltimore, or the significance of Hickok's time there, in either of the published collections which do provide excerpts from ER's and Hickok's correspondence. Only one of Hickok's letters from this time frame is included in *Empty Without You*, mailed from the Lord Baltimore Hotel on November 2, 1934. In this letter, Hickok reacts to recent newspaper reports which covered ER's speech in New York City, yet focused on ER's attire more than the content of her presentation.

God damn it, Hickok writes, *none of us ought to be wearing velvet dinner gowns these days. Not when . . . 4,000 Baltimore children couldn't go to school in September because they didn't have clothes.* Hickok's frustration with economic inequality in Baltimore includes criticism directed at ER, and Hickok is quite frank in her articulation of the contrast between ER's privileged attire and the vast poverty in the city: *[T]he thought of you in a blue velvet dinner gown—even though you are my friend and I love you—irritated me profoundly. Sometimes I get so sick of this whole damned mess! . . . Darling—in a blue velvet dinner gown or out of it—I love you.*

Requests for ER's and Hickok's correspondence from the FDR Presidential Library and Museum National Archives coinciding with Hickok's stay in Baltimore in late 1934 produce a collection of thirty letters: three from Hickok and twenty-seven from ER. Hickok's three letters are all written on Lord Baltimore Hotel stationery. ER's letters are penned on stationary from various addresses, including The White House; 49 East 65th Street, Manhattan, New York; Hyde Park-on-Hudson, New York; and Warm Springs, Georgia.

The previous year, in 1933, ER had dined at the Lord Baltimore Hotel in the company of another pioneering woman—Amelia Earhart. On April 20, 1933, Earhart "broke up a White House dinner party" by inviting ER and guests (ER's brother, the president of Eastern Air Transport, and the parents of author Gore Vidal) to accompany her on a roundtrip flight to Baltimore. The party landed in Baltimore, and then dined at the Lord Baltimore Hotel before returning to the White House.

Only five of ER's and Hickok's Baltimore-based letters from late 1934 are included in Streitmatter's *Empty Without You*: the November 2, 1934 letter from Hickok and four late fall 1934 letters from ER: 1.) an undated letter 2.) a letter dated November 3, 1934 (on The White House letterhead) 3.) a letter dated November 3, 1934 (on Val-Kill Cottage/on Hyde Park-On-Hudson letterhead) 4.) a letter dated November 22, 1934 (on Georgia Warm Springs Foundation letterhead).

Faber's *The Life of Lorena Hickok* contains a few selected lines and paraphrases from ER's and Hickok's Baltimore-based letters, and *One Third of a Nation: Lorena Hickok Reports on the Great Depression*, contains the November 21, 1934 letter written to ER by Hickok. The majority of ER and Hickok's Baltimore communication, however, is unpublished and inaccessible, except through an individual FDR Library and Museum National Archives appointment and/or paid request for print copies via postal mail.

Hickok's letters are lengthy and legible. ER's letters are shorter and often illegible, as ER's handwriting is extremely difficult to read, with heavily slanted cursive letters that are hard to differentiate and decipher. Streitmatter confirms that "[m]any of [ER's] sentences ramble on and on and on with many twists and turns, comma splices, misspelled words, and challenges to coherence." Due to this translation challenge, as well as the overwhelming amount of correspondence by ER and Hickok (which discourages timely archiving and indexing), the majority of ER's and Hickok's communication is inaccessible and/or untranslatable. Yet, the letters supply a wealth of resources, not only regarding ER and Hickok's relationship, but also in revealing historical views of cities, such as Baltimore, through the internal documentation of outsider perspectives.

While Hickok's published correspondence (to Hopkins via her FERA work) furnishes compelling information about Baltimore during the Depression years, it is Hickok's personal correspondence which provides a more passionate view of the city and its residents. For example, Hickok's November 13, 1934 Baltimore-based letter to Hopkins, included in Lowitt and Beasley's *One Third of a Nation*, discusses wages for various local businesses, such as Bethlehem Steel, Glenn Martin, and stenographers for the Equitable building, as well as her observation that people are refusing jobs because wages are less than the government relief.

Eight days later, in her November 21, 1934 letter to ER, Hickok describes her thoughts about the challenges of issuing emergency relief to a city that is resistant to new federal programs. Hickok also quotes the principal of one of the most economically-challenged schools in Baltimore when describing the conditions of the city: *We give free lunches to the children here—only to those who are the worst off, because we haven't enough money to feed all those who may be hungry . . . Never have we had enough bread . . . so that there was enough for each child to have all it could eat!* Hickok's intimate communication to ER contains not just her own voice, but multiple voices and views of the city, meshing insider and outsider perspectives in joint frustration of the state of child hunger in Baltimore in 1934.

In addition to illustrating the pervasive state of poverty in the Baltimore City schools to ER in her November 21, 1934 letter, Hickok recounts details about her recent meeting with the Maryland A. F. L. leader, Joseph P. McCurdy. Again, Hickok paraphrases a local official's words to convey the urgency of the situation: *"[L]awyers generally, he says, are advising them to ignore the NRA and the other New Deal regulations, on the ground that they are un-constitutional, and that industry can go to court and 'hear the game'.*

Lowitt and Beasley cut the remainder of McCurdy's words (or rather, Hickok's re-quoting of McCurdy's words) from this particular letter in *One Third of a Nation*, though readers would not know this unless they had also ordered a copy of the original version of the letter from the FDR Library. The following excerpt by Hickok, included in her original letter, is replaced with ellipsis in *One Third of a Nation*:

How in God's name, he said, You're going to inculcate in people
the desire to do the right things is something I don't know. You
can't legislate it into them . . . It looks to me as though the only
way might be for the President to get the boys together and say:
"If you'll be decent about this, I'll help you to save some of what
you've got. If you won't, you'll lose—and, by God, I'll help 'em to
take it away from you!"

Cutting this section of Hickok's letter from the publication deletes an insightful glimpse into the unfiltered opinions of union leaders toward city and federal officials during the Great Depression. Moreover, this editing reinforces the reality that what Lowitt and Beasley (and other editors, including this author) may view as unimportant or distractive in personal communication may be viewed quite differently by other readers. As well, the editing highlights the constantly shifting political and economic trends which continue to affect publishing and scholarship priorities.

Other unpublished finds in ER's and Hickok's Baltimore-based communication stored within the FDR Library include Hickok's November 23, 1934 letter. In this letter, Hickok summarizes the recent national news of *the President's executive order pulling all the various representatives of the Government out in the states together into a body*, and responds with a bit of an "I told you so": *Remember how I was pleading for something of the sort a few months ago?*

Hickok's frustration with national and local governments and officials permeates her letter, as she recounts how she *called up the Baltimore relief administration today and asked him who was head of the NRA compliance board here, and he didn't know!* Much of the dysfunction in Baltimore, Hickok finds, is due to administrative bureaucracy, and she spends a good part of her November 23, 1934 letter to ER listing grievances connected to the grid-locked city.

Case in point, Hickok explains to ER that *[i]n the last few months two Baltimore companies—one of them Glenn Martin airplane manufacturers, with a lab of Government orders—announced they were going to raise wages. And the Baltimore Association of Commerce requested them not to do it!* Hickok's view of Baltimore commerce leaves much to be desired, as she admits to ER that *[t]his morning I met the only intelligent businessman I've encountered so far in Baltimore,* reinforcing the city's continuing stereotype as a town of economic incompetence.

ER's letters mailed to Hickok at The Lord Baltimore Hotel are much more difficult to analyze in their routing, due to their lack of legibility. ER's letters add a new challenge to the study of intimate letters: indecipherability. Streitmatter does manage to decipher one of ER's letters from the fall of 1934 in *Empty Without You: Hick my darling/ That cry of 'I want something all my own' is the cry of the heart and I was near to tears last night. You told me once it was hard to let go but I found it was harder to let go and yet hold on . . . for I love you and you've made of me so much more of a person just to be worthy of you.*

Interestingly, Streitmatter leaves off the last line of this letter in *Empty Without You.* That line, as viewed in the original document available from the FDR Library, reads: *If you can come on [untranslatable word] I can put my arms around you tonight.* However, general readers would not know this unless they had a copy of the original letter with which to compare while reading Streitmatter's published version. Regardless of the editorial intention behind this decision, both the decipherable and the undecipherable words in ER's 1934 letter to Hickok demonstrate an unfiltered desire for female intimacy in no uncertain terms.

In 1936, two years after leaving her temporary position in Baltimore, Hickok "began retrieving the letters she had written to Eleanor; between that year and 1968 when [Hickok] died . . . she purposely destroyed hundreds of letters," including "all of her letters to Eleanor written prior to November 26, 1933." Streitmatter explains that Hickok "burned the most explicit of the letters, dramatically dropping them, one by one, into the flames of a fireplace," so that "[w]e can only imagine what has been lost."

The intimate letters of ER and Hickok housed in the FDR Library are, then, a mere trace of a much larger body of communication that will never be found or translated. ER's and Hickok's preserved letters, even if only partially preserved in their original content and scope, still serve to represent the historical personal intimacies and language of women which continue to lack full accessibility and clarity to date, even when written by prominent and privileged women.

Eleanor Roosevelt's and Lorena Hickok's Baltimore-based letters, in particular, showcase much more than intimate communication routed through a particular geographical setting. Their letters, published and imagined, underscore the private needs of public figures, the role that society continues to play in policing relationships and determining validity, and the history of cities from *within*—a history only able to be told through the relationships that remained outside of limits and boundaries.

Chapter Five

Unpublished Words and Uncovered Visions

Mark Twain's Letters to Olivia Langdon Clemens

***Mark Twain**
1877/Frank Millet*

***Olivia Langdon/** October 1869*
Twain immediately fell in love with Langdon after viewing this picture in an ivory miniature in Langdon's brother's stateroom aboard his 1867 voyage to Europe and the Holy Land on the steamer, Quaker City.

IF NOT DELIVERED WITHIN 10 DAYS,
TO BE RETURNED TO BALTIMORE, MD

Mrs. Saml L. Clemens
Hartford, Conn

Guy's Monument Hotel
on the European plan
Monument Square
Samuel C. Little, *Proprietor,*

Baltimore, *April 26, 1877*

. . . I am so given to forgetting everything that I resolved
I would tell you something about this wonderful establishment
before I had a chance to forget it. . .

Ever Yours in Earnest

Saml.

A half-century earlier, before Eleanor Roosevelt and Lorena Hickok created an intimate correspondence route through Baltimore, another set of prominent correspondents, Mark Twain and his wife, Olivia Langdon Clemens, wrote to one another for support and companionship via another historical Baltimore hotel: Guy's Monument Hotel, which was formerly located half a mile north of the Lord Baltimore Hotel on Monument Square. The Battle Monument Square, situated on North Calvert Street between East Fayette and East Lexington Streets, still houses exclusive hotels and homes only available to economically-privileged Baltimore residents and visitors.

Twain and Langdon wrote regularly when Twain traveled and lectured away from their home in Hartford, Connecticut. Within their vast correspondence, three preserved Baltimore-based letters Twain wrote to Langdon uncover not only a man dedicated to intimate communication with his wife, but also an unfiltered behind-the-scenes documentation of the home of one of the United States' first multi-millionaires and locomotive and engine designers. Twain's intimate letters to Langdon bring this lost Baltimore landmark and its former owners to life, as Twain's storytelling enables Langdon to also view the visionary people and settings he discovers while visiting the city.

Two Baltimore-based letters written by Twain to Langdon in April 1877 are publicly accessible through the University of California's *Mark Twain Project* digital archives. Twain's Baltimore-based November 1884 letter is only available through direct Microfilm transcript request via the University of California and has never been published in either print or online format—neither has it been accessible to the general or academic public, nor released to or circulated within the Baltimore community.

Twain first visited Baltimore in 1872 while on a lecture circuit; however, "[n]o letters written between 20 and 26 January 1872 have been found." There are newspaper accounts, but no current preserved first-hand correspondence by Twain, documenting his stay in Baltimore in 1872. *The Baltimore Sun* reported on Twain's lecture, "Roughing It," which was held at the main hall of the Maryland Institute on January 23, 1872. *The Sun* noted Twain's "comical appearance as he entered alone, [and] at once excited laughter, and his gestures and speech, which are of an apparently lazy character, with his humor and paradoxical ideas, kept his audience in the best humor for over one and a half hours."

Part of the entertainment factor of Twain's 1872 lecture appeared to be his own long introduction of himself, which criticized typically flattering introductions and admitted "the only public introduction that had ever delighted [Twain] was by a man who, when doing so, said he knew nothing about Twain except that he was never in a penitentiary, and that he could not understand why not."

Five years later, Twain returned to Baltimore to view the rehearsal of a play in Baltimore's Ford's Theater (also known as Ford's Grand Opera House) he was co-writing with Bret Harte, called *Ah Sin*, which was due to open in Washington, D.C. on May 7, 1877. As was the case with many of Twain's relationships, tension mounted between Harte and Twain, as well as among Twain and the production's actors. Twain wrote to his lifelong friend, author and critic William Dean Howells, from the rehearsal in Baltimore on April 27, 1877, observing: *There's a combat going on . . . between two men in every-day clothes, who rave & roar & fell each other with imaginary chairs & shoot each other with imaginary pistols . . . [and] all the other actors & actresses sit within 6 feet of them & calmly converse about the reasonable price of board in Baltimore!*

Twain mailed two letters to Langdon during this 1877 trip. The letters uncover an extraordinarily intimate epistolary relationship that not only connected Twain and Langdon across state lines, but also enabled them to share the vision of some of the remarkable inventions and industry being constructed in Baltimore in the late-nineteenth century.

Twain's April 26, 1877 letter to Langdon is written on letterhead from Guy's Monument Hotel, "on the European plan, monument square, Samuel C. Little, Proprietor, Baltimore," which was formerly located at the corner of Calvert and Fayette Streets, and rented rooms for $1.25-$2.00/day and had, only fourteen years earlier, housed the military provost-marshal's quarters.

Monument Square, Calvert and Fayette Streets
Former site of Guy's Monument Hotel

The letter is a 32-page manuscript in itself, primarily detailing, through literary descriptions and visual sketches, the eccentric compound of "Alexandroffsky," a residential property which formerly faced Hollins Street and was located between Fremont Avenue, Poppleton, and Baltimore Streets. The property was built by millionaire Thomas DeKay Winans, who was the son of Ross Winans—"one of America's first multi-millionaires and a pioneer of railroading technology and development."

However, time took its toll and "[b]y 1929, the wreckers were pulling down the great chimney [of "Alexandroffsky"]. The city rejected buying the site for a park, and it remained a vacant lot for decades." The "Alexandroffsky" property is now part of the University of Maryland biotech park site near Hollins Street.

Many of the eccentric and pricey items from "Alexandroffsky" were auctioned off in the 1920's. The estate's lion statues were moved to the Baltimore Zoo in Druid Hill Park, where children continue to climb and pose on them for keepsake photos. "Crimea" was converted into Leakin Park, and the Orianda House, designed in 1857, survives to this day.

Ross Winans designed and built an array of transportation innovations, including the first successful locomotive used on the Baltimore and Ohio Railroad, the eight-wheeled rail car system, and newly designed "axels, bearings[,] trucks and carriages." Ross Winans's sons, Thomas and William Louis, continued their father's legacy in railroad expansion, helping to

71

engineer the first Russian railroad line between St. Petersburg and Moscow in 1843. The influence of spending many years in Russia was reflective in the names of Thomas Winans's homes in Baltimore: "Alexandroffsky" (in tribute to the Czar) and "Crimea" (his summer estate consisting of over a thousand acres in West Baltimore).

Twain's awe at "Alexandroffsky" is apparent throughout his entire letter to Langdon, as he tours the sprawling property and shares his discoveries. Another literary giant, Jules Verne, was equally inspired by the Winans family inventions and modeled his submarine in *Twenty Thousand Leagues Under the Sea* after Ross Winans's cigar boat.

Twain begins his narrative of "Alexandroffsky" by recounting his first unsuccessful attempt to enter Thomas Winans's home, during which time *[t]he porter & his wife said Mr. Winans was out, & that all the young gentlemen were absent from the city.* Obviously, the porter is describing only the upper-class, white "young gentlemen" in the city, as the working-class men are still present on Winans's property, as Twain shortly views first-hand. Twain's access to "Alexandroffsky" was only possible because of his privileged status as a prominent nineteenth-century man of a particular social class and race, which he recognizes, noting, *it costs money to run that place & pay those 30 or 40 workmen & servants.*

Not long after Twain's first unsuccessful attempt to enter "Alexandroffsky," he is approached by a carriage coupé from within which Winans hails Twain and invites him to tour the grounds as a guest. Once inside the estate, Twain describes the entryway, party room, and saloon to Langdon, noting particularly interesting inventions, such as automated water and central heat and gas lighting systems. In addition, Twain includes drawings of various unusual utilities and home fixtures to help Langdon to visualize the scene. Some of the early sketches in the letter include a fireplace with logs that are restricted from tumbling forward, triangular tables which fit to form hexagon-shaped card tables, and self-lighting gas burners for illuminating Winans's saloon—which was capable of seating 250 People. Twain uses the second person voice in his tour of the house which directly invites Langdon into the setting: *If you wish to go down cellar to see the wilderness of water tanks*

& various sorts of pipes . . . you turn a knob, & a table & a couple of chairs make you shudder by proceeding to turn slowly & solemnly down on their sides to the floor. In this way, Langdon is a fellow companion in the discovery of the many unexpected inventions at "Alexandroffksy"—such as water-powered musical organs and indoor fish hatcheries—just as much as Twain is.

Twain then moves Langdon *up a winding stairway of so slight a slant that water molasses wouldn't have flowed down it,* taking her into a workshop that looks like it *had been struck by lightning,* as the room has *all manner of tools & traps & contrivances in it, & among other things a large, long-necked inverted glass funnel filled with infant brook-trout.* Again, Twain follows his description with a drawing, this time of a funnel with a stream of water at the bottom and a spout from the side near the top.

Twain's amazement at the eccentric Baltimore property is impressive, especially considering scholars and historians usually consider Twain to be the epitome of eccentricity. Twain declares to Langdon: *Everywhere you go in this house you find mysterious knobs, springs, cranks & other sorts of automatic deviltries . . . & similar creatures fairly swarm in every nook & upon every coign of vantage.* Winans's inventions, like live creatures, are reborn through Twain's personal letters to Langdon, as they take life and action once again when reaching Connecticut—and again, historically, upon reaching readers in the twenty-first century.

We entered Mr. W.'s (bedroom), Twain continues on page twelve of his April 26, 1877 letter to Langdon. *Chaos is no name for it! Yet it was orderly to him. He knew where to put his hand on each of the million things in it.* Twain also notes Winans's unusual heating system for his bedroom, contained in a water tank installed directly under the bed, and two cords—one which, upon being pulled, introduced different levels of air (street, ventilated, house temperature) and one which unfolded a sign outside of Winans's bedroom door, which read: *Asleep.*

The marvels continue to reveal themselves inside the estate, as well as in Twain's letter, including a little steam-engine run by water-power and *a thing which you could step on, & instantly your weight was registered on a dial.* Twain's vision and observations drive the letter, yet Langdon remains the motive behind Twain's eyes—his second lens in viewing Winans's one-of-a-kind home. Twain holds Langdon's hand (metaphorically and epistolary-wise), as he walks her through "Alexandroffsky." In this way, Twain's love for Langdon guides his capture of the extraordinary qualities of this former Baltimore estate, as much as his pen does.

Final stops on Twain's physical and epistolary tour of the Winans property include a carpenter shop, a library and music room, a cellar/furnace room, an outdoor piping room, a machinery shop, an indoor horse arena, a skating rink, an artist's quarters, stables (containing multiple carriages and horses), and a garage. Inside the garage, Twain is particularly fascinated by Winans's coupé, with its *plate-glass top—an invention of his for getting sunshine without snow, in winter.* Again, Twain invites Langdon directly into the scene, further depicting the carriage's sunroof customization: *You pull a string & slide a blue silk curtain along if you want to temper the sunshine.*

As the "tour" ends, Twain excuses himself, stating, *I am so given to forgetting everything that I resolved I would tell you something about this wonderful establishment before I had a chance to forget it.* Readers remain grateful that Twain did take the time to recount his experience at the Winans estate for his wife in the form of a personal letter.

In contrast with Twain's lengthy April 26, 1877 "Alexandroffsky" letter, Twain's second piece of correspondence mailed to Langdon from Baltimore—the very next day—is a short, double-sided correspondence card dated April 27, 1877. On the postcard, Twain states that he *had a jolly adventure last night with a chap from the 'Eastern Shore'—you must remind me to tell you about it when I get home.* Due to Twain's decision not to write about this particular day in detail to Langdon, readers remain in the dark about Twain's adventure with the Eastern Shore "chap" and his *4 hours in the State Prison to-day, after rehearsal.* Unlike Twain's April 26, 1877 letter, the only details about Twain's April 27, 1877 day that remain are his admittance to Langdon that *it would take a book to hold all I saw & heard. Am too tired (to-night) to write.* We can only imagine the invaluable descriptions and sketches that Twain would have provided of Maryland's State Prison in 1877 if he had not been too tired to write to Langdon that night.

Seven-and-a-half years later, Twain returned to Baltimore for a short stop during a four-month reading tour with writer and critic, George W. Cable.

Photograph of writers Mark Twain (left) and George Washington Cable autographed by both, from their "Twins of Genius" lecture tour of 1884-1885

The (Baltimore) Morning Herald reviewed one of Twain and Cable's Baltimore readings:

> Mark Twain no sooner put his head outside the flies than the audience began to laugh as well as applaud. There was something indescribably droll about the very look of the man. He, too, wore the conventional swallow tail. He came forward with a lazy air. It was as much as he seemed able to do to drag one foot after another. His dark, iron-grey hair was brushed back. He has a heavy brownish moustache. As he walks he stoops slightly. He never smiles. When he says anything that creates laughter, he simply pauses, throws his head a little on one side and peers sleepily out of the corner of his eye. His favorite use of his hands is either to scratch the back of his head or with the outside of his thumb to rub his half-closed eyes.

Cable wrote a personal letter to his wife during this Baltimore stop on November 28, 1884, in which he describes Twain and "Southern" Baltimore: *Nov. 28, 1884; Baltimore/ I am again in the retiring room. Mark is making the house roar as only a Southern audience can. It is an immense house too, although the rain has poured all day long.*

Twain follows suit in writing to Langdon from Baltimore the next day. His November 29, 1884 letter begins with the mention of the recent departure of Ross Revillon Winans from his company. Ross Revillon Winans was the son of Thomas DeKay Winans (the guide of Twain's tour seven-and-a-half years earlier through "Alexandroffsky") and grandson of Ross Winans. Twain then uses his typical sarcastic word play to downplay the importance of Baltimore's most prominent academic President at that time: *[W]e dine with President Gilman of Johns Hopkins University, or President Hopkins of John Gilman University, darned if I remember which.*

Twain's November 29, 1884 letter also provides updates on the marriage statuses of the Winans and Whistler families and includes information about an upcoming meeting with R.M. Johnston, the author of the *Dukesborough Tales*. In addition, Twain informs Langdon *that dam Goddard has called with some social proposition or other, which we can't accept,* referencing the famed reporter and civil rights activist who was also the president of Baltimore's Shakespeare Club at that time.

The letter ends with Twain's expression of gratitude for family pictures that Langdon has included in a recent letter. On the reverse side of the letter is a dual apology/explanation regarding Twain's correspondence schedule: *I don't write every day, but often I write twice a day to make up.*

In a letter dated January 10, 1870, sent from Albany, New York, Twain admits to Langdon, *[b]ut I am blessed above my kind, with another self—a life companion who is part of me—part of my heart, & flesh & spirit—& not a fellow-pilgrim who lags far behind or flies ahead or soars above me.* And, three days later, in a January 13, 1870 letter, pledges his loyalty to Langdon, which includes her approval regarding one of his favorite vices: *I shall treat smoking just exactly as I would treat the forefinger of my left hand; If you asked me . . . to cut that finger off, & I saw that you really meant it, & believed that the finger marred my well-being . . . I give you my word that I would cut it off.*

Twain kept all ten of his fingers throughout their marriage, yet it hasn't been until recent decades that Langdon's major role in Twain's life (as evident through their intimate letters) has been seriously validated by scholars and historians. The preservation of Twain's personal letters to Langdon has been center stage in this effort, allowing Twain's and Langdon's relationship and Langdon's identity to be more clearly defined.

Newly discovered letters between Twain and Langdon were released as recently as 1995 by the University of California Press, prompting a "new" Langdon to emerge, which broadens perspectives of Twain to include a man perpetually influenced by his heart and love for Langdon. In "The Olivia Myth: Letters Reveal a Truer Picture of Samuel Clemens' Wife; Her Influence on His Work," Gretchen Kell reviews the most recent volume of Twain's published letters, edited by Michael Frank, who explains that it wasn't until the mid–1990s that "we get a sense of [Twain and Langdon's] mutual dependence, of their real partnership. They had a strong, lasting marriage . . . until she died in 1904."

Frank asserts that Langdon has "changed from being perceived as a 'passive, sickly, prudish individual who was a censor of [Twain's] work and had no sense of humor' to a 'wife supportive of her husband's writing, an equal and active marriage partner and a young woman with great vitality, despite the sickness and tragedy in her life'." Before that time, "Olivia Clemens [had] developed in a legendary sort of way," due to the fact that "[n]o one had the facts," and no one was looking to intimate letters as a legitimate venue for locating evidence.

Twain's Baltimore-based letters to Langdon continue to uncover this new vision of their marriage, as well as new and unfiltered views of a late-nineteenth-century port city that held innovative discoveries, wonders, and mysteries for its prominent and privileged residents and visitors—whether in the chaotic invention hoarding of the Winans's eccentric estate, in the onstage and offstage drama of the city's rehearsing actors, or in all of the other local sights that Twain did not have the time or energy to document.

Twain's descriptions and sketches of what he saw in Baltimore during his short visits highlight the city's unique mixture of tradition and invention, public and private enterprises, and social and geographical landscapes and inequities. Twain's quote about Thomas DeKay Winans's bedroom—*Chaos is no name for it! Yet it was orderly to him*—mirrors Baltimore's history as a city of contradictions. Twain's letters to Langdon capture this juxtaposition, and in doing so, allow us, as readers, to also accompany Twain (and Langdon) on his outsider's tour of Baltimore's former insiders' visions.

Chapter Six

Unfiltered Words and Unconvinced Perspectives

Letters between Ralph Waldo Emerson
and Lidian Jackson Emerson

Lidian Jackson Emerson and Edward Waldo Emerson/*1840*

Ralph Waldo Emerson/*1846/Johnson*

Ralph Waldo Emerson
Barnum's City Hotel
Monument Square
Baltimore, MD

Lidian Jackson Emerson
Concord, MA

---

*Have the good angels, or that more sombre Spirit that loves you so well,
Prevailed over your thought by night & by day?*

-Ralph Waldo Emerson, Jan 8/9 1843

Lidian Jackson Emerson
Concord, MA

Ralph Waldo Emerson
c/o Charles Bradenbaugh, Esquire
President of the Mercantile Library Assoc.
Baltimore Street and Holliday Street
Baltimore, Maryland

**My turn of expression is so very happy that I think you
must believe the time of my breaking forth into verse is
at hand.**

-Lidian Jackson Emerson, January 10, 1843

Thirty-four years before Twain wrote to Langdon to share his view of Baltimore, another nineteenth-century prominent writer and thinker wrote to his wife to declare his perspective of the city while touring and lecturing through the Mid-Atlantic states. That writer was Ralph Waldo Emerson, who visited Baltimore while speaking about New England in 1843. Not only did Emerson, like Twain, share his vision of nineteenth-century America to his audience in Baltimore, but he also created his own history of the port city through his direct accounts of his observations during his lecture tour. Through their intimate letters to their wives, born in the same block of Monument Square, Emerson and Twain preserved Baltimore's lack and excess of vision, capturing an early American city that presented surprises and voids at every street corner.

Ralph Waldo Emerson's desire to find new and welcoming philosophical and literary audiences and contemporaries in the Northeast and Mid-Atlantic regions brought him to Baltimore in January of 1843, where he addressed the Mercantile Library Association on the merits of "New England," and the "Customs, Genius, and Trade of New England." In "Emerson and Baltimore: A Biographical Study," George E. Bell notes that this date was sixteen years after Emerson visited Baltimore for the first time, at age twenty-three, during "a winter's health trip of several months in the *South*—Emerson's first trip outside New England."

The Baltimore American and *Commercial Advertiser* attempted to capture the highly philosophical and intellectual level of Emerson's January 17, 1843 lecture:

> The subject was "New England." We cannot attempt a synopsis of the lecture. It abounded in thoughts of a deeper kind than are usually embodied in popular addresses—in views comprehending a large range—and it was marked by a felicity and propriety of diction and manner well calculated to secure the favourable estimation of the listener.

While in Baltimore, Emerson stayed at Barnum's City Hotel in Monument Square. Barnum's City Hotel, located at the southwest corner of Calvert and Fayette Streets, was considered "the country's most renowned hostelry at the time" and helped to establish Baltimore as a trendy and notable city during the nineteenth century. The hotel was built in 1825 and torn down in 1889, replaced by the Equitable Building (Baltimore's first sky scraper) in 1891. Some of Barnum's City Hotel's most renowned guests included Washington Irving, John Wilkes Booth (and co-conspirators), John Quincy Adams, and Charles Dickens. In fact, in 1842, the year before Emerson's visit, Dickens declared it "the most comfortable of all hotels in the United States."

Former site of Barnum's City Hotel (Equitable Building)
Monument Square

Emerson's letters, including correspondence to Jackson, were initially published by Columbia University Press in 1939, whereas selected letters of Jackson, including some correspondence to Emerson, were not published until 1987, by the University of Missouri Press. Viewed together, the letters exchanged between Emerson and Jackson reveal a relationship that extended past one of domestic husband and wife, as their communications regularly discuss transcendentalist aims alongside familial and career issues and logistics. In Emerson's letters, accounts of lectures and travel intertwine with concerns for family and associates at home. Jackson's letters depict not only a concerned and supportive wife and mother, but also a skeptical participant within the Transcendentalist movement. Emerson's and Jackson's correspondence showcases a sharing of societal criticism and analysis, visionary applications, and literary knowledge, as well as the desire by both parties to remain intellectually connected, in spite of their long-distance geographical separations during Emerson's travels.

Upon his Baltimore arrival in 1843, Emerson immediately reports on his accommodations to Jackson in a letter dated January 8/9: *I am very well lodged & fed in what I believe Dickens called the best hotel in America.* Dickens, as well, mailed letters from Baltimore, though he did not leave any preserved *intimate* letters along his path, as his wife traveled with him during his stay in the city.

The March 23, 1842 issue of the *Baltimore Patriot and Commercial Gazette* noted Dickens's stay at Barnum's City Hotel less than a year earlier, during the same time that Washington Irving was passing through the city on a lecture tour:

> Charles Dickens.—This distinguished author has been in Baltimore for the last two days, and left this morning in the Susquehanna Railroad line for Columbia. Mr. and Mrs. Dickens received at their rooms at the City Hotel the ladies and gentlemen who extended to them the courtesies of social intercourse, and were entertained privately, as far as their limited sojourn with us would admit. Washington Irving was also in Baltimore, and left this morning for New York, whence he sails for Madrid early in April. It was very pleasant to meet in the social circles these distinguished representatives of American and English literature. Mr. Dickens made a visit yesterday to the Maryland Hospital and Penitentiary, as he takes a deep interest in studying human nature in such receptacles of misfortune and crime. The civilities extended to him in Baltimore were very quiet and unostentatious, and such as must have been gratifying to his feelings as a man.

Baltimore offered a combination of urban innovation and small town setting for many nineteenth and early-twentieth-century prominent figures, including Henry James, who described the city in his 1906 article, "Baltimore": "[T]he natural pitch of Baltimore, the pictorial, so to speak, as well as the social, struck me, once a certain contact established, as that of disinterested sensibility." Like many other visitors, James immediately noted the contradictory nature of Baltimore as a city caught between the North and the South; in fact, James remaps the location of Baltimore and the amalgamation of the North into the South not as a question of *where*, but of *when*. James observes:

Wonderful little Baltimore, in which whether when perched on a noble eminence or passing from one seat of the humanities, one seat of hospitality, to another—a process mainly consisting indeed, as it seemed to me, of prompt drives through romantic parks and woodlands that are all suburban yet all Arcadian—I caught no glimpse of traffic, however mild, not spied anything 'tall' at the end of any vista.

Like James, Emerson struggles to find an accurate manner to depict and differentiate Baltimore from other cities.

The Catholic influence Emerson finds, in contrast to the Protestantism permeating New England, is central in his vision of the city: *high mass in the Cathedral here, & with great pleasure . . . It is well for my Protestantism that we have no Cathedral in Concord . . . I should be confirmed in a fortnight. The Unitarian church forgets that men are poets. Even Mr. Frost himself does not bear it in mind.*

Other contrasts that Emerson notes in his Baltimore-based letters to Jackson include climate and vegetation observations: *Here is today the mildest climate, we left the snow half way between N.Y. & Phila. And here canary birds cages hang outside of the windows and myrtle trees or something looking very like myrtle grow in the open air in a neighboring yard.* Emerson regularly uses "Massachusetts' culture as his yardstick" in viewing Baltimore *through* New England, and in sharing that comparative map of the city with Jackson.

Emerson does not hold back in confessing the lack of enlightenment in Baltimore to Jackson: *I cannot hear of any poets, mystics, or strong characters of any sort.* Emerson's search for intellectuals within Baltimore society leaves him disappointed in both the lack of leaders and in the lack of extraordinary qualities in the city, and he suggests to Jackson that *[p]erhaps there is nothing very distinctive in the population.*

Emerson emphasizes his intellectual dismay through a question-and-answer recounting of his initial inquiries into Baltimore's 1843 literary and scholarly scene:

Have you any libraries here—"None"
Have you any poet?—"Yes; Mr McJilton."
Who?—"Mr McJilton."

Any scholar?—"None."

In addition, Emerson declares the once prominent history of Baltimore—via its prominent men—now in decline: *Charles Carroll the [last surviving] Signer [of the Declaration of Independence] is dead, & Archbishop Carroll is dead, and there is no vision in the land.*

Bell clarifies that when "in the evening of January 7, 1843, Emerson arrived in the Baltimore and Ohio Railroad depot on Pratt Street, he was aware that Charles Carroll was dead. [Emerson] was also sensitive to the change that had occurred and was occurring in the nation, the change which was to bring about between 1840 and 1861, what Carl Bode termed the 'modern shape' of the nation's culture."

"Though couched in humorous satire," Bell explains, "Emerson's view of Baltimore and her people belied a deeper disaffection for the South; and his dark attitude, first evidenced in [his] Baltimore [letters] and later confirmed in his trips in the South, continued over the years." Like many other prominent figures of his time, Emerson's consideration of Baltimore as a southern city coincided with his residence north of the city's borders and his own comfort with New England culture and geography.

As Emerson's vision of Baltimore is conditionally filtered by his relationship to Massachusetts, so is his January 8/9 1843 letter to Jackson: *[H]ow is all with you at home? those two young things that are left there with you? . . . How fares my gracious mother? And how my sister dear? And Henry brave & good? And how did Charles Lane speak to the Lyceum?* Here, Emerson is referring to Charles Lane, a social reformer who promoted transcendentalism and the utopian community of Fruitlands, a 90-acre farm community Lane purchased in Harvard, Massachusetts in 1843. The Lyceum movement, popular in New England during the nineteenth century, established regular meetings which combined instruction and entertainment with educational and social topics.

Emerson's concern for home includes correspondence inquiry about his prominent New England contemporaries, as well as desired health updates from Jackson, who suffered from perpetual depression, anxiety, and hypochondria, in addition to physical and psychosomatic ailments. His January

8/9 letter asks about Jackson's mood, via metaphorical means: *[H]ave the good angels, or that more sombre Spirit that loves you so well, prevailed over your thought by night & by day?* Emerson remarked later in their marriage that "the Lord made [Jackson] curiously. She is so sharp & dignified with her morale, and keen as a mathematician on some points—and yet she has many holes in her mind." One of Jackson's doctors theorized that Jackson "was diseased from a nonhygienic life, meaning irregularity in eating, sleeping, and exercising . . . [sustaining] an introverted practice of watching an organ, thereby perverting drugs from having any effect on it."

When Emerson reaches his Baltimore hotel five days later on the evening of January 14, 1843 after a visit to Washington, D.C., he finds two letters waiting from Jackson, prompting him to complete the letter he started on the train earlier that afternoon. The in-transit portion of the letter includes a summary of his Washington, D.C. visit to the Patent Office's United States Exploring Expedition Exhibit, where Emerson describes fascinating artifacts from around the world, including *stones & sand & volcanic scoriae from the Antarctic Continent* and *coming from our friends the Feejees, tattooed heads & baked heads.* His view of the Capitol, he states to Jackson, is that of *a homeless place a kind of hotel the whole town & very well accommodated hotel showy and comfortless, a pic nic party in winter.* In dramatically larger letters, Emerson temporarily interrupts this letter to Jackson to write to their daughter, Ellen. He asks: *Is Ellen a good girl? Papa thinks of her in Bal-ti-more,* underscoring early evidence of the stressed pronunciation of the city's name—from an outsider's perspective.

It took another half century after Emerson's letters were released for Jackson's letters to find a publisher, not unlike the delayed and/or neglected publication of many other women, wives, and less prominent historical correspondent partners. It is not surprising that Jackson's January 10, 1843 letter to Emerson is actually addressed to another prominent man: Charles Bradenbaugh Esquire, the President of the Mercantile Library Association. *The Notes Supplementary to the Johns Hopkins University Studies in Historical and Political Science* clarifies that "[a]t the time of its organization in 1839, the [Mercantile Library] Association occupied rooms at the corner of

Baltimore and Holliday streets, but in 1848 its library was removed to the basement of the Athenaeum building, on the corner of St. Paul and Saratoga Streets, where the most active period of its existence was passed."

My dear Husband, Jackson begins her January 10, 1843 letter to Emerson, *Your letter came to day and contents us well, except that we are sorry to find you can give us no good news of the foot, so soften the ill news as you may be turning it into a jest. If Baltimore air does not heal it perhaps a Baltimore doctor will. We will look for a better account of it soon.* Jackson's letter not only addresses Emerson's physical health, but her own mental health, as well, equating manic expression with literary creation: *[m]y turn of expression is so very happy that I think you must believe the time of my breaking forth into verse is at hand.*

Like Emerson, Jackson's letters regularly rely on figurative expressions to provide much more than logistical information about health and family; the letters produce their own metaphorical conventions, linking Emerson's and Jackson's lives to their literature. For example, Jackson concedes, *I wish I had some new stories to tell you of our beautiful poem Edith, and our excellent prose Ellen; but have none.* The children join the literary offspring being produced by Emerson and Jackson in their prominent house and home front in Concord, Massachusetts, in addition to their published and unpublished writing.

Dolores Carpenter admits in the introduction to her anthology of Jackson's collected letters that "[e]xtensive cutting of household trivia has been made." A primary aim of the book, Carpenter acknowledges, is to provide public accessibility of Jackson's letters not just for Jackson's sake, but also to "shed light on notable contemporaries" in Jackson's time (xxviii)— that is, predominantly prominent *men* in Jackson's time.

Jackson highlights these "noteable contemporaries" in her January 10, 1843 letter mailed to Emerson in Baltimore, recounting that *[w]e had a meeting of the wise men and their admirers on Sunday evening—(Mr Wright was in Boston) and though I do not believe many were edified all must have been amused.* Jackson's sarcasm regarding "the wise men and their admirers" exposes a woman who was much more than an extension of Emerson, his contemporaries, and their vision of the future for the human race. Her skepticism of Charles Lane's proposed "Fruitlands" is evident in her depiction of his Utopian vision: *[T]he poor human race are to be allowed in the future, if they would walk in innocence, to walk in no clothing but white linen spun by their own hands . . . when we are innocent there will be no need of warm cloaks boots or umbrellas—we shall be at such perfect liberty so independent of times and seasons, that we can well wait within doors till the weather be fine & the walking good.*

In her letter to Emerson, Jackson recreates her previous conversations with the "wise men," including Bronson Alcott, the father of Louisa May Alcott: *Mr Alcott was descanting on the iniquity of formal exchange—"brother should give to brother all superfluity—brother should be free to take whatever he wanted of brother wherever he could find it" &c- I answered "that might do, Mr A if there were but two people in the world".*

Jackson's critique of Bronson Alcott's ideas is unapologetic and slightly contrary, as she tells Emerson how *Mr Alcott proposes to abridge labour and live a life of ease and independence by certain ways of proceeding, one of which is to make your own chairs in a form of simple elegance and cover them with linen of your own spinning and weaving.* Jackson's response to Alcott's proposal is cleverly crafted, yet still discounted by Alcott in his final determination of the actions and decisions of the "wise men": *When I said with a sigh that I would rather be excused from washing those linen covers preferring to dust common painted chairs, he said "O but we will contrive a way to simplify washing[").*

The voices of New England's prominent, nineteenth century "wise men" dominate Jackson's letter, not only in content and her summary of their words, but also in their obvious influence on her life, and American culture at that time. Jackson's reference to all of the attendants by "Mr." or "Dr." demonstrates the gender norms and formal separation in public stature, between herself and the men at the meeting, and Jackson's commentary provides tremendous insight into not only the prominent men of her time (including her husband), but also a woman who was allowed inside the realm of prominent and privileged men, but was required to remain an outsider because of her gender and perspective.

At the end of her lengthy January 10, 1843 Baltimore letter to Emerson, Jackson's voice takes on a more managerial tone. She updates Emerson on his traveling and lecturing schedule and offers alternative options, as well as financial trepidations. Jackson then follows her business updates and advice with an apology: *I wish I had resolution to write better*—ironic self-effacement, especially since Jackson's humility contrasts with her confident voice and competent narrative skills, as well as with her ability to manage Emerson's career decisions by mail from several states away.

In Robert D. Habich's review of Carpenter's *Selected Letters of Lidian Jackson Emerson*, he notes how "[b]eset by depression and morbidly obsessed with impending death and illness, [Jackson] could also be witty, acerbic, sociable, and passionately committed to the reform movements of the day, from animal rights to abolitionism." Jackson's introverted tendencies and dissociated perspective seem to vanish when she was freed from the boundaries of her external society and its public writing standards, at least such is viewed in her Baltimore-based letters. Within the safety and structural freedom of her personal communication, Jackson's oversensitivity found a literary route and temporal home away from the judgments of those prominent figures around her in Concord. The intimate letter form gave Jackson a wider societal and literary map in which to be a solid debater, thinker, and writer, contrasting with her reputation as a life-long weak and semi-invalid woman.

Carpenter explains that behind Jackson's oppositional tendencies, stood a woman with a "philosophic mind and [unfiltered] deep emotions," though evidence is primarily only visible through the preserved proof of Jackson's personal letters. In constructing her epistolary words to Emerson, due to the need to transmit familial, social, and career management information, Jackson likely did not realize that her own intimate letters would provide the same movement—private transference of public knowledge—to future audiences wanting to know more about the Emersons' private lives, and the settings that housed them.

The anonymous writer of an 1849 article, "Emerson as a Lecturer," inaccurately predicted Emerson's future, precisely because the article's writer neglected the intimate letter as a legitimate venue for preserving history: "We wonder if he will ever die like other men? It seems to us he will find some way of slipping out of the world and shutting the door behind him before any body knows he is going. We cannot believe he will be *translated*, for this would be too gross a method of exit."

In searching for appropriate transcendental post-life translation, Emerson's life-time readers and listeners did not consider the future publication of Emerson's (and Jackson's) unpublished words: "He is more likely to be evaporated some sunshiny day, or to be exhaled like a perfume. He will certainly not be seen to go—he will only vanish." Luckily for Baltimore, the rest of the world, and posterity, intimate letters by Emerson and Jackson were preserved and eventually published. Emerson and Jackson have not *vanished* from the literary and historical landscape; their literary perfume still exists for generations of future critical thinkers and writers to inhale.

Emerson's preserved letters, especially those intimate ones to Jackson, and Jackson's preserved letters, especially those intimate ones to Emerson, have allowed Emerson—and Jackson—to linger more deeply in the world than most. By composing personal letters which lived in private spheres during their physical lifetimes (and continue to communicate through public spheres during their literary and historical lifetimes), Emerson and Jackson transcended their own life spans in a way they likely never imagined. The final translation of Emerson—and Jackson—may not be one from language to language, but from the private sphere to the public sphere in mapping an unfiltered and convincing vision of a future world, which briefly considered Baltimore to be within the acceptable scope of its boundaries.

Chapter Seven

Unfolding (and Unspoken) States

Letters between John and Abigail Adams

John Adams, *1766/Benjamin Blyth*

Abigail Adams, *1766/Benjamin Blyth*

Mrs. Adams

At Mr. John Adams's

Braintree

For
The Honorable John Adams Esq.
at
Baltimore
in Maryland

The century before Emerson and Twain noted their observations of Baltimore while touring along the east coast, the symbol of the city was not represented by a large marble monument dedicated to the country's first President in Monument Square, but in the small and growing community that was quickly and not so quietly developing around Baltimore's harbor. John Thomas Scharf's *History of Baltimore City and County* describes how "[t]he adoption of the Declaration of Independence was nowhere received with livelier demonstration of joy than in Baltimore. On the 11th of July [1776] it was printed in the Maryland Gazette, and on the 29th it was proclaimed at the court-house in the presence of the independent companies and militia, amid the loudest applause, accompanied with salvos of artillery." Soon after the adoption, Congress aimed to strengthen its military forces and began to include many men from the Baltimore area in its army.

As tension and fighting escalated over the next few months, the Congress, fearing an attack on its Philadelphia meeting location, moved its winter session to Baltimore on December 20, 1776. Within this unfolding and newly independent government landscape, a group of significant intimate letters was exchanged between John Adams and Abigail Adams—composed while John traveled for congressional duties and Abigail remained on their farm in Braintree, Massachusetts.

The Adamses's intimate letters provide much more than an extended timeline regarding the congressional and military events unfolding during the late 1770's. In fact, it is Abigail's role as an active correspondent that enables their private letters to transform into an active history encounter, what Joseph J. Ellis refers to in the foreword of *Dearest Friend: Letters of Abigail and John Adams*, as a "recover[y] [of] the messiness of history-as-it-happens." As opposed to filtered public narrative, the Adamses's letters provide "a historically correct account of the American Revolution [which] would emphasize the utter confusion of the actors in the drama, including himself, who were making it up as they went along."

John and Abigail Adams are unique in the vast amount of letters that they wrote and in the preservation of their letters (about 1,160) during the late 1700's and early 1800's. Ellis feels it is "[i]n part the size of the full correspondence [which] makes it the most revealing exchange between a publicly prominent husband and wife in all of American history." Compared to other early Presidential couples, this is quite remarkable, as "Martha Washington destroyed all but three of the letters she and George exchanged." Abigail, too, suggested this demise early on for her correspondence to John in 1774: *You will burn all these letters, least they should fall from your pocket and thus expose your affectionate Friend.* Yet, many biographers and critics have theorized that the Adamses likely knew that their letters would be archived; thus, the role of that knowledge in the careful preservation of their correspondence.

In "First Thoughts: Life and Letters of Abigail Adams," Gelles emphasizes that "[l]etters, then became the lifeline of Abigail's relationship with John," as their correspondence became their main communicative network during John's chronic and lengthy absences. However, John's and Abigail's letters were not always exchanged through a regulated postal system, especially since the postal system was also newly developing, often unreliable, and vulnerable to interception.

The Adamses's letters were regularly delivered within the first consistent circuit of US correspondence delivery, that is—communication transported due to the geographical movements of prominent men. Such is the case with the Adamses's Baltimore correspondence, which is available in the *Adams Family Papers: Electronic Archive* through the Massachusetts Historical Society.

Tis a great grief to me that I know not how to write nor where to send to you, Abigail begins her January 26, 1777 letter: *I know not of any conveyance. I risk this by Major R[ic]e who promises to take what care he can get it to you.* John, too, informs Abigail of their short-term correspondence delivery network in his February 15, 1777 letter, written 2 weeks after his arrival in Baltimore: *Mr. Hall, by whom this Letter will be sent, will carry several Letters to you, which have been written and delivered to him, several Days. . . You may write to me, in Congress, and the Letter will be brought me, wherever I shall be.*

The receipt of letters helped to confirm safety and wellness, especially when external factors were influencing daily, weekly, and yearly events for the Adamses, as well as the rest of the new country. Abigail admits such in her January 2, 1777 letter: *I long to hear of your arrival and to get one Letter from B[altimor]e. The Situation will be New and afford me entertainment by an account of it. At all times remember in the tenderest manner her whole happiness depends upon your welfare.* John, too, demonstrates personal anxiety over the lack of communication from Abigail on February 10, 1777: *It is now a Month and a few days, since I left you. I have heard nothing from you, nor received a Letter from the Massachusetts.*

John's ability to write regularly to a confidante outside of his public sphere allowed him the freedom to express his frustration with the unfolding country's leadership and his own doubts about the future. His February 17, 1777 Baltimore letter notes how *My Disposition was naturally gay and cheerful, but the (awful [crossed out]) Prospects I have ever had before me and these (illegible) cruel times will make me melancholly.* Much of John's Baltimore correspondence to Abigail includes his articulation of his struggle to stay positive and well among a country and people who often seem incapable of integrity, optimism, or sustained health. Additional Baltimore-based letters by John include suggestions for the unfolding country and its Congressional leadership on economic, leadership, military, and medical fronts, as one might expect from the man who would become the second President of the United States . . . 20 years later.

John's observations of and suggestions for Baltimore stem from his Congressional time in the city, written while Congress temporarily housed itself in a large building located on the southwest corner of Sharpe and Baltimore Street from December 20, 1777- February 27, 1777. The house was owned by Henry Fite, and was the house farthest west in town, and one of the largest in 1777.

Henry Fite House/"Congress Hall"
Courtesy of the U.S. State Department

John's impressions of the unfolding city fill his pages to Abigail. His first letter written to Abigail from Baltimore on February 2, 1777 confirms his safe arrival, the day before, even with *the longest Journey, and through the worst Roads and Worst Weather.* His reaction to the city is mixed, and he explains to Abigail that *Baltimore is a very pretty Town, situated on Petapsco River, which empties itself into the great Bay of Chesapeak. The Inhabitants are all good Whiggs, having sometime ago banished the Tories from among them.* Yet, he notes, *[t]he Streets are very dirty and miry, but every Thing else is agreeable except the monstrous Prices of Things. We cannot get an Horse kept under a Guinea a Week.* Horse parking is not the only overpriced item in Baltimore in the late-eighteenth century. John does not hold back his dissatisfaction with the cost of lodging in his next letter, written five days later on February 7, 1777. Yet, the same letter also emphasizes his desire to raise the interest rate in the country, in addition to initiating taxes.

John's desire to understand Baltimore's religion, laws, and culture—from its Catholic majority to its particular customs—prompts him to compare himself to Ulysses in his heroic quest for diversity and moral transcendence beyond his home setting and traditions. Within this quest, he is directed to *a Place called Fells Point, a remarkable Piece of Ground about a mile from the Town of Baltimore,* as he writes in the first of two letters written on February 10, 1777.

Fell's Point is a key feature within John's depiction of Baltimore, as he observes, records, and translates the landscape to Abigail—*a Bason before the*

Town . . . a Fortification erected, on this Point with a Number of Embrasures for Cannon facing the Narrows which make the Entrance into the Harbour. John takes significant time in his letters to recreate Fell's Point and its surrounding features through detailed explanations so that Abigail, like so many other female spouses of prominent men, can also "see" the city in which he is temporarily living. This remapping sends another chapter and charting of John's journey along the Eastern states and toward the presidency, directly to his most trusted reader and "dearest friend."

Reading the Adamses's Baltimore-based letters, however, we quickly see that there is another unfolding event which is causing just as much anxiety and uncertainty for the Adamses, as the unfolding state of the country, Congress, and the city of Baltimore. *I am sure no separation was ever so painfull to me as the last*, Abigail states in her January 26, 1777 letter, explaining that *[m]any circumstances concur to make it so—the distance and the difficulty of communication, the Hazards which if not real, my imagination represents so, all conspire [to] make me anxious, as well as what I need not mention.* Editors Margaret A. Hogan and C. James Taylor of *My Dearest Friend* note Abigail's use of "circumstances" "[i]n keeping with eighteenth-century norms that disapproved of explicit mentions of pregnancy in letters (the polite euphemisms were 'in circumstances' or 'stately'), [and] neither Abigail nor John directly mentioned the situation until Abigail came close to 'her time'."

John is extremely concerned about Abigail's pregnancy, yet he is unable to directly state this, even in his private communication to her: *I am anxious to hear how you do. I have in my Mind a Source of Anxiety, which I never had before, since I became such a Wanderer*, John writes in his February 10, 1777 letter. *You know what it is. Cant you convey to me, in Hieroglyphicks, which no other Person can comprehend, Information which will relieve me. Tell me you are as well as can be expected.*

The fact that John, in his intimate letter, must utilize additional layers of privacy to receive information about the wellbeing of his pregnant wife seems a bit ridiculous when John is directly and critically discussing government figures, strategies, and future plans in the same letter. Gelles explains the discrepancy within a cultural framework, as "[t]he epistolary tone [of the eighteenth century] established varying degrees of intimacy." "Religion, for instance, was so acceptable a topic that people would write without hesitation, establishing a basis of consensus that would connect rather than alienate them," Gelles clarifies, yet, "[f]eelings on the other hand, would be more selectively expressed, and medical conditions or pregnancy, hardly at all." Thus, Abigail's pregnancy remains unspoken on the literal and public levels of the letter, yet the letter's private level—that of symbolic and indirect information—still speaks of its existence.

John's final letter written from Baltimore to Abigail on February 21, 1777 remains hopeful for the emerging country, its governing forces and cities, and his growing family, even amidst his concern and doubt. He ends this letter expressing parental hope—contrasting his frustration with the uncertain states unfolding around him with optimism for his sons' future: *I wish my Lads were old enough. I would send every one of them into the Army, in some Capacity or other. Military Abilities and Experience are a great Advantage to any Character.*

Little did John know his son, John Quincy Adams, would visit Baltimore 42 years later, in March of 1819, and pen the following observation in his own private diary: *The soldiers are good men and true. But the officers? The commanders! What with want of honesty in some and want of energy in others, the political condition of Baltimore is as rotten as corruption can make it.*

Additionally, John could not have known that five months later, on John Quincy Adams's 10th birthday— in the summer of 1777—Abigail would deliver a stillborn baby girl named Elizabeth, who would be their last child. This reality makes the Adamses's Baltimore-based letters even more poignant in the foreshadowing painted by both John's and Abigail's anxiety about the pregnancy, which is still unfolding through the correspondence as we read it in the twenty-first century, even if it is still "unspoken" on the page.

Ellis theorizes that even today, "(i)n most histories these personal factors are airbrushed out, leaving the outstanding public events to stand alone as the spine of the story. But the real story, told here, has multiple dimensions that defy any purely linear narrative." In fact, Ellis asserts, "John's [and

Abigail's] letters provide the clearest window that we have into the zigzazzy course of a revolution in the making" (ix). John's and Abigail's Baltimore-based letters, in particular, showcase a prominent outsider's view of the city and the country, and the influence of his communication within the course of unfolding history across public and private fronts—both needed and necessary to truly see unspoken history in its fullest reflection.

Part Three
Valves: Epistolary Medicine
Letters as Alternative Homes

Johns Hopkins Hospital, 1903

One need not travel far into Baltimore to find geographical markers related to its most famous writers. In turn, one need not travel far into Baltimore to find the imprint and impact of its world-renown medical institutions, especially Johns Hopkins Hospital. However, the role that intimate letters played in connecting these pivotal twentieth-century writers to the Baltimore medical community is less evident in the city's landscape.

The inability for Baltimore's top medical institutions to adequately treat serious physical and mental illnesses during the twentieth century indirectly caused partners to create alternative shared homes found only in the transporting pages of their correspondence. The same medical institutions also housed hidden communication which was written due to the need of support, validation, and companionship of its own staff and administrators. Navigating a physically and emotionally intense, elite, male-dominated field, letters were often the only medicine available to alleviate the ailments of the minds, bodies, and souls of women in early American science.

Chapter Eight

Literary and Physical Sanctuary

Letters by H. L. Mencken and Sara Haardt

H. L. Mencken/*Ben Pinchot, photographer*
Theatre Magazine, August 1928

Sara Haardt/*1920-1929*

H. L. Mencken
1524 Hollins Street
Baltimore, Maryland 21223

Miss Sara Haardt
Maple Heights Sanitarium
14913 York Road
Sparks, Maryland 21152

Sara Haardt Mencken
424 Union Memorial Hospital
Baltimore, Maryland 21218

Henry Louis Mencken
704 Cathedral Street
Baltimore, Maryland 21201

H--
704 Cathedral Street
Baltimore, Maryland 21201

Mrs. H. L. Mencken
Johns Hopkins Hospital
Baltimore, Maryland 21287

The Bad Boy of Baltimore. The Baron of Baltimore. The Sage of Baltimore. The German Valentino. The Lover. These are just a few of the labels that Henry Louis Mencken, the world renowned editor of *The Smart Set* and *The American Mercury* (predecessors of *The New Yorker*) and journalist for *The Baltimore Sun*, received during his lifetime from 1880 to 1956—the majority of it spent residing at 1524 Hollins Street in Baltimore, Maryland.

1524 Hollins Street
Childhood home of H. L. Mencken

Mencken once summarized his residence at Hollins Street: "I have lived in one house in Baltimore for nearly 45 years. It has changed in that time, as I have—but somehow it still remains the same . . . It is as much a part of me as my two hands. If I had to leave it I'd be as certainly crippled as if I lost a leg." Mencken's prediction would prove bittersweet, as less than five years after marrying Sara Haardt and moving to Cathedral Street, he would lose Haardt to complications due to tuberculosis. After Haardt's death, Mencken returned to live at his house on Hollins Street, eventually becoming severely disabled from a stroke that left him barely able to read, write, or speak for the last eight years of his life.

Jon Winokur notes in *The Portable Curmudgeon* that the fact that Mencken "was deprived of his ability to read and write [after his stroke] was a grotesque irony that wasn't lost on Mencken himself: shortly before Mencken's death on January 29, 1956, a visitor mentioned the name of a mutual acquaintance who had died in 1948 [the same year of Mencken's stroke]. Mencken thought for a moment and finally said, 'Ah, yes, he died the same year I did.'"

Mencken's public reputation as a Baltimore bachelor whose definition of love was "the delusion that one woman differs from another" also differs with the private man seen in the intimate letters he devotedly wrote to Haardt throughout their courtship and marriage. Mencken's early intimacy philosophy, that "the great secret of happiness in love is to be glad that the other fellow married her," would prove to be in direct contrast with the private reality of a man who composed intimate letters to one woman for over twelve years and then constructed an extensive tributary archive for her after her death.

Haardt and Mencken's letters are housed in the Special Collections Archives at Goucher College in Towson, Maryland, along with bound collections of Haardt's stories, notes, school notebooks, publications, scrapbooks and other literary artifacts. There are published and unpublished materials in the collection. For example, an unpublished homemade Valentine's Day tri-fold card made by Haardt is constructed from a collage of cut-out magazine pictures and includes a short message from Haardt which reads: *I worship you, H. M. / Guess who?* Another unpublished handwritten note by Haardt rests in the 1931 file, delivering an unfettered and daily glimpse into Haardt and Mencken's marriage: *Darling/ I have gone out for a while. / I will be back in time to fix your supper.* It is this contradiction between Mencken's public irreverence and private acceptance of intimacy that makes his and Haardt's letters so intriguing.

Who was the real Mencken? Was he really Baltimore's "Bad Boy" or just Baltimore's "good boy" in waiting—for a woman who could match his intellectual and literary capabilities? Do Mencken's unfiltered and private intimate letters paint a more honest picture of him than his public and professional works? Mencken scholar and author Marion Elizabeth Rodgers echoes the flaws of traditional biography in attempting definite representations, citing Mencken, who declared that people's "personalities, so to speak, are not revealed brilliantly or in the altogether, but as shy things that peep out, now and then, from inscrutable swathings, giving us a hint, a suggestion, a moment of understanding." Mencken and Haardt's letters can surely be mapped as "inscrutable swathings," giving contemporary readers a fresh understanding of Baltimore's heart as an epistolary sanctuary for literary and health desires.

Pre-Haardt, Mencken had the attention of many early Hollywood screen actresses, as well as stage actresses and dancers, and he was known to particularly enjoy the company of blonde women. In fact, it was an evening with Mencken that inspired Anita Loos to write *Gentlemen Prefer Blondes*, as she felt that Mencken was ignoring her conversation because of the fair-haired distractions around him.

How, then, did the young, Southern brunette win Mencken's heart? Was it Haardt who transformed Mencken? Or was it Mencken, himself, who secretly shifted his personal stance from *The Bad Boy of Baltimore* to *The Loving Fiancé of Hollins Street*? Regardless of the pivotal shift, Fred Hobson and many other scholars confirm that "by the late 1920's it [was] clear that America's most notorious bachelor [was] smitten." In reply to his shocked public, who wondered how Mencken could be embracing the very institutions he formally insisted on dismantling, Mencken stated "with mock seriousness: 'I formerly was not as wise as I am now . . . the wise man frequently revises his opinions. The fool, never'." Mencken's contradictory stances, including those related to intimacy, continued to sustain him and his writing throughout his life—but only if he revised them into new contradictions.

Mencken met Haardt in 1923 after giving a lecture at Goucher College, where Haardt was teaching after recently graduating from the college. Haardt was an unlikely match for Mencken in many ways; for one, she was 18 years his junior and was from Montgomery, Alabama—a state Mencken regularly ridiculed. Additionally, Mencken, a fifteen-year old 1896 valedictorian graduate from Baltimore Polytechnic Institute, "missed few opportunities to disparage the higher education that he had spurned."

Yet, Mencken and Haardt were actually quite similar, as both were extremely smart, witty, productive, and maintained astonishing work ethics when it came to their writing. As well, both writers pushed themselves to produce, even while suffering from physical pain. Mencken had debilitating bouts with hay fever, and Haardt was often admitted to Baltimore hospitals for long-term residencies because of various illnesses which plagued her from birth. Indeed, the majority of Mencken and Haardt's personal letters, dated from May 1923 to April 1935 (the month before Haardt's death), revolve around their health issues and the necessity of their letters in sustaining their marital relationship and literary production.

Mencken and Haardt's early letters document secret Prohibition-era drinks and meals at Baltimore restaurants, such as Fritz Baum's and Marconi's. Their lunch and dinner dates blossom into a "slow and uneven" courtship, which some speculate "was partly due to the 40-something Mencken living with his mother at the family home on Hollins Street." During all of Haardt's repeated hospitalizations, she and Mencken exchange literary advice, support, and encouragement through their letters. Mencken initially takes on the role of mentor in his correspondence with Haardt, though Haardt's role quickly transforms from mentee into that of an intellectual and literary peer.

Mencken's identity, too, shifts as his relationship with Haardt unfolds. Sara Mayfield notes in *The Constant Circle: H. L. Mencken and His Friends*, that "[t]he carapace of H. L. Mencken, the hardboiled critic we soon discovered, had been developed as a defensive mechanism by an extremely sensitive man." That critic, the Mencken who had supporters believing his written voice could dismantle or transform any institution or condition around him, was helpless to achieve what was likely his most challenging iconoclastic desire: to dismantle the pending terminality of his wife.

In the end, Mencken's well-crafted and persuasive words proved ineffectual in stopping Haardt's premature death, even within the privileged care of Baltimore's highly regarded doctors and medical facilities. Mencken was unable to subvert the public health ill known as tuberculosis. He remained helpless to watch his wife succumb to the disease. No amount of wit can mask the devastation present at the end of Mencken and Haardt's letters, stopped short, mid-conversation, between Mencken and Haardt in April 1935, a month before Haardt's death. Mencken and Haardt's intimate letters cease, without closure or a clever rejoiner, just as abruptly as their letters began in Baltimore twelve years earlier, with one person reaching out for the other through epistolary means—in search of literary and physical connection. Mencken's personal diaries (unsealed twenty-five years after his death in 1981) expose the depth of his loss, including his admittance years after Haardt's death, that "[i]t is a literal fact that I still think of Sara every day of my life, and almost every hour of the day."

While Haardt is the one who initiates their correspondence, Mencken is the one who writes the last preserved entry to Haardt at Johns Hopkins Hospital, a message lacking an epistolary response—and a message leaving Mencken with a broken self. While Mencken's public persona might initially seem contradictory to the person revealed in his letters to Haardt, a closer look at Mencken and Haardt's correspondence uncovers a communicative realm functioning independently of public society. Viewing Mencken and Haardt's letters as a singular alternative home and sanctuary enables the correspondents to un-problematically form contradictory selves, as the letters function under intimacy standards, versus public expectations of early twentieth-century Baltimore.

Haardt first writes to Mencken twelve days after attending his tongue-in-cheek lecture on "How to Catch a Husband" at Goucher College on May 8, 1923: *Before I get stuck in Alabama for the rest of the summer I want you to get me straight on this short-story business,* she begins the letter before asking, *How does one do it? I mean, see you.* Haardt's appreciation for Mencken's academic irreverence is clear from the start of their correspondence. Immediately, she establishes her commonality with Mencken in wanting *to write something and I am wondering if anything could come out of a Baltimore second-story back or a messing with elephant-eared academics.*

Goucher College, St. Paul Street, 1920
Sara Haardt's Employer and Alma Mater

Known at Goucher as "Soulful Highbrow," Haardt is also the one who secures the time and place of their first lunch date at _Domeniques_ in her second letter to Mencken, dated May 26, 1923. Haardt admits that she, too, is bored by the mundanity within Baltimore's academic circles: _These have been dog days at college and I am looking forward to the meeting as the only inspiring thing that could happen._

Before long, Haardt and Mencken are exchanging letters at a rapid rate, Mencken initially taking the lead in providing Haardt writing and publishing advice, in addition to suggesting proper methods and places for drinking. The willingness of many Baltimore restaurants to ignore the Prohibition rules provides Mencken a welcome setting to develop his relationship with Haardt, and to reinforce one of his "favorite doctrines that 'the whole world would be better if the human race was kept gently stewed'."

Mencken's early letters to Haardt follow her from Goucher College on St. Paul Street to Maple Heights Sanitarium, in Sparks, Maryland, where she was hospitalized for acute bronchitis and tuberculosis in 1924. Never completely removed from his role of editor and reviewer, Mencken suggests reading material to Haardt in his letters while she is hospitalized at Maple Heights. His correspondent role gradually shifts from mentor, to peer, to intimate partner.

Former Maple Heights Sanitarium, Sparks, Maryland
Residential Treatment Facility for Sara Haardt

Mencken downplays Haardt's experience, and health challenges, in his letters by exaggerating the potential fictions that could be taking place at Maple Heights: *Has the janitor yet tried to kiss you? It is coming! Also, you say nothing about the nurses getting drunk. What is the matter with them? Again, nobody has yet stolen your shoes. Be patient!* As with almost all of his letters, Mencken's humor steals the show and reveals intellectual sarcasm intent on surpassing institutional boundaries and physical chambers. His recommendation for Haardt: *[D]on't let a small flare-up alarm you . . . I suspect that my own temperature ranges between 85 and 108. It is never over 92 on Sunday mornings, when the church bells ring.* Within the sanctuary of his personal letters with Haardt, another Mencken quickly surfaces, one at odds with the self who was often credited with saying, "[m]arriage is a wonderful institution, but who would want to live in an institution?"

Mencken and Haardt continued to date from 1927–1930, writing regularly while Mencken edited the *American Mercury* out of New York, and Haardt temporarily moved to Hollywood in an attempt to make some money from screenwriting. 1928 saw Haardt's return from a frustrating and unprofitable stay in Hollywood, while Mencken continued to travel and write, spending time in Chicago at the Democratic and Republican National Conventions of that year's Presidential Campaign. 1929 brought the stock market crash and the beginning of the Depression, as well as Haardt's extended stay at Union Memorial Hospital after she had her tubercular kidney removed.

Union Memorial Hospital
Residential Treatment Facility for Sara Haardt

By the end of 1929, Haardt's "health was on the decline, [and] so too was Mencken's popularity." The couple, amidst the shifting of public opinion toward Mencken and Haardt's increasing debilitating health issues, became engaged to be married in late August 1930.

On April 25, 1930, Mencken writes to Haardt while she is visiting her family in Alabama to inform Haardt of his family's reaction to their engagement. Mencken states that his family received the news well and he is *as happy as the boy who killed his father.* He ends the letter: *I bust with love!* Mencken's words are a far cry from his initial public position on marriage, that "[t]he worst of the marriage is that it makes a woman believe that all other men are just as easy to fool."

Two months before their official union, Haardt writes to Mencken concerning the progress of new home furnishings at their new house—704 Cathedral Street—the home they will soon be sharing as husband and wife. Haardt's last letter sent to Mencken at his Hollins Street address spills with excitement as she discusses the new flooring and furniture arrivals for the house: *It is all very thrilling,* she pens, *and I think the place is going to be sweet. And it will be perfect with you!*

704 Cathedral Street
Marriage Home of H. L. Mencken and Sara Haardt

Haardt continued to struggle with her health after their marriage, and Mencken continued to travel while editing *The American Mercury*. During these separations, Haardt's fluctuating temperature is a recurring theme in many of their letters, becoming a regulator as it functions as a public measurement of Haardt's health status and a private gauge of her and Mencken's marital and literary status. For example, while battling pleurisy at Union Memorial Hospital on March 10, 1931, Haardt highlights a moment of temporal ease: *Last night my temperature was normal for the first time (it was your kiss).*

Even after Haardt is officially released from Union Memorial Hospital later that year to recover at home on Cathedral Street, she continues to feel detached and disconnected, as Mencken is often away on out-of-state assignments. Haardt's loneliness permeates her perception of their house, as seen in her June 12, 1932 letter to Mencken, who was covering the Republication convention in Chicago at that time, letting him know that *[i]t has rained, a fine drizzle, since early morning, and the house is as quiet as a tomb.*

Much to Haardt's dismay, Mencken returned to Baltimore after the close of the Republican Convention in June 1932, only to leave for Chicago, once again, to cover the Democratic Convention. Haardt writes an extremely emotional letter to Mencken on June 21, 1932, beginning with her admittance that *[i]f I weren't patriotic, and a born Democrat, I'd be weeping. I could scarcely bear for you to go this time.* Haardt's desire for Mencken is unable to be contained with customary words in this letter. She spells *I Love You/Love You* horizontally and vertically on the page, ending her letter with three rows of X's and the number: *1,000,000,000,000,000,000,000,000.*

Two years later, Haardt took what would be her last physical trip to her childhood home in Montgomery, Alabama to visit her dying mother. This time, Mencken is the one left alone in their home on Cathedral Street, and he is not happy about the separation, writing in his September 6, 1934 letter to Haardt: *If there is no letter tomorrow morning I'll begin to pitch and heave. It now seems a month since you left, and the house begins to be as lonely as the ruins of Carthage.*

The comparisons between Mencken and Haardt's half-empty home and other places of death and despair begin to heighten in intensity and frequency at this point in their letters. Yet, while Mencken regularly laments Haardt's absence, he still finds time to update Haardt on his beer adventures: *Tonight I am going down to Highlandtown with Buchholz to try Hausner's beer.* Mencken's delivery of such discoveries, however, is now met with a much weightier last call, as he admits *I hate to think of coming home to the empty house. This love business wears me down.* Mencken was also being worn down at this point in his life by his opposition to FDR, who skillfully played Mencken's words against him about the incompetence of journalists at the Gridiron Dinner in December 1934, which FDR attended after returning from his Thanksgiving holiday in Warm Springs, Georgia with his wife, Eleanor Roosevelt.

Haardt is admitted to Johns Hopkins Hospital a few months later and is diagnosed with meningitis. Mencken, too, continues to be plagued with respiratory issues during this time. The Cathedral Street house meant to be a marriage home becomes a constant reminder of physical separation, rather than a geographical union.

Johns Hopkins Hospital
Residential Treatment Facility for Sara Haardt

Mencken and Haardt's letters circulate back and forth from 702 Cathedral Street to Johns Hopkins Hospital during early 1935, discussing health, writing, reading and alcohol. A deeper sense of parallel suffering and longing emerges in their letters. For example, Haardt writes to Mencken from Johns Hopkins Hospital on March 31, 1935, updating him on her temperature (*normal*) and her displeasure with the thought of him alone in their house. The next day, Mencken updates Haardt on his blood pressure (*very good for an old boozer*) and his displeasure that *[t]he house is horribly lonely and gloomy.*

Haardt's health rapidly declined throughout April and May of 1935. Mencken's brother, August Mencken, noted Mencken's "attitude toward doctors and medicine would be roughly parallel to a Catholic's attitude toward priests . . . He thought they could do miracles . . . as a matter of fact, sometimes they do, but not as often as he thought." By the end of April, Haardt had only a month left to live, yet she composes a telegram on April 30, 1935, relating time-sensitive information concerning Mencken's forthcoming article galley for *The New Yorker*.

The last published letter by Mencken, addressed to Haardt at Johns Hopkins Hospital in April of 1935, is also minimal in content—yet exponential in its heartbreak. Mencken cannot deny the undisputable shift of intimacy and spousal geography at this point in his and Haardt's lives, even in his letters. His letter contains a mixture of practical help and lyrical exposition. No longer does he write about Haardt's temperature or his latest alcohol discovery; he does not offer any clever or witty words to camouflage the inevitability of Haardt's death.

In the letter, Mencken merely provides instructions to Haardt for the connection of a record player, with the declaration that, after successful installation, *[y]ou will then bathe in art.* Mencken's directions for the record player are simple, lacking literary pretense or flair, and his closing line is bleak and final in its metaphorical reach, exposing the mourning "Henry" found in mid-town Baltimore—the man behind the public artifice known simply by the last name "Mencken": *The house is a desert./ H.*

Mencken's life would continue to be a personal desert without Haardt. After Haardt's death, Mencken's public persona would once again become his dominant identity, as he would acknowledge that "I was fifty-five years old before I envied anyone, and then it was not so much for what others had as for what I had lost." Mencken's loss of Haardt, for all intents and purposes, was also the loss of his intimate self, as evidenced through his and Haardt's letters.

Mencken's and Haardt's mutual understanding of each other's literary desires, as well as their negotiation of a private life which differed from the expectations of their public society, is the underlying Baltimore love story found within their letters. Mencken, the man who once said, "If I ever marry, it will be on a sudden impulse—as a man shoots himself," would spend the rest of his life wishing for his "wound" to return. For a few long years, yet short in the time of a life-span, Mencken and Haardt's letters would provide a sanctuary in the midst of their separated Baltimore addresses, a home where the compromised human body was secondary to intimacy and where a personal Baltimore literary society (made up of only themselves) determined its own iconoclastic standards and expectations.

Chapter Nine

Literary and Mental Sanctuary

Letters by F. Scott and Zelda Fitzgerald

F. Scott Fitzgerald/ *1921, Gordon Bryant*

Zelda Fitzgerald/ *1922, Metropolitan Magazine*

Mme. X
Phipps Clinic
1800 Orleans Street
Johns Hopkins Hospital
Baltimore, Maryland 21287

Dearest D.O.
La Paix
York Road
Towson, Maryland

Scott Fitzgerald
1307 Park Avenue
Baltimore, Maryland

Zelda Fitzgerald
Sheppard and Enoch Pratt Hospital
6501 N. Charles Street
Baltimore, Maryland 21204

F. Scott and Zelda Fitzgerald often crossed paths with H. L. Mencken and Sara Haardt in Baltimore's small literary scene during the 1930's. In fact, in *Mencken & Sara: A Life in Letters*, Marion Elizabeth Rodgers notes accounts of "early morning visits of F. Scott Fitzgerald [to 704 Cathedral Street], demanding [Mencken and Haardt] listen to portions of his new novel, *Tender Is the Night*." "Often this would occur just when Sara had drifted off to sleep," Rodgers clarifies, "and then Fitzgerald would write an apologetic note to 'The Venus of Cathedral Street'."

Scott and Zelda's intimate letters, like those of Mencken and Haardt, provide a window into the epistolary homes built apart from physical houses in Baltimore—literary rooms constructed because of long-term residencies in Baltimore's medical institutions. Scott and Zelda's letters passed through Baltimore's postal system during the winter and spring of 1932, while Zelda was a resident at the Phipps Clinic at Johns Hopkins Hospital, and from May 1934 to April 1936, during which time she received care at Sheppard and Enoch Pratt Hospital. Constantly striving for literary and mental sanctuary, the Fitzgeralds' letters unveil the desperate and passionate people behind the iconic "Fitzgeralds" and the epistolary living spaces created to contain those lives.

Scott and Zelda first met in July 1918 in Montgomery, Alabama, where Zelda grew up with Sara Haardt. Zelda had recently graduated from high school and Scott, almost 22 years old, was stationed at Camp Sheridan, Alabama as a lieutenant in the infantry. The two were quickly engaged, but they soon broke up after Scott accidentally received a letter Zelda had intended to mail to another suitor. They became reengaged in November of 1919 and married in April of 1920. The 1920's was a decade-long whirlwind for the couple, as Scott published six books, and Zelda, one of the most well known flappers of her time, quickly became known as the "it" girl of the era.

The popular couple relocated constantly within the United States during this time and often vacationed abroad in Europe. The Fitzgeralds also spent two extended stays in Hollywood, in 1927 and 1931, in hopes that Scott would gain financial and screen writing success. Zelda had her first severe breakdown in 1930, as she and Scott were in the process of moving to Paris. Soon after, Zelda entered the Prangins Clinic in Nyon, Switzerland, where she stayed until September 1931. After a short return to Montgomery, Alabama, the Fitzgeralds relocated to Baltimore in January 1932, where H. L. Mencken referred Scott to Adolf Meyer, chief of Psychiatry at Johns Hopkins School of Medicine, and Zelda was checked into the Henry Phipps Psychiatric Clinic of Johns Hopkins Hospital.

Henry Phipps Building, Johns Hopkins Hospital
Residential Treatment Facility for Zelda Fitzgerald

Scott and Zelda lived apart from one another for the majority of their married lives after 1930 (including most of their time in Baltimore). Their intimate letters provided a shared home they could still both inhabit while Zelda received full-time residential psychiatric care—that is, until Scott died at age 44 from alcohol, heart, and tuberculosis-related issues.

Kendall Taylor explains in *Sometimes Madness is Wisdom: Zelda and Scott Fitzgerald, A Marriage* that Scott and Zelda were "[c]o-creators of their own legend in which fantasy and fact often blurred. They found it increasingly difficult to perceive or accept reality." The Fitzgeralds' manic creative strengths and debilitating psychiatric and physical weaknesses created a powerful geographical and metaphorical storm which was intensified because of their inability to live together in a traditional marital home. Nowhere is this magnetism better viewed than in their letters.

During Zelda's first stay in Baltimore at Johns Hopkins Hospital, in the winter of 1932, Scott returned to their rented home in Montgomery,

Alabama so that their daughter, Scottie, could complete her academic year. During these months, while visiting Zelda in Baltimore, Scott "usually stayed at the Rennert Hotel, only a short walk from Mencken and Haardt's house on Cathedral [Street], and often stopped by to discuss Zelda's condition." Sara Haardt's health condition, at this point, was also in decline.

"What is extraordinary is that the years of Zelda's greatest discipline as a writer," Sally Cline notes in *Zelda Fitzgerald: Her Voice in Paradise*, "coincided exactly with those years when she was first hospitalized, and then diagnosed with schizophrenia." Zelda actually finished her autobiographical novel, *Save Me the Waltz*, only a month into her program at Johns Hopkins Hospital.

In one of Zelda's first letters written to Scott from the Phipps Clinic in February 1932, she describes Baltimore from beyond the window in her room: *The row of brick houses from the window at night present a friendly conspiracy to convince us of the warmth and pleasantness of life—but its cold here and there is no communication yet between the swept chilly pavements and the sky.* Here, Zelda captures the meeting point of contradiction in her description, the urban warm-coldness of the city, breaking open the community façade that pretends to care when visible.

Zelda daydreams while on chaperoned downtown excursions, finding some of the décor she views to be *perfect for the house that we'll never have*. That house is the imaginary rendezvous spot that Zelda continually desires throughout her life, both in and outside of her letters. It is the house where longing and satisfaction room together—a place, Zelda explains, caught between dreams and reality.

Zelda was not naïve in acknowledging her struggle with sanity. In keeping in line with Mark Twain's analysis, "When we remember we are all mad, the mysteries disappear and life stands explained," the majority of Zelda's Baltimore letters to Scott regularly attempt to depict and clarify the challenges of her daily living. One of her February 1932 letters is particularly acute in its capture of her mental and physical status and her surprise at finding her own face reflected in the mirror, as opposed to a visualization of ancient and spiritual suffering—the internal countenance that she faced on a daily basis. By finding the accurate words to articulate what she is feeling, Zelda attempts repeated justifications in being the cause behind her physical separation from Scott.

Zelda's mental and physical confinement, via her hyper-sensitive mind and her institutional housing, is often counterbalanced in her letters to Scott with observations and analysis of the people and places outside of her pre-scribed boundaries. Zelda draws tangible links between her contemporary experience and historical landscapes as she depicts the Baltimore wharves as *Whistlerian*. Baltimore becomes Zelda's connection to the past as she links herself to the genealogical traces of the city's early European American immigrants, validating her place, along with Scott, in twentieth century America. Her observations of the city usually contain both analytical and metaphorical constructions, giving her letters to Scott a mixture of unfil-tered narrative and critical manipulation.

Since the present moment was a consistently restless and transitory place for Zelda, her sensory descriptions are grounded in the unrelenting longing of a perpetual outsider plagued with unattainable desires. Zelda's kinship with Scott was built on this joint need for a shared, unconventional, creative life which would admit and actively pursue these desires. In a letter written in February and March of 1932 from the Phipps Clinic, Zelda reflects on Scott's role as the guide in their atypical history and existence as she tries to find some balance in their separated lives. She emphasizes: *I wish we had a house, dear.*

At the mercy of mental illness and an institutionalized schedule, Zelda views her physical rooms, mind, body, and life like a tourist. Baltimore, too, provides her with a lodging ticket whose dates of stay are temporary and indefinite. A February/March 1932 letter to Scott admits Zelda's fancy for the city and its potential as a future entertainment outlet for herself and Scott. Indeed, Zelda can't help but to fantasize a future in which her and Scott's problems will diminish or disappear, and they will be able to enjoy the luxu-ries of the city as traditional residents. Another February/March 1932 letter to Scott depicts Zelda's view of Baltimore as *a marvelous place, a prosperous, middle-age distinguished lawyer with many artistic hobbles [sic] sort of place.*

Zelda's descriptions of Baltimore are prisms of magnified evidence of "life stands explained" from her own unique set of internal binoculars. However, Zelda's vision held a prescription unavailable and unattainable to most in her society, including her doctors at Phipps. Zelda's creative lens, while intellectually and artistically stimulating, failed to cushion the brutal consequences that her hypersensitivity caused for herself and for those around her. Scott Donaldson states in *Fool for Love: F. Scott Fitzgerald* that it was during Zelda's initial stay in Baltimore that she shifted from offering herself in "tender disguises" in her letters to Scott to "identifying 'her plight' with that of the 'crazy people' she saw in Phipps."

An early March 1932 letter is a prime example of Zelda's instinctual ability to break categorical boundaries to create a home where polarized effects were the norm, not the deviance. In this letter, she compares her life to *a vast black shadow* that she must *swallow* as she accepts the fact that there are creative worlds that, as hard as she might try, are impossible to fully reach and comprehend. By recognizing there is a further existence beyond her psychological reach, Zelda's justifies her madness within a larger spectrum of human experience.

Zelda's continual desire to define and represent her extreme states produces striking metaphors in her letters to Scott. Another March 1932 letter describes how *[s]ometimes I feel like a titan and sometimes like a three-months abortion.* An additional March 1932 letter describes Zelda's internal disconnect and powerlessness, as she clings to tangible and concrete figures and images in an attempt to provide some sense of clarity for Scott. She writes, *my spiritual carcass is being gnawed by superior vultures to myself and I am bleak in spirit and sometimes I don't care that I am a bitter wretch and sometimes I don't care that I am most unusually happy.* Zelda is aware of the extremity of her mania and, while often displeased with her institutionalized status at Phipps, she never writes that she has been wrongfully committed or incorrectly diagnosed.

"[W]hile [Zelda] complained about the hospital's environment," Taylor explains, "inwardly she was grateful for the clinic's protection [from herself]." For Zelda, true madness was enforced inactivity. Even when Zelda was physically confined and medicated within the Phipps Clinic, it was impossible for her mind to rest. Her letters depict the hospital staff as part of the institutionalized walls and furnishings around her. Nameless nurses carry out their duties as Zelda documents their actions in her letters to Scott. For example, Zelda's March 1932 states that *there's a nurse who sticks her head in the door to see that I don't strangle myself on the shadows every five minutes or stab myself with the rays of light.*

Zelda's intensity is both her weakness, as it takes its physical and mental toll on her health and relationships, and her strength, as it provides the ability to create stunning descriptions and figures of speech in her writing. Caught between the world of the imagination and the world of reality, Zelda constantly struggles to locate herself in her life and in her words.

While Zelda resided at the Phipps Clinic during 1932, Scott rented a fifteen-room Victorian house in Towson, Maryland named La Paix. In *Zelda: A Biography* Nancy Milford describes the property in vivid detail: "It had gables and porches, fifteen or sixteen rooms, and it was full of night sounds, dark and rather down at the heels." The house was located on York Road near Sheppard Station. La Paix was raised in 1962 to "clear the land for St. Joseph Hospital." Fitzgerald actually found the property with the help of Edgar Allan Poe, Jr., a relative of the famous writer and a Princeton classmate of Scott.

La Paix Cottage, Towson, Maryland
Rented home of F. Scott and Zelda Fitzgerald
(Courtesy of the Maryland Historical Society, Image ID# PP105.07)

La Paix provided a transitional existence for Zelda, as she was allowed to visit La Paix during the mornings and return to Phipps in the afternoons. What was intended to be a smooth reentry into society, however, turned out to be an intensification of emotional battles for Scott and Zelda. While living at La Paix, Scott continued to drink and battle chronic tuberculosis, and Zelda resented the strict schedules that Scott tried to enforce to stabilize her erratic behavior.

Complications and tragedies mounted at La Paix, as Zelda mourned the lack of success of her novel, *Save Me the Waltz*, which received poor reviews and sales when it was released in October 1932. Then, "there was a fire at La Paix [in 1933], which apparently started when Zelda burned some old clothes in a neglected upstairs fireplace," which left "the house badly damaged." To add to the turmoil, Zelda's brother committed suicide in August of 1933, and a month later Scott and Zelda's friend Ring Lardner died.

Scott's letters to Zelda during their La Paix years are often didactic; he attempts to explain Zelda's behavior to her in an authoritative manner, providing organizational and stabilizing advice for her life. His letters reveal his desire for direction, in regard to Zelda's behavior, through their content and their structure. Commanding and declarative paragraphs, lists, and analytical questions regularly address Zelda's actions and their consequences. The questions attempt to identify and categorize Zelda. Structured like an unconventional and ongoing graphic organizer, Scott tries to format and impose logic within Zelda's non-orderly mind.

In a letter written to Zelda from La Paix in 1932, Scott charges Zelda with not taking any responsibility in the enormous toll that her irrational behavior is placing on their entire family. He explains the unhealthy way that Zelda is morphing into her art, *becoming the dark tragic destiny of being an instrument of something uncomprehended, incomprehensible, unknown* and how Zelda *succeeded merely in crashing [her]self, almost me, + Scotty, if I hadn't interposed.*

Scott often dons the role of interventionist in his letters to Zelda, which is a bit of a paradox since he (as an artist and husband) also inhabited the dangerous realm between excessive creativity and self-destruction. Many biographers, including Cline, have noted how Scott and Zelda's marriage and writing were "dominated by Scott's increasing alcoholism and [Zelda's] own mental suffering, each of which nourished the other." Nowhere is this co-dependency more visibly captured than in their Baltimore-based letters.

Scott's desperation is clear in a letter written to Zelda in the summer of 1933. He discourages Zelda from "*shut[ting] yourself away,*" thereby causing the entire house to feel her tension and depression. In contrast with Zelda's letters from this time period, which express her desire for external urban adventure and shared creative experience with Scott, Scott's La Paix letters strive for internal psychological transformation (mainly on the part of Zelda), so that the couple might one day permanently reside within a physical home. *The schedule*, as Scott repeats in a letter written to Zelda in the summer of 1933, was the primary measure prescribed by Zelda's doctors to help her sustain a balanced existence. Scott explains that *the best protection is the schedule and then the schedule and again the schedule.*

The "schedule" did not work. In December of 1933 Scott and Zelda moved from La Paix to a smaller rented house in Baltimore at 1307 Park Avenue. Soon after, Zelda suffered a third nervous breakdown and had to be readmitted to the Phipps Clinic in February 1934. She remained at the Phipps Clinic until March of 1934, after which she was transferred to Craig House in Beacon, New York. In May of 1934, Zelda returned to Baltimore and resided at Sheppard and Enoch Pratt Hospital in Towson for the next two years while Scott continued to rent at 1307 Park Avenue.

1307 Park Avenue, Baltimore
Rented home of F. Scott Fitzgerald

Zelda's mental state fluctuated from 1934–1936, from productive mania to depressive silence, and she often heard voices. During this time, Zelda's simultaneous longing for and fear of Scott mirrored her own polarizing feelings about herself as a friend and enemy. She continually struggled to find sanctuary between the woman she wanted to be (on the page and in her mind) and the woman she saw in the mirror at Sheppard Pratt.

Sheppard Pratt Psychiatric Hospital
Residential Treatment Facility for Zelda Fitzgerald

Scott continued to direct and interpret Zelda's life for her during her residence at Sheppard Pratt, especially in regard to her daily habits, stressing the importance of organization and structure. Scott freely admits his anxieties caused by Zelda's institutionalization and their separated relationship, as evident in his May 31, 1934 letter, yet feels relieved to know Zelda is *within hearing distance again.* 1307 Park Avenue and Sheppard Pratt might have been within hearing distance, but the psychological distance between the spouses at these addresses continued to grow during 1934 and 1935, as well as any remnants of a possible future shared home.

Zelda's letters to Scott at 1307 Park Avenue from 1934–1936 are full of declarations of loneliness and longing, especially throughout the first weeks of her residence at Sheppard Pratt, during which time Scott was forbidden to visit her. Zelda is acutely aware of the mental and physical toll of her creativity, and she articulates this unabashedly in her letters. The artistic process, Zelda's June 14, 1934 letter from Sheppard Pratt demonstrates, is one not of selfish intention, but of shared human honesty.

Seldom is Zelda apologetic for these artistic leanings. She frequently uses descriptions of the natural world to create epistolary locations and situations where she is accepted without bias, just for being who she is. In this realm of landscape-presence, as John Wylie explains in "Landscape, absence, and the geographies of love," "self and world come close together, and *touch each other* and then go beyond even that, and become *part of each other*, intertwined in a 'phenomenological collapse of self and world'." Within this space, Zelda can intertwine Sheppard Pratt with her mind, combining synesthesia and personification in completely unique and unexpected routes and presentations.

On the one hand, Zelda's visionary scope is extremely impressive and holds the confidence and acuity needed to chart new territories of intimate geography. On the other hand, Zelda's visionary threads are fragile and frayed, and the stability of her mind is often sacrificed for a brilliant color choice or unpredictable shifts in design. The following excerpt, from a letter written to Scott in October 1934, shows Zelda's articulation of this trade-off through a self-inventory: *1.) I am lonesome. 2.) I have no relatives or friends and would like to make acquaintance with a Malayian warrior. 3.) I do not cook or sew or commit nuisances about the house.*

Within this context, rests the uncharted setting of Zelda's Baltimore residence: *The Sheppard Pratt hospital is located somewhere in the hinter-lands of the human consciousness and I can be located there any time between the dawn of consciousness and the beginning of old age.* Zelda explains to Scott, in surprising clarity, the crux of her predicament: *Life is difficult. There are so many problems. 1) The problem of how to stay here and 2) The problem of how to get out.*

Zelda's mental and physical state deteriorated during the summer of 1935. As Nancy Milford notes, "[t]hroughout June, July, and August she persisted in whatever ways were open to her to try to harm herself. She refused to talk about herself to anyone on the staff—her letters to Scott were her only release." In one of Zelda's letters from this time period, written in the fall of 1935, she beautifully captures the temporal qualities of life by admitting her inadequacy in sending anything *from an empty world,* especially in the fall season, a time of year which exemplifies the reality that *all times are sad from their transience.*

Time, for someone who could never feel comfortable in her own skin or in the present moment, was a constant reminder of her inability to attain full mental and physical health or satisfaction. Instead of seeing and experiencing people and places in the present time, Zelda immediately began to mourn their inevitable departures from her life upon their arrival. Living primarily in the metaphorical past or hypothetical future, Zelda continued to spiral into further hopelessness and confusion throughout 1935.

Zelda was transferred to Highland Hospital in Asheville, North Carolina in April of 1936, where she lived exclusively for the next four years. At this point, Zelda requests that Scott bring some of her memories from Baltimore: *a sense of the Baltimore streets in summers of elms and of the dappled shade over the brick, and of that white engulfing heat.* She, in return, will look for a small natural wonder for Scott, found somewhere hidden between the hills of North Carolina.

Zelda's perpetual hunt for that missing piece was her amazing strength and her tragic flaw, an unattainable desire which carried her from childhood to death in its personal embrace. Zelda wanted to discover the home of wonder, and the inevitable failure of its capture and sustainability is what fueled and destroyed her. Zelda's letters to Scott contain the closest approximation of the line between genius and madness that is likely able to be articulated. Zelda's ability to see, what Wylie describes as the "coinciding of [human and] landscape, of unifying the visible and the invisible, seer and seen, [not because of lack of access, but because it is] in fact the precondition" is what set her apart from others and continues to define her letters as extraordinary.

Scott eventually relocated from Park Avenue in Baltimore to Grove Park Inn in Asheville, North Carolina, so that he could be closer to Zelda at Highland Hospital. Scott's friends and family speculated that this was the point when Scott realized that he and Zelda would likely never live together again, prompting a deep depression.

In 1939, Zelda was stable enough to take an extended leave from the hospital. She and Scott traveled a bit during this year, including a trip to Cuba, which proved disastrous. After the Cuba trip, in April of 1939, Zelda wrote to Scott in New York City (where he was staying with his sister and brother-in-law) from the Hotel Stafford in Mount Vernon, Baltimore while in route back to Highland Hospital. The short note is typical Zelda, expressing extreme apology, intense gratitude, and exaggerated optimism—all at the same time. Less than two years after the note was mailed, Scott was dead. Eight years after Scott's death, Zelda perished in a fire in Highland Hospital at age 48.

No matter where Zelda lived, she remained a floating body, even while the people around her constantly built up blockages, hoping that resistance, schedule, and consistency would be enough to stop her from rushing down the seductive stream of self-destruction. Author Jeanette Winterson explains how "[p]art of our strangeness of being human is our need of boundaries, parameters, definitions, explanations," as well as "the need for them to be overturned." Zelda exemplifies the consequences of overturning—in beautiful depth and debilitating breadth—of a life which could not be lived without breaking boundaries.

Zelda and Scott's Baltimore-based letters grant readers the privileged ability to also see the visionary landscapes of epistolary residence and sanctuary that Zelda and Scott created in their minds and in their letters. Through a heartbreaking and exhausting journey into her own mind and body, Zelda's letters provide one of the strongest sources "committed" to understanding the creative condition. Scott's letters, as well, allow readers additional windows into his own struggle for self and spousal wellness within a literary life.

Like H. L. Mencken and Sara Haardt, F. Scott and Zelda Fitzgerald are typically viewed through their public works and their shared societal identities, versus their private communications and independent internal relationships. Remapping the famous literary couples' geographies through their intimate letters creates new homes within Baltimore that reveal the literary and health sanctuaries required for their temporary survival—a visceral map neglected on current websites and walking tours due to its location beyond the city's external boundaries.

Chapter Ten

Seeking Medical Sanctuary

Letters from Dr. Esther Loring Richards
to Dr. Abby Howe Turner

Esther L. Richards
by unidentified photographer
Courtesy of The Alan Mason Chesney Medical Archives
of The Johns Hopkins Medical Institutions

Abby Howe Turner

Dr. E. L. Richards
The Johns Hopkins Hospital
North Broadway
Baltimore, Maryland

Miss Abby H. Turner
Mount Holyoke College
South Hadley
Massachusetts

While Zelda Fitzgerald was a patient at the Henry Phipps Clinic at Johns Hopkins Hospital, writing intimate letters to her husband, F. Scott Fitzgerald, one of the directors at the Phipps Clinic, Esther Loring Richards, was also mailing her own intimate and confidential letters—to Abby Howe Turner, a fellow doctor also navigating the challenges and pressures of being a woman in early American science. It is more than likely that Zelda's letters sent to Scott, mailed to La Paix cottage in Towson, Maryland, physically touched inside the same postal bin that temporarily housed Richards's letters on their way to Turner at Mount Holyoke College. Perhaps, Richards was one of the nameless staff members that Zelda describes to Scott in her letters. These speculations occur, in part, due to the historical lack of archival research and preservation of women's letters and women in early American science. The lack of in-depth biographical and critical research on Richards and Turner, in particular, opposed to many of their literary and political contemporaries, immediately highlights the academic and public preferences for histories of prominent figures in the humanities and social sciences, versus those in the medical and traditional sciences.

Esther Richards and Abby Turner initially met at Mount Holyoke College, where Richards was an undergraduate student and Turner was a professor. Turner graduated from Mount Holyoke College in 1896 and served on its faculty from 1896–1901 and from 1904–1940. Richards graduated in 1910 from Mount Holyoke College, the same institution that Emily Dickinson attended for one year, from 1847–1848, at age sixteen. Miriam R. Levin notes in *Defining Women's Scientific Enterprise* that even though Dickinson did not graduate, she "drew on [Mt. Holyoke's] knowledge of the natural world to create [her] artistic works," much as Richards would draw on artistic frameworks to inform her contributions to the natural world and her correspondence.

Richards and Turner established an intimate friendship which continued for years and was nurtured by their extensive long-distance correspondence. Many of Richards's letters to Turner are accessible through the *American History and Genealogy Project* and span 1915–1932, the years during which Richards was a graduate student and faculty member at Johns

Hopkins Hospital. During this time, Turner was founding and advancing the physiology department at Mount Holyoke. Richards's letters to Turner, only published during the last decade due to the voluntary efforts of Mount Holyoke College alum, Donna Albino, share Richards's desire for female connection within the male-dominated world of early twentieth-century American science.

The Alan Mason Chesney Medical Archives of the Johns Hopkins Medical Institutions holds Richards's professional papers in "The Esther L. Richards Collection." While the archive is not digitized, the website describing the archive does list a small amount of biographical information about Richards, as does the "David Richards Family Papers"—a familial archive connected to the Massachusetts Historical Society. Esther Loring Richards was born in Hollison, Massachusetts in 1885 to David Richards and Esther Loring. After receiving her undergraduate degree from Mount Holyoke College in 1910, Richards earned her M.D. from the Johns Hopkins University School of Medicine in 1915 and then joined the psychiatric faculty at the Johns Hopkins Henry Phipps Psychiatric Clinic in 1917, where she was psychiatrist-in-charge of the outpatient department of the Phipps Clinic from 1920 until 1951. "The Esther L. Richards Collection" states that "[i]n addition to her medical and academic responsibilities, Richards was very active on the lecture circuit and gave a great deal of her time to community service."

Henry Phipps Building, Johns Hopkins Hospital
Employer of Dr. Esther L. Richards

The recipient of Richards's letters—Abby Howe Turner—was born in 1875 in Nashua, New Hampshire, to George Turner and Emeline Cogswell Turner. The "Turner Papers, ca. 1896–1960," from the *Mount Holyoke College Archives and Special Collections*, and the "Abby Howe Turner 1896" correspondence, accessible through the *American History and Genealogy Project*, contain the bulk of available biographical information about Turner. After receiving her undergraduate degree from Mount Holyoke in 1896, Turner studied at a variety of top tier institutions, including the University of Pennsylvania, the University of Chicago, the Harvard School of Public Health, the University of Copenhagen, and Radcliffe College. She became a full professor of physiology and zoology at Mount Holyoke College in 1913, where she founded the department of physiology and taught until her retirement in 1940.

Like many women of their time, Richards and Turner devoted weekly, if not daily, time to letter writing. Turner's diligence and devotion to the personal letter is evident from her vast correspondence collection exhibited in the *American History and Genealogy Project*. "Letters from Abby Howe Turner 1896" includes a short history of Turner's correspondence habits and several sender/recipient categories. Donna Albino notes that Turner "liked to write to her friends when she was away from campus. She kept carbon copies for herself, fortunately, and they are displayed here." Richards's letters to Turner are included in "The Esther Richards Letters," although no pre-served correspondence has been found to date that was written by Turner to Richards.

"Women's letters rarely just exchange information," Lisa Grunwald and Stephen J. Adler explain in *Women's Letters: America from the Revolutionary War to the Present*, "[i]nstead, they tell stories; they tell secrets; they shout and scold, bitch and soothe, whisper and worry, console and advise, gossip and argue, compete and compare. And, along the way, they usually with-out meaning to—write history." The history of (and found in) Richards's and Turner's letters (and of/in many of their female contemporaries' let-ters), including the role that women's colleges played in initiating countless long-term female/female intimate epistolary relationships, is sorely missing from current academic scholarship.

Albino explains that "some of [Turner's] correspondents returned her letters to them at some point (or their next of kin did) . . . [However, there are not any preserved copies of] the letters that [Turner] wrote to [Richards]." *Mount Holyoke College's Archives and Special Collections* also "could not locate any letters . . . [in their] correspondence materials in the files for both Esther Richards '10 and Abby Turner '98."

The experience of attending a liberal arts women's college was life-changing for Richards and Turner, and it propelled them to maintain a strong relationship with Mount Holyoke for the remainder of their lives—Turner, through her faculty appointment at the college, and Richards, through visits and correspondence. Richards and Turner's long-distance relationship, set into motion after Richards graduated and moved to Baltimore, was contingent on their continual cycle of correspondence. Their letters became a stable means of communication and a place of safety for expressing female intimacy, support, and companionship within their male-dominated fields of psychiatry and physiology. Viewing Richards's letters to Turner (and acknowledging the known, but unpreserved, letters from Turner to Richards) allows a much clearer, wider, and unfiltered glimpse into what it was like to be a pioneering American woman in the sciences during the early decades of the twentieth century.

Margaret W. Rossiter's *Women Scientists in America: Struggles and Strategies to 1940* includes Richards as part of "a colony of talented women scientists, employed and unemployed, formed around Johns Hopkins University in the 1920's and 1930's." Rossiter sites Baltimore as containing "an unusually rich group" of women scientists in the early twentieth century, stressing that "[e]ven the limited success that women scientists had attained by 1940 had required the best effort of a host of talented women, who, seeing how both science and women's roles were changing around them, took steps to carve out a legitimate place for themselves in the new order" they struggled to establish.

Research inquiries regarding additional information about Richards and Turner (outside of their small archives at their career institutions, Johns Hopkins Hospital and Mount Holyoke College), do not produce many findings. Turner is briefly mentioned in *Defining Women's Scientific Enterprise: Mount Holyoke Faculty and the Rise of American Science* by Miriam R. Levin, and Margaret W. Rossiter's *Women Scientists in America: Struggles and Strategies to 1940* includes a few references to Richards and Turner, but only in listing the women as scientific faculty at Mount Holyoke College and Johns Hopkins University, among "notable female scientists at seven major women's colleges," including Barnard, Bryn Mawr, Goucher, Mount Holyoke, Smith, Vassar, and Wellesley.

Additionally, because the norm for cataloguing and archiving preserved correspondence has traditionally been through the more prominent and/or male correspondent, the situation of the Richards/Turner correspondence proves interesting, as both correspondents were women and both were "prominent" in their scientific fields during their times. Consequently, while Richards and Turner both attended Mount Holyoke College as students, their collected papers are found separately at their places of employment, and Richards's letters to Turner are held in the Mount Holyoke-based archive. The specific case of the Richards/Turner correspondence not only spotlights the public neglect of early pioneering women and their private letters, but it also demonstrates the need to develop a non-patriarchal and hierarchal framework for mapping prominent same-sex correspondents who fall outside of standard archival categorization fields.

Johns Hopkins Hospital's role in the Baltimore community and Richards's life is notable, beginning with its pronounced return address on the majority of Richards's envelopes contained in the online archive. Early on in her employment at the Phipps Clinic, Richards recounts a local Baltimore preacher's words in her February 27, 1916 letter to Turner, expressing anger at the preacher's doubt of the Phipps Clinic's legitimacy: *The Rev. said 'If Onesimus had lived in Balt. today people would have considered him the product of his heredity & environment, & sent him to the Phipps Clinic to be investigated.' That made me hot too.* Richards's emotions guide her portrait of

Baltimore throughout her letters to Turner, painting a combustive picture of a city grappling with poverty, mortality, institutional dysfunction, and fast-paced cultural shifts.

Due to Richards's regional outsider status, her words depict a different geographical network from that of an insider, especially regarding Johns Hopkins Hospital and its immediate surroundings. *It has been warm here*, Richards writes to Turner on August 7, 1917, *but the patients have not minded it much. You see they are southerners.* While adjusting to living in a slightly warmer climate than her native New England, Richards's early correspondence to Turner often refers to the humidity and physical drain of Maryland's summer months. Richards's August 7, 1917 letter admits that *[t]he heat is so hard on your spirit, I know from past summers.* The mid-Atlantic seasons not only appear in the content of the correspondence, but also in their reflection of a medical career which is consistently and constantly cycling, blurred with the weight of perpetual precipitation, transition, and challenge. Baltimore is a place, Richards reinforces on August 7, 1917, *where the children have suffered fearfully, & their lives are snuffed out easily.*

Richards's mapping of Baltimore includes paths into Johns Hopkins Hospital not found on street signs or directories—a preserved region of the children she hears *cry[ing] at night, and in the daytime when they trudge by the clinic over the hot & dusty walk*— transporting routes only revealed in an epistolary key.

Richards's letters regularly critique the gender-biased and elitist medical community in Baltimore, as well as the country at large. Richards's earliest archived letter, sent to Turner on March 10, 1915, while Richards was still a graduate student, describes her displeasure at a conversation during a recent Johns Hopkins Medical dinner, in which the hostess *told [Richards] [h]ow many maids she carried abroad with her when she first went after marriage.* This early glimpse of Hopkins society is a bitter pill Richards must swallow in order to carve out her reputation as a woman in early American science. Her correspondence to Turner provides a place for unfiltered venting about Baltimore's upper class, especially those in high ranking positions at Hopkins. Richards's March 10, 1915 letter to Turner ends with a perfect example of such elitism, a quote from the Hopkins dinner hostess: *She was interested to know how I survived such close & continuous contact with the "masses."*

Richards's outsider status, not just in terms of her home region, but also in terms of her gender and class, influences many of her letters to Turner. Richards often relays variations of her message written on September 4, 1920: *[t]he battle with me is pretty much alone.* Within this long-term state of isolation, Richards's armor becomes the words and letters exchanged between herself and Turner, in addition to her communication with other female peers and friends, many originating from her time at Mount Holyoke College. Richards's September 4, 1920 letter to Turner is clear in its declaration of the correspondence necessary for her survival: *Please write me often. I need your letters.* The network of letters from women provides Richards with the support and validation that she neither receives from Johns Hopkins Hospital, nor from medical communities elsewhere in the nation, even while being one of their pivotal figures.

Richards's words to Turner on September 29, 1924, written while Richards was in Sherborn, Massachusetts, still ring with her anger: *How slip-shod they do things at the Harvard Medical & that nice discrimination against our sex! Pleasant isn't it. I've often longed to put a bomb under that noble University, blow it sky high, & begin again with something less conservative & aristocratic.* Free from career and collegiate restraints and requirements in the epistolary form, Richards can critique the medical field, in quite violent metaphor, without fear of retaliation.

Richards's correspondence to Turner actually becomes its own medical university curriculum proposal, enabled, because of its unique genre status, to exist separately from the systemic inequities of Richards and Turner's time. Clearly organized, defended, and debated back and forth across multiple states—for close to two decades, Richards's desired medical university is only found on paper, its "less conservative & aristocratic" elements tucked neatly inside envelopes, its enrollment limited to two corresponding members.

Richards, the once idealistic pioneering female student, gradually grows disenchanted with her former alma mater, the psychiatry field, and her patients. Her February 22, 1917 letter admits that *[Mount Holyoke] seemed ideal when I left 7 yrs ago, and now it might suffocate me if I stayed there long enough.* Richards's desire for humanistic connection and faith increases as she ages, and Richards often relates her analysis of the current state of the country to Turner, as seen in her February 13, 1932 letter: *Education does not educate emotions of selfishness, & greed & Ego striving. Only the Grace of God does that, & people don't believe in that any more. We are sold to service & culture.* Even with Turner's missing correspondence, Richards's portion of the communication exposes a search for identity, meaning, and integrity beyond the medical field, as the world quickly changes around her and the other women trained and based in late-nineteenth and early-twentieth-century customs and ideologies.

The developments of Richards's and Turner's epistolary network fostered the communication, analysis, criticism, and growth necessary to directly support them, as well as to indirectly bridge opportunities and advancements to other women in early American science, as noted in the many letters in which early American sister schools are referenced. For example, Richards's February 17, 1920 letter updates Turner on a newly formed alum organization at Johns Hopkins and an education rally *in conjunction with Smith, Goucher, Mt. H. Bryn Mawr for endowment campaign interest.*

Over a century later, Richards's preserved personal correspondence to Turner (and Turner's unpreserved personal correspondence to Richards) remains the clearest evidence of their intimate relationship and the communicative support necessary for them to sustain long-term careers as women in early American science. Yet, their fascinating connection and body of correspondence remain missing from standardized histories and publications, as it does for so many other women outside of preferential fields of study.

Part Four: Ventricles
Networks of Intimacy and Need
Letters as Lifelines

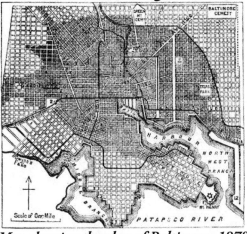

Map showing the plan of Baltimore, 1878
unknown cartographer

Beyond the veins and arteries, beyond the atriums, and beyond the valves, Baltimore's ventricles pulse, circulating the city's blood as they send words throughout the city's intricate network systems. Unlike the historical significance of the city's origins, the prominent markers of the city's established residents and visitors, and the reputation of its esteemed medical community, Eastside and Westside Baltimore loom in the background, secondary in their recognition and attention compared to other circulatory urban markers, even though they are just as large and integral as the other chambers.

Without these chambers, the life of the city would not function, as each chamber contributes to the work necessary for the urban heart to continue beating. Each ventricle fills with blood, and is then forced to contract before pushing the blood back into the heart and body or releasing it into the lungs. As well, the Eastside and Westside of Baltimore contain intimate communication which documents this process, again and again, throughout the city's history—continuing to fight for life, love, respect, and rights.

Chapter Eleven

Unrequited Love and Language

Letters by Edgar Allan Poe

"The Sleeper"/ Illustration to a poem published by Poe
1900/W. Heath Robinson

Edgar Allan Poe

Virginia Poe/ Watercolor Painted After Her Death in 1847

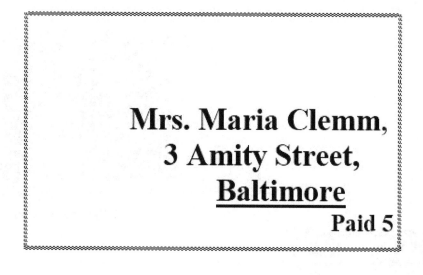

**Mrs. Maria Clemm,
3 Amity Street,
<u>Baltimore</u>**

Paid 5

*Let me have, under her own hand, a letter, bidding
me good bye—forever—and I may die—my heart
will break—but I will say no more.*

Edgar Allan Poe to Maria (and Virginia) Clemm.
August 29, 1835

144

To say that there is some ambiguity and confusion regarding the intimate letters of Edgar Allan Poe is an understatement. In the same vein that Baltimore and various other cities declare "Poe" to be one of their cities' writers, studying the surviving letters (and acknowledging the letters that didn't survive) of Poe and his intimates only seems to complicate existing theories about him, his work, and his correspondents. Thus, scholars have been trying, for decades, to find the "real" Poe through layers of confusions, contradictions, and unreliable sources. That endeavor seems as preposterous as uncovering the "real" Baltimore. However, Baltimore's role in the route of Poe's epistolary body is "real," especially in regard to Poe's correspondence to his cousin Virginia, who would become his only wife at age 13 in 1836, and to her mother—Poe's Aunt Maria.

While Baltimore hosts important sites of Poe's scattered life, including his home on 3 Amity Street and his gravesite at 515 W. Fayette Street, both located on the Westside, his letters often remain uncharted. Yet, that epistolary mapping, when viewed in the context of Poe's constant need for intimacy and validation from women, reveals an addiction of the heart *and* the epistolary form, as well as personal correspondence scars left by Poe's unrequited love for people and the page.

Thomas Ollive Mabbott's opening introduction to an 1831 edition of poetry by Poe recounts some of Poe's thoughts regarding love: "It was my luck to fall in love only with women from whom age, death, and marriage to others separated me." "Luck," or rather lack of "luck," surely influenced Poe's path, especially concerning unmet and intimate literary desires; yet, this unrequited love also fueled Poe's dark and emotional stories of the human psyche that are still read and treasured today.

In order to examine Poe's intimate letters in connection to Baltimore, we must first note Poe's early and temporary stay in the city with his grandparents, David and Elizabeth Poe, and then an elderly nurse, while his parents toured with a theatre group during the first year of his life. A friend of the family later reported that the nurse gave Edgar and his sister, Rosalie, bread soaked with gin and laudanum "to make them strong and healthy" and "to put them to sleep when restless." Thus, Baltimore was, from the time Poe was five weeks old, a place where chemical substances and guardians were provided as substitutes for Poe's familial care and attention.

By the time Poe was three years old, his father had abandoned the family and died and his mother had passed away from tuberculosis. Poe's inability to write to his mother as a young child and man, at least at an earthly address, would influence the rest of his life. Poe's early letters to his mother were likely only recorded in his head, sent to a location he had to create within his own mind, as opposed to finding it on a printed map. Poe's perpetual need to be "closely associated with some woman who could play the role of mother to him" would dominate the rest of his life. Yet, this impossibility—of rekindled maternity—only enhanced Poe's inability to find and capture, through physical and epistolary means, a sustainable relationship in which he could accept himself.

The interception of early letters that Poe wrote from the University of Virginia to his fifteen-year-old girlfriend/fiancée in Richmond, Sarah Elmira Royster, by her father (who was not too keen on their relationship) foreshadowed Poe's long-term epistolary and infidelity drama. Stable correspondence relationships and exchanges seemed to always be out of reach for Poe, just as much as his attainment of an ideal woman and companion was. The interference of other parties was a staple theme in Poe's correspondence life, as well as the reality that the drama was often instigated by Poe himself.

After Poe was discharged from the U.S. Army in 1829, he applied to West Point and boarded near his Baltimore relatives, his Aunt Maria Clemm and her family (Maria's son, Henry, and daughter, Virginia; Poe's grandmother, Elizabeth Poe and Poe's brother, William Henry), who lived on Mechanics Row, Wilks Street (what is now Eastern Avenue) until his appointment came through in March 1830.

Records also show that Poe was in Baltimore on December 10, 1829, when he sold a slave belonging to Maria Clemm in the Baltimore slave market, a fact that is often intentionally left out of public narratives or Baltimore references to Poe. In "Amorous Bondage: Poe, Ladies, and Slaves," Joan Dayan explores the contradictions in Poe's "dilemma of bondage, with both slavery and the constructed ideal of 'the ideal lady,' who is 'elegant, white, and delicate,'" yet who is repeatedly degraded by Poe as he presents "ladies," in his stories, "who turn into revenants and lovers who turn into slaves."

Researchers have also confirmed that Poe was living in Baltimore when his second volume of poetry, *Al Aaraaf, Tamerlane, and Minor Poems* was published in December 1829 by Hatch & Dunning. Poe's return to Baltimore in March 1831, after being expelled from West Point, was welcomed by Maria Clemm and her family, who offered Poe a home in their small quarters at 3 Amity Street, where he would live for the next four years.

3 Amity Street
Home of Edgar Allan Poe and the Clemm Family

Jeffrey Meyers describes Poe's Baltimore years fittingly as, "the least documented and most obscure period of his life." There is record of a letter Poe wrote to John Allan (his foster father) during this time, requesting money for debt which Poe claimed contributed to his arrest. Meyers states that while Poe scholars lack the proof of an actual arrest to confirm Poe's claim, "(i)n 1832 half the prisoners in the Baltimore City Jail were insolvent debtors." Historians do agree that during Poe's years in Baltimore he "lived in humble and desperate circumstances" and forged "intense emotional attachments to both Maria and Virginia Clemm." To this day, Poe's four years in Baltimore are primarily inaccessible in traditional preservation terms, with much conjecture as to his activities, his personal life, and his state of mind during this time.

There is a letter, however, that Poe mailed to Maria and Virginia Clemm in Baltimore after he left the city to work as an assistant editor of the *Southern Literary Messenger* in Richmond, Virginia. The letter's urgency stems from the fact that Poe had recently heard that his male cousin, Neilson Poe, who was living in Baltimore, "had offered to take [Maria] and Virginia into his home, support them, and, in addition, provide for Virginia's education."

Poe was extremely distressed by the news and wrote to Baltimore in hopes of persuading Maria and Virginia to decline Neilson Poe's offer and join him, instead, in Richmond. The bulk of Poe's letter is addressed to Maria, with a short note to Virginia attached to the end. The correspondence is high-drama, focused on the potential breaking of Poe's heart and the need for Maria (and subsequently, Virginia) to have mercy in their own hearts. Poe immediately expresses his distress in the opening sentence of the letter, stating, *I am blinded with tears while writing this letter —I have no wish to live another hour . . . My bitterest enemy would pity me could he now read my heart.*

While Poe is the one who has physically moved to a new state and city, Maria and Virginia are the ones who must relocate to fulfill his emotional longing. Poe warns, *[you] have both tender hearts—and you will always have the reflection that my agony is more than I can bear—that you have driven me to the grave—for love like mine can never be gotten over.* Poe's immortal love assigns its own guilt to the correspondents, displacing the responsibility of his potential death directly into Maria and Virginia's hands and hearts.

The tension between earthly and unearthly needs plays out throughout the letter like a closing argument. In a world Poe perceived to be perpetually against him, with *not one soul to love me,* as Poe expresses at the end of the second paragraph of this letter, and a fear of infidelity of love *and* letters, as he admits in the third paragraph—*I am afraid to trust it to the mail, as the letters are continually robbed,* Poe has only language as his faithful soul mate.

Poe repeatedly professes his lack of power in influencing Maria. *I cannot advise you,* he stresses, *Ask Virginia. Leave it to her. Let me have, under her own hand, a letter, bidding me good bye—forever—and I may die—my heart will break—but I will say no more.* Poe's rhetoric reinforces his desperation, including his direct address to Virginia at the end of the letter: *My love, my own sweetest Sissy, my darling little wifey, think well before you break the heart of your Cousin, Eddy.*

The battle for validation of the heart continues even after his letter closes, as Poe notes his need to re-open the letter and add an enclosure of $5 to confirm his financial integrity, acknowledging that he has *just received another letter from [Maria] announcing the rect. of mine.* Poe's reaction: *My heart bleeds for you.*

Poe's persuasive letter was successful, as "Mrs. Clemm rejected Neilson Poe's offer . . . [and] she and Virginia joined Edgar in Richmond in October, where they lived temporarily at the boarding-house. . . Edgar and Virginia were married there on 26 May 1836." Recognizing what historians know now—that the rented house Poe raved about in the letter "proved too small to accommodate them," and that the owner of the *Southern Literary Messenger* grew unhappy with Poe due to his conflicting ideas and his periodic drinking, it is easy to scoff at Poe's inflated language. Still, his reach for Maria (as a nephew and soon-to-be son-in-law) is impressive in its intensity and intimacy.

In fact, Richard P. Benton asserts in "Friends and Enemies: Women in the Life of Edgar Allan Poe," that "Maria Clemm herself . . . was perhaps altogether the most important woman in Poe's life. She looked after and cared for him with devotion and loyalty from the time he was twenty-one until the end of his life." Like Poe, Maria simultaneously played multiple roles; hers included caregiver, confidante, and fan—in addition to mother-in-law, aunt, interceptor, and instigator.

Maria's desire for Poe to maintain status within mainstream society, however, was challenged, as Poe was not destined for charted territory. He maintained the role of visitor in all of his addresses, as well as within his own body and mind. Benton admits that "Mrs. Clemm did her best to care for her 'Eddie' and to help him with his affairs, but she could not save him from himself, and their relationship was to terminate with his death in Baltimore on 7 October 1849."

Poe shared intimate correspondence with a variety of other women both before and after Virginia passed away in January of 1847. Fanny Osgood and Elizabeth Ellet, two women on the literary circuit in New York, were extremely jealous of each other's and Poe's affection (including Poe's letters and their letters to him), which eventually spared a fight between Poe and Ellet's brother. Sarah Helen Whitman and the widowed Sara Elmira Royster Shelton also played large roles in Poe's epistolary life after Virginia's death.

The toxic ramifications of Poe's dependence on women, chemical substances, and intimate letters surely burdened Virginia, even if she was aware of his relationships and personal communication with other women. Poe wrote that "My poor Virginia was continually tortured (although not deceived) by [Ellet's] anonymous letters, and on her death-bed declared that Mrs. E. had been her murderer." Evidence of Virginia's exhaustion and frustration with rumor and gossip is found in "the only poem Virginia is known to have written," penned on February 14, 1846, which expresses her desire to find a refuse from *the tattling of many tongues*, where *[l]ove alone shall guide us. . . [and] heal my weakened lungs*.

As well, there remains only one surviving independent letter, written by Poe to Virginia (Clemm) Poe. The letter was written on June 12, 1846, a few months before Virginia's death, in which Maria is directly referenced within the letter as Poe assures Virginia that *[o]ur Mother will explain to you why I stay away from you this night. I trust the interview I am promised, will result in some substantial good for me, for your dear sake, and hers.*

Alas, none of the women Poe courted before and after Virginia's death were able to fill Poe's desire for a *soul-life*. Longing for an integrated body and mind—his own and others—he could never obtain, Poe could not settle for the strengths one woman could realistically provide. As Poe confessed to Maria Clemm in a letter written from New York on July 7, 1849: *I was never really insane, except on occasions where my heart was touched.*

Meyers explains that "Poe liked to worship women from afar, in letters and in verse. When he drew dangerously close to them, he became overwrought and insecure, and deliberately – if unconsciously – ruined his chances of marriage." Long-term, Poe's desire for unattainable women and words both sustained and destroyed him, as his earthly female intimates remained out of his reach, due to "ill-health, nervous temperament, difference in age, financial considerations, family responsibilities, parental opposition, religious beliefs or married state." Yet, Poe's letters were able to feed his addiction and provide a means to be, at least temporarily, and within the first few minutes and hours of their mailings, the stimulation and assurance that he would one day receive satisfaction of the heart.

"Poe constantly recycled the feelings," Meyers suggests, "if not the actual words of his love letters, just as he had recycled his love poems." Poe's dependence on women for his own self-worth and on the letter form as a unfiltered release of that desire provides a window into the only living language and body that welcomed and accepted Poe in the long-term. His letters, in the end, were his only faithful and requited "soul-lives." In them, he was granted the freedom to send desire out in multiple directions, to multiple destinations, to multiple women, and in that reach, attempt to chart the unattainable parts of himself that he yearned to meet and reconcile.

The details regarding Poe's return to Baltimore on September 27, 1849 (in transit to Philadelphia and New York from Richmond), and his death less than two weeks later on October 7, 1849, remain blurry and unverifiable. Accounts range and paint various possibilities for his death, from "delirium tremens," to "a lethal amount of alcohol," to "congestion of the brain," to "cerebral inflammation," to "encephalitis."

There are differing accounts concerning the whereabouts of a "trunk Poe brought from Richmond . . . containing. . . a packet of letters from Elmira Shelton." Confirmations and denials of the discovery and existence of these letters and the trunk housing them in Baltimore continued after Poe's death, as well as the whereabouts of the letters by a majority of intimates throughout Poe's life. Sarah Helen Whitman even attempted to continue her correspondence with Poe after his death, recording his psychic letters "sent" from the other side: *Pray for me, Helen; pray for me.*

Nearly every page of the numerous Poe biographies published to date mentions his personal letters and the relevance of correspondence in researching Poe and the complex relationships he had with women. Like the interlocking chambers of the heart, Poe's communication network extended past himself, and required, for its sustainability, reaction from the people and places around him.

Maria Clemm's influence on Poe's intimate relationships, both before and after her daughter's death, was highly formed by her actions regarding his personal letters. "Indeed she said that after his death she destroyed hundreds of letters written to him by 'literary ladies'—as she knew he wished her to do." Maria was a major engineer in selecting and editing the work we now know as Poe's epistolary body. In her later years, Maria "had countless requests for samples of [Poe's] writing from friends who had loved and appreciated him. In answering them, she had given away the letters he had written to her."

Maria passed away on February 16, 1871 at Church Home in Baltimore, located at Broadway and Fairmont Avenue, a charity home for the elderly which had once been called Washington Medical College—the same location where Poe died 22 years before.

Poe's intimate epistolary history, including early routes and a final stop in Baltimore, proves unable to be neatly charted into conventional chambers, including the Westside. In Poe's correspondence life, physical setting was secondary to internal location and narrative, creating a mapped line that, much like floaters in the eye, disappears when chased. As such, Poe remains everywhere and nowhere—perpetually both inside and outside of Baltimore. Solidifying the unrequited love that Poe desired in his life and through his literary work, the soul of Baltimore's "tell-tale" heart still continues to beat, even when standard methods fail to hear or locate it.

Chapter Twelve

Protected Private Letters of Public Lives

(Missing: Thurgood Marshall's Letters to Vivian Burey Marshall)

Thurgood Marshall, between 1930-1945

Vivian "Buster" Burey Marshall

The National Bar Association

(Incorporated)
Thurgood Marshall, Secretary
4 East Redwood Street
Baltimore, Md.

Vivian Marshall

1838 Druid Hill Ave.

Baltimore, Maryland

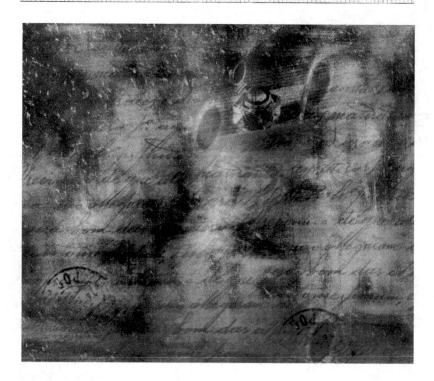

Baltimore's Westside includes many important civil rights figures and landmarks often absent from conventional city timelines and tours. Unless one is familiar with twentieth-century Baltimore civil rights history, it is virtually impossible to identify geographical locations which once housed leading civil rights figures and their pivotal political decisions and actions. Unlike the many state and city-funded memorials dedicated to Baltimore historical figures, especially in the downtown area, the Westside remains lacking in public tribute, acknowledgement, and restoration of its contributions. Born within the racial and economic inequities that have persisted within the Westside, a void of intimacy lingers below the surface of its streets: a protected view of public figures' personal communication for the sake of privacy and reputation.

Supreme Court Justice Thurgood Marshall depicted his view of the city in a 1966 interview with the *Baltimore Sun*, stating that "he left Baltimore in the 1930s and was 'glad to be rid of it forever'." Marshall's early years in Baltimore, however, present a network of familial, educational, and geographical influences which demonstrate the importance of personal relationships and communication in furthering civil rights. Locating the role of intimacy in that mapping, though, is quite another matter. For example, Marshall's letters to his first wife, Vivian "Buster" Burey Marshall, with whom he lived in Baltimore from 1930 to 1938 are not traditionally preserved. There is actually only one publicly known and accessible intimate letter written by Marshall to Burey, composed several years after they moved from Baltimore.

Instead of dismissing the role of intimacy in Thurgood Marshall's climb from West Baltimore to the highest judicial bench in the country, it serves the Baltimore community, and the country, to view Marshall's sole preserved letter to Marshall not as a stand-alone artifact, but as a representative piece of the missing map of intimacy hidden within the Westside chamber of Baltimore—a map which remains covered, to this day, by layers of self-preservation.

The muting of much of Marshall's personal life and intimate correspondence is a by-product of his public identity as a pioneering African

American leader. This silence includes actual missing letters and personal communication, as well as intimacy that did and does not align with public expectations. In order to preserve public reputation, intimacies and more controversial levels of authenticity are often purposefully muted within minority groups, contributing to what Walter R. Allen explains as a consequential "tendency to gloss over important within-group differences; thus, monolithic, stereotypic and inaccurance portrayals of Black family life are common"; furthermore, intimate relationships and communications that go against the public grain are routinely ignored.

Intentional and unintentional subversion makes the process of researching intimate letters by prominent African Americans often as gripping as finding actual letters. This research journey, while only seldom successful in unveiling literal letters, regularly uncovers other societal and historical discoveries contained within the voids and silences that exist in place of preserved letters.

The only printed collection of Thurgood Marshall's early letters is *Marshalling Justice: The Early Civil Rights Letters of Thurgood Marshall*, edited by Michael G. Long. Additional correspondence by Marshall can also be found in the *Thurgood Marshall Papers* and the *NAACP Papers*, which are housed at the Library of Congress and available online. Library of Congress archivist Patrick Kerwin states, "the [LOC online] collection contains little material from [Marshall's] pre-judicial career." The archive is based on "career" letters and Marshall's public years, from 1949–1991, a good decade after Marshall's move from Baltimore.

Long's edition provides a thoughtfully constructed epistolary trail of Marshall's early career letters from 1935-1957, but only one letter to Burey is included. Long's collection also does not include any letters addressed to Cecelia Suyat Marshall, Marshall's second wife, whom he married ten months after the death of Burey on February 11, 1955, even though the collection spans Marshall's letters through 1957. Marshall's letter to Burey was written in 1940, during the time Marshall was traveling through the Deep South to meet with local NAACP leaders. Four years prior to the letter's date, Marshall and Burey had moved from Baltimore to New York after Marshall had accepted the position of Assistant Special Counsel of the NAACP.

The letter from Marshall to Burey is included in Long's edition as a small supplement within other May 1940 correspondence written by Marshall to Walter White, who was executive secretary of the NAACP from 1931 to 1955. Long notes that Marshall wrote to send Burey "handwritten news of the trip" he was taking through the Deep South. The letter to Burey, Long explains, "is one of the few extant letters to [Marshall's] first wife." Long clarifies that "[t]he letters to Vivian seem few and far between," as during the research process for his book, he "found nothing more substantive than what appears in *Marshalling Justice* . . . [and] suspect[s] [Burey's] family has a box of letters somewhere, and if [found] . . . would be one of the best finds in research about Marshall." As of the completion of this project, no additional letters between Marshall and Burey have been found. Long's suspicions, though, confirm that the lack of tangible letters between Marshall and Burey does not negate their existence or the possibility that they are privately archived.

Long emphasizes the lack of personal preserved correspondence by Marshall in *Marshalling Justice* and the striking intimacy of Marshall's letter to Burey compared to the rest of his career letters, noting "[Marshall's letter's] tenderness is rarer still." Long's use of the term "tenderness" is fitting to describe this letter, especially in comparison to Marshall's other preserved letters to national organizations and high ranking political figures, which still read publicly, even if initially intended to be private.

In Marshall's letter to Burey, he addresses her with an intimate nickname before summarizing his recent activities while traveling through the Deep South: *Dearest Shooksie:/ This is really beautiful country down here. A. Maceo Smith drove us over 400 miles yesterday in eight and a half hours. The trip was fine and the scenery was swell. Maceo's wife came along with us so we will be good.* Marshall's mischievous side peeks through the update in his admittance of the need of a chaperone (Maceo's wife) in order to *be good.*

Marshall continues his update to Burey, acknowledging a letter which Burey previously sent—a letter that still remains missing from Marshall's public epistolary body: *I have been eating so much that I am sure I have gained more weight. The trip as a whole is more than interesting. Thanks so much for your letter. Don't worry because one of these days I will be able to stop traveling so much and we will be together.* We can see, in these few short sentences, a much more universal and relatable "Marshall," who, in his intimate moments, resembles the rest of us. While Marshall's intimate letter to Burey is rare, it still provides a wide window into the private life of the public Marshall, offering intimacy as part of a stronger vision of the whole "Marshall."

Marshall's early years in Westside Baltimore were paramount in laying the foundation for his later success in advancing civil rights. A pivotal source for detailing Marshall's early life in Baltimore is *Young Thurgood: The Making of a Supreme Court Justice* by Larry S. Gibson, Professor at University of Maryland Francis King Carey School of Law. Gibson includes a foreword in his book by Marshall's son, Thurgood Marshall, Jr., who states that Gibson's "sleuthing has led him to courthouses and clerk's office records as well as professional and personal correspondence in countless locales" in order to collect the primary sources needed to accurately represent Marshall's early life and influences.

As was the case for this author, Gibson had to become his own customized search engine, locating historical information and social and familial links through non-academic sources and metaphorical mappings, eventually contesting the "popular belief [that] Marshall hated Baltimore." Through his research, Gibson concluded that a love/hate dichotomy was inadequate to describe Marshall's early relationship with Baltimore, claiming that "while Marshall did have some bad memories of Baltimore's stifling racial segregation, he still spoke mainly with affection for the city where he was born and raised." Gibson's interviews with Marshall's personal friends and family quickly proved "[t]his early period of Marshall's life had shaped his personality, attitudes, priorities, and work habits."

Thurgood Marshall was born "Thoroughgood Marshall" on July 2, 1908 and was named after his paternal grandfather, who also altered his original name—to "Thorney Good Marshall." Both of Marshall's grandfathers owned large grocery stores in Baltimore. His paternal grandfather's store was located on the southeast corner of Dolphin and Division Streets and his maternal grandfather's store stood on 63 Orchard Street and Denmead Street (now 20th Street). After Marshall's birth, Marshall's father, William Marshall, temporarily relocated the family to Harlem while he worked on the New York Central Railroad. Before Marshall started school, however, "the family returned to Baltimore and moved in with [Marshall's mother's] brother Fearless Williams at 1634 Division Street."

For the next two decades, Marshall's father worked various waiter jobs, including positions at the Maryland Club and the Gibson Island Club. When Marshall's father was not working food service jobs, he "went to the courthouse in Baltimore and watched civil and criminal trials. At home, Marshall's father and his sons frequently discussed politics, race relations, and news events." Marshall's interest in law and policy bloomed within these charged hours inside his childhood home, as Marshall's father exposed him to a legal and political world that extended well past the boundaries of their Baltimore row home and neighborhood.

It was in large part, Marshall's father's contradictory traits, being "at the same time ornery and affable, stern and softhearted," that contributed to Marshall's ability to become a successful lawyer and judge. Marshall credited his father with balancing advocacy with competitive debating, as "by teaching me to argue, by challenging my logic on every point, by making me prove every statement," Marshall explained, "[h]e never told me to be a lawyer, but he turned me into one." It is these same conflicting traits, prized in the courtroom, that prove problematic when trying to map intimate historical connections, particularly for prominent political figures whose careers hinged on untarnished reputations.

Gibson carefully crafts Marshall's early history through familial and geographical lenses in *Young Thurgood*, stating that "Marshall, unlike his more outgoing classmate, the future entertainer Cab Calloway, preferred the safety and security of his family and neighborhood." In fact, Gibson, asserts, "[t]here was never a time while growing up when Thurgood Marshall felt disconnected from his family. He remained regularly in touch with several intelligent and attentive relatives." Within this communicative and intimate Baltimore framework, the young Marshall grew.

After attending Henry Highland Garnett School (Public School 103), Marshall attended the Colored High School, which was originally a German-American [Elementary] School at Pennsylvania Avenue and Dolphin Street in Old West Baltimore. Marshall's class was the last class to use the building, as a new Junior/Senior High School (named Frederick Douglass High School) was built for African American students in 1925, located at Calhoun, Baker, and Carey Streets. A well known story about Marshall's early legal training includes the actions of his high school principal, Mason Hawkins, who regularly punished him by "sending him to the basement and requiring that he memorize portions of the Constitution." Marshall-biographer Juan Williams notes that Marshall later recalled, "Before I left that school, I knew the whole [Constitution] by heart."

Marshall excelled on the debate team and on the student council. He also excelled at "maintaining his reputation as a cutup and prankster," Williams reports in *Thurgood Marshall: American Revoluntionary*. One of Marshall's classmates, Charlotte Shervington, "remembered Thurgood acting up one day when the teacher left the classroom: 'Thurgood was full of the devil. He threw a piece of chalk and hit me in the eye. He didn't aim to hit me in the eye, he just threw the chalk. He was mischievous'." Marshall's desire to instigate trouble and distract others, as is often the case with many ambitious and restless young leaders-in-the-making, manifested in mischief—self-initiated entertainment to keep Marshall occupied when he was not satisfied with the status quo around him.

After graduating from high school in 1925, Marshall entered Lincoln University, the first degree-granting historically black university founded in 1854, in Chester County, Pennsylvania. It was during Marshall's final year at Lincoln that he met his first wife, Vivian "Buster" Burey. Marshall initially planned to marry Burey a few years after graduation, but that plan quickly changed. Burey elaborated in a May 8, 1954 *Chicago Defender* article: "First we decided to get married five years after I graduated, then three, then one, and we finally did just before I started my last semester."

160

After graduation, newlyweds Thurgood and Burey moved into Thurgood's parents' house at 1838 Druid Hill Avenue, which was already housing Marshall's parents, Marshall's brother and his brother's wife and son, and Marshall's brother's mother-in-law.

Former site of 1838 Druid Hill Avenue
Early home of Thurgood Marshall, Vivian Burey Marshall, and other family members

Since The University of Maryland schools did not admit African Americans at that time, Marshall did not apply to The University of Maryland School of Law in Baltimore—which would have been only a few miles from his house. Instead, he attended Howard University in Washington, D.C.

Marshall commuted from Baltimore to Washington, D.C. for the next three years, excelling at Howard, passing the bar, and becoming what the law school dean at Howard, Charles Houston, deemed a "social engineer." One of Marshall's first long-distance separations from Burey was a trip with Houston, "to document and photograph the stark differences between black and white schools" in the Deep South. Marshall would take two additional road trips with Houston in the 1920's. The existence of Marshall's May 1940 travel-based letter to Burey, written more than a decade after his travels with Houston, suggests it is more than probable that Marshall regularly corresponded with Burey during these early road trips, even if we do not have actual preserved traces of those letters

The Baltimore landscape would play a vital role for Marshall and Burey after Marshall passed the bar and throughout the 1930's, as Marshall opened his own law practice, began to work for the Baltimore branch of the NAACP, and collaborated with Charles Houston to win the first major civil rights case—*Murray v. Pearson.* Burey made her own mark on the advancement of civil rights within Baltimore by participating in the City Young People's Forum, which included speakers such as Zora Neale Hurston, Sterling Brown, and W. E. B. Du Bois. Burey was also the president of the Opportunity Makers Club, described by Gibson as "a group of educated young women that sought to assist its members in finding employment and starting small businesses."

Compared to Marshall's legacy, however, Burey remains a distant shadow in Baltimore's and the country's history. Part of this is due to her early death, at age 44, from lung cancer, as well as from the lack of descendents from Marshall and Burey. However, anyone would be hard pressed to deny the influence and need of Marshall's early family and intimate relationships, including his marriage to Burey, in establishing the necessary foundation for his eventual role as the first African American Supreme Court Justice. Burey's decision not to tell Marshall about her terminal lung cancer diagnosis in 1954 until after the Brown v. Board of Education case was decided demonstrates the extremity of Burey's private sacrifice of silenced personal communication for the sake of Marshall's public commitment to civil rights.

Marshall's impact on the advancement of civil rights was contingent on his passion, which is evident through his published letters and courtroom testimonies. His emotionality is also preserved in the desperate voices of anonymous letters that, Long explains, Marshall "would forward . . . not only to law enforcement officials but also to the national media, with the hope of drawing attention to the problems he dealt with every day." By forwarding personal letters to the media, Marshall hoped the unfiltered and raw feelings of the anonymous correspondents would speak directly to the public. In this way, Marshall could depict the atrocities happening to African Americans through primary personal accounts other than his own.

Marshall's private reputation remained at stake for the rest of his life—and even after his death, especially in regard to his personal letters. *New York Times* reporter Neil Lewis covered the provocative release of Marshall's private papers just two years after his death and describes the reaction of the court to the release: "In an angry letter on behalf of a majority of the Supreme Court, Chief Justice William H. Rehnquist accused the Library of Congress today of bad judgment in releasing the papers of Justice Thurgood Marshall so soon after his death, and he warned that Justices might no longer donate their papers to the Library." Rehnquist's warning is an example of the controversy that continues today over the public accessibility of private correspondence by historical figures and the repercussions that often occur when family members or colleagues feel violated by the disclosure of information in those letters.

The resistance against making Marshall's private correspondence public, due to Marshall's role as a Supreme Court Justice, and as an African American trailblazer, is more than understandable. One cannot dismiss the serious implications of publicizing intimate materials and the often significant consequences of that action. Negotiating these often conflicting identity groups can be extremely difficult, as Anita L. Allen notes in "Privacy Isn't Everything: Accountability as a Personal and Social Good": "[a] public figure may be accountable in one sense and to one degree to the general public, but in further senses and to further degrees to members of his or her identity group." Decisions to release private papers are likely to awaken emotions in one or more groups connected to the correspondent's often overlapping identities. Allen reinforces that "[t]he late Supreme Court Justice Thurgood Marshall was accountable for his personal life, not simply to the public, but also, and critically, to his African-American public," which included his private friends, family members, and colleagues. Marshall's identity (including his written communication—both public and private), therefore, held multiple layers of expectations that he had to constantly negotiate in his position as a Supreme Court Justice and that others continue to feel obligated to negotiate for him, even after his death.

Subsequently, consent from family members is often a requirement, as was the case with Marshall, when publishing personal letters after the death of a prominent figure. Family members often feel a violation of intimacy will take place by the public exposure of personal letters, as Dena Goodman notes in "Old Media: Lessons from Letters," and the figure and/or family members will be forced into vulnerable public positions.

After the release of Marshall's papers, Supreme Court Justice William Rehnquist articulated his desire for new protocols regarding the release of personal materials by Supreme Court Justices to include "career family" approval, as well as traditional family consent. Neil Lewis explains:

> Justice Rehnquist's letter said the library misinterpreted the agreement Justice Marshall signed with Mr. Billington in 1991 for the disposition of his judicial papers. The Chief Justice said that while the library had discretion to make the papers available, it had an obligation to consult with other members of the Court and Justice Marshall's family. Had the library staff done so . . . it would have understood the need to keep the materials private for a longer time.

Rehnquist's statement stresses the ambiguous line between public and private ownership in determining the library's right to publish private papers of a public individual, as well as the library's responsibility in observing an appropriate delay and standard in that release. This desired delay is complex and variable, often unnecessarily pitting historians against families.

However, as Goodman clarifies, "that is what historians do; at the very heart of our work is reading other people's mail." Therefore, coming to terms with the often inevitable exposure of private materials within the public sphere is a process many families of prominent figures must address and unwittingly accept. Each prominent figure's correspondence history is different, however, making untenable a standard waiting period for disclosure.

The publication of intimate letters will continue to be controversial, as will the intimate letter's inherent component of complex and often problematic content. The risk factor in intimate letters, while sometimes uncomfortable for correspondents and/or their families if the letters are made public, is often the prime reason that intimate letters are written. In fact, as Emily Bernard emphasizes in "Love Letters, Straight from the Heart," "letters show us that our intimate ties are what make it possible to face the dangers the larger world has in store for us."

The intimate letter regularly creates and nurtures the first brave words and steps of visionary and leading thought. Marshall, himself, fluctuated on his reaction to requests for his personal papers throughout his life. Debra Newman Ham recalls that "[w]e [the Manuscript Division at the Library of Congress] initially asked for his papers around 1965 [and] [a]t that time he wrote us back and said that he did not have any papers." A second request was made in 1977 Ham notes, to which Marshall did not respond, but after which "we began to hear rumors that Justice Marshall was planning to destroy his papers and that he was not going to keep them." It was not until after Marshall's retirement in 1991, with a third request from the Library of Congress and a meeting between Marshall and several Library head personnel, that Marshall agreed to donate his papers—which arrived at the Library in the fall of 1991, a little under two years before he died on January 24, 1993.

The history of Marshall's personal papers speaks to many of the discrepancies and conflicts regarding the public accessibility of prominent figures' intimate materials. Even when Marshall granted the Library permission to publish his papers posthumously, controversy still festered over the "when" and "where" of their public disclosure. Furthermore, the fact that Marshall wanted to destroy his own papers at one point highlights the contradictory desires found, even within a singular self, regarding the release of private material and the unanswerable question—Are some things better left unknown about a historical figure's personal life, even if the information would better the social good of the public?

Marshall, "the man," embodies many of the same contradictions found in the study of the intimate letter, which is why, even with an ambiguous mapping, his part in the formation of the intimate chamber of Westside Baltimore is so important. Gibson notes how Marshall "fought for racial justice without becoming a racist," was "simultaneously idealistic and pragmatic," and was "a passionate advocate, yet he maintained friendly relationships with his opponents."

Williams also describes the public/private contrast of Marshall, "the figure," as being part of the disconnect between today's youth and the civil rights history that Marshall helped create: "The combination of [Marshall's] reclusiveness and his standing in popular culture as an elderly, establishment figure blinded much of the nation to the importance of his legacy. Young people were especially uninformed about the critical role Marshall had played in making history." Furthermore, as Williams declares, many people do not know "that Marshall laid the foundation for today's racial landscape"—a societal map which stemmed from Marshall's personal experiences growing up in West Baltimore. The missing and muted intimate letters by African Americans, including Marshall—from early America, to the civil rights period, to today—remain invaluable to the public, even if that material resides in the shadows of its own existence.

Remembering Marshall through his intimate words to his first wife allows the portrait of a prominent man to become human, as well as legendary. Lucy D. Suddreth, Chief of Support Operations for the Library of Congress, recounts that "[d]uring his last news conference in June 1991, after announcing his retirement, Justice Marshall said that he wished to be remembered with 10 words, 'That he did what he could with what he had'." When it comes to intimate letters, a similar saying rings true: Scholars do what they can with what they have—including what they don't have, but know was once there. This stands true, especially for the Westside of Baltimore, including the missing intimate letters between Thurgood Marshall and his first wife, Vivian Burey Marshall.

Chapter Thirteen

Unprocessed and Unpublicized Correspondence

Clarence Mitchell, Jr.'s Letters to Juanita Jackson Mitchell

Mitchell Family: Juanita Jackson Mitchell,
Clarence Mitchell III (standing),
Clarence Mitchell, Jr., and Keiffer Mitchell
Paul Henderson, undated.
Courtesy of the Maryland Historical Society, HEN.00.B1-041.

One civil rights couple who remained out of the shadows of Baltimore's history and influence are Clarence Mitchell, Jr. and Juanita Jackson Mitchell. The Mitchells' political and familial influence continues to be deeply routed in the city's landscape to this day. Locating the intimate routes of the Mitchells' lives in the Westside is easily completed; however, accessing that intimacy through private and preserved sources reveals another hidden mapping within Baltimore's ventricles.

There are select intimate letter excerpts between Mitchell and Jackson referenced in Denton Watson's *Lion in the Lobby: Clarence Mitchell Jr.'s Struggle for the Passage of Civil Rights Laws*. These selections, as noted by Watson, are pulled "from the personal collection—love letters written by Clarence—that are in the private collection controlled by Michael Mitchell." The Mitchell/Jackson family is not alone in their desire to keep the intimate letters of deceased relatives in private archives; many prominent families separate intimate letters from their non-intimate letter siblings before releasing them to the public.

The *Mitchell Family Papers*, not to be confused with the private collection, were donated to the Library of Congress in 1997, at which time librarian James H. Billington announced the donation "to be the most important unprocessed archive on the modern civil rights era." Mitchell's intimate letters to Jackson, though, were not included in this donation, highlighting the current and continuing resistance to include private materials in publicly accessible venues. Yet, it was Watson's exposure to Mitchell's intimate letters to Jackson that dramatically shaped the biographical portrait he painted of the young Baltimore couple and of Mitchell's later actions as a civil rights lobbyist and director of the NAACP Washington Bureau. This intimate knowledge also contributed to Watson's ability to emphasize Jackson's influence and legacy as a part of both Jackson's and Mitchell's stories.

Unlike Thurgood Marshall, most sources deem Mitchell's and Jackson's Baltimore influence as inseparable from their identities as prominent civil rights figures. Two of today's landmarks which pay tribute to Mitchell's influence include The Clarence M. Mitchell, Jr. Courthouse on North Calvert Street and the Clarence M. Mitchell, Jr. School of Engineering at Morgan

State University, though it is telling that neither of these major tributes are on the Westside of Baltimore, where Mitchell lived during his formative years and where he courted Jackson from her family home at 1216 Druid Hill Avenue, just a few blocks from Thurgood Marshall's early marital home with Vivian Burey.

1216 Druid Hill Avenue
Former home of Juanita Jackson and her family, prior to marrying Clarence Mitchell, Jr.

In contrast, current Baltimore residents and visitors would be hard pressed to find such large public tributes to Jackson, even though she was known as "the matriarch of one of Baltimore's oldest civil rights families" and was the first African American woman to graduate from the University of Maryland School of Law and to practice law in Maryland. Unbeknownst to many current Maryland residents and visitors, "the school desegregation suits championed by [Jackson] made Maryland the first Southern state to integrate its school system after the 1954 Supreme Court decision in *Brown v. Board of Education* of Topeka, Kansas." Jackson's role (as with many prominent female figures) was, and continues to be, overshadowed by the public contributions of her husband.

Born on March 8, 1911, Mitchell spent the first few years of his life in a small house on Stockton Street near Pressman Street in West Baltimore before moving to 553 Bloom Street. Mitchell attended Public School 103 on Division Street with Thurgood Marshall, though Marshall was three years ahead of Mitchell in age and studies.

Thurgood Marshall Elementary School: Formerly Henry Highland
Garnett School
Public School 103/Division Street School—1315 Division Street.
(Photographed before the fire in 2016)

Part of the reason that Mitchell and Marshall did not know each other during their childhood years, Watson suggests, was their three-year age difference. "A more important reason, though," Watson claims, "was the difference in their social status [as Marshall] lived 'on the other side of the tracks' in western Baltimore." Marshall's "home was on prized Druid Hill Avenue, commonly dubbed by some lower-class whites as Bread and Tea Avenue," Watson explains, since "[t]hey thought that the black residents there were having such a difficult time making ends meet, in their effort to live up to their new social status, that they could hardly afford more than bread and tea for food."

The young men would eventually meet at Douglass High School, and then again at Lincoln University, where Mitchell became a part of the debate team with Marshall. Douglass High School was also the site of another vital connection: that of Mitchell and Jackson, who met while performing in a school production of *Sleeping Beauty*. However, it was not until Mitchell was a senior at Lincoln University that he and Jackson would cross paths again.

Two years younger than Mitchell, Jackson was born on January 2, 1913 to Lillie Carroll Jackson and Keiffer Jackson in Hot Springs, Arkansas. Lillie Carroll and Keiffer Jackson met at the Sharp Street Memorial Methodist Episcopal Church, married in 1910, and led an early life on the road "showing religious and educational motion pictures in churches and schools from town to town." Watson notes how Kieffer Jackson's "pioneering endeavor provided blacks with a welcome alternative to the generally demeaning depictions of the race that were then prevalent in the movies." Lillie Carroll Jackson was also considered a mother of the civil rights movement, as she pioneered the non-violent tactics of the civil rights movement during the 1960's and headed the Baltimore chapter of the NAACP from 1935–1970.

After traveling on the road as a family for eight years, the Jacksons moved to 1326 McCulloch Street in order that their children would have a stable address during their schooling years. Watson stresses that Carroll demanded "her girls maintain a very high standard of decorum" and "made it clear that the girls could not dare look at boys until they were out of college." In fact, Carroll's repeating refrain to her girls was "Boys and books don't go together." Mitchell later admitted, "Juanita's parents had an iron-clad prohibition against her socializing with boys. I knew her but I kept my distance."

In 1927, Lillie Carroll Jackson withdrew her daughter from Morgan State College during her sophomore year, in hopes of finding placement for her in an out-of-state accredited college (as the segregated Maryland schools were not accredited at that time). Carroll then challenged the Dean of the University of Pennsylvania to admit Jackson and accept her credits from Morgan; Jackson would reconnect with Mitchell soon after her transfer from Morgan, before graduating from the University of Pennsylvania in 1931.

Jackson recounted that "Mitchell swept her off her feet with his 'silver-tongued oratory,'" being someone who was "not only a smooth talker in private . . . [and] knew how to hold an intelligent woman's attention, but was also a forceful and eloquent public speaker." Mitchell's oratory skills, evident in his intimate letters and in his public speaking, helped to simultaneously advance his public civil rights aims and his personal desire of creating a union and a family with Jackson.

Watson describes the Baltimore that Mitchell and Jackson returned to after college as the same "mean" and contradictory city that they had left; the same city that Marshall referred to as "up-South Baltimore." Andor Skotnes notes in "'Buy Where You Can Work': Boycotting for Jobs in African-American Baltimore, 1933–34," that in 1931 "[t]he *Afro-American* found . . . that Black-owned clothing stores in the community were outnumbered by white-owned stores seven to one, shoe-menders two to one, confectioners five to one, grocery stores thirteen to one, and eating establishments two to one; there were no Black-owned hardware stores." Skotnes stresses that "[t]he segregationism under which African Americans in Baltimore lived at the end of the 1920's was ubiquitous . . . [there were] nominally integrated public places in the city, [although] the White power structure still made it clear that it considered Blacks outsiders." Jackson and Mitchell saw these inequalities first-hand and immediately began to work on civil rights reforms after completing their degrees.

Soon after, Jackson founded the City-Wide Young People's Forum, and Mitchell headed the NAACP's publicity program. Behind their public roles, however, intimacy and communication held Mitchell and Jackson together as a unified force. This intimate force was based in Jackson's faith in Mitchell, as Watson notes Jackson "believed in him . . . [and] he found himself 'thinking and doing things [he] would never otherwise dream of doing'." Mitchell's future developed into a collaborative journey and vision, as he wrote to Jackson that *whatever else there is before me now is your dream not mine.*

In "Don't Write Any Letters," Roger Rosenblatt declares that "[l]etter writing, while a sign of civilization, is also a high-risk occupation." The danger is that "[l]etters conceal almost nothing, which accounts for their power . . . [as] one looks for things to be said in letters that are not said elsewhere, expecting truth most of all." An example of a lack of concealment is evident in a letter Mitchell wrote to Jackson in 1937, while attending the Atlanta School of Social Work as an Urban League Fellow, in which Mitchell states his *intoleran[ce] of cowardice in others,* as he expresses his dismay at the media's silence regarding the recent unjust sentencing in Atlanta of a fourteen-year-old boy who received twenty years on the chain gang.

In the letter, Mitchell criticizes Atlanta's media accounts of the sentencing to Jackson without hesitation, emphasizing his view of the newspapers in Atlanta as venues lacking in truth and justice. Mitchell's truth and justice, as presented to Jackson through his intimate letter, is the knowledge of injustice and the bravery required to express that knowledge in public—a contradiction which the intimate letter both promotes and hides.

The "ultimate" intimate letter that is expressed publicly, many would argue, is the marriage vow. Mitchell spent significant time writing and memorizing his vow to Jackson, which is included within a letter titled, "By Your Husband to Be," which is paraphrased in *Lion in the Lobby*. In the letter, Mitchell utilizes the metaphor of a rose with a small thorn to testify his admiration for and devotion to a woman as strong and supportive as Juanita—a *rare fragrance*. Through the metaphor, Mitchell admits the benefit of pain and self sacrifice in developing an intimate union between two trailblazers, as well as the beauty and richness of that transfer.

Due to their public roles, Mitchell and Jackson "were Baltimore's dream couple . . . [they] represented a generation of their race that had pledged their lives to the service of their people." The couple was welcomed with open arms into elite society circles, as Watson confirms "[t]he older generation supported [Mitchell and Jackson] as they developed a new blueprint for freedom."

Henry Louis Gates, Jr. notes the importance of unpublished and unrecognized communications in fostering societal changes, crediting Mitchell with being the man responsible for much of the behind-the-scenes writing and action needed to advance civil rights in America. "Let me shorthand it this way," Gates explains, in "Who Was the Unsung Hero of the 1964 Civil Rights Act?," "[i]f Netflix were to green-light a *House of Cards* prequel set in that era, Mitchell would be a star character at every stage of the legislative process—the man even the president called at night." Yet, scholars and historians still tend to neglect communication performed "at night" and/ or within intimate venues, even though those communications are typically the primary forces directing public histories.

Mapping this evasive communication is extremely difficult, due to the fact that many intimate exchanges, including letters, are not accessible. For example, Juan Williams predicted that the release of The *Mitchell Family Papers* would "give the Mitchell family and Baltimore a more prominent place in civil-rights history." However, as Marilyn McCraven exposes in "The Mitchell Papers: New Revelations," it turned out that "Williams was able to make only limited use of the papers in his research [for *Thurgood Marshall: American Revolutionary*] because [the Papers were not] properly catalogued and filed." Two decades later, The *Mitchell Family Papers* are still being processed for the public and Mitchell's intimate letters still remain tucked away in a personal family archive, accessible and viewable only with private permission.

Chapter Fourteen

Destination Compromise

*"Du Bois Cottage" Letters between W. E. B. Du Bois
and Nina Gomer Du Bois*

W. E. B. Du Bois in front of Baltimore home, ca. 1945
*Courtesy of the W. E. B. Du Bois Papers, 1803-1999,
Special Collections and University Archives, UMass Amherst Libraries*

W. E. B. Du Bois and his wife Nina Du Bois, ca. 1945
*Courtesy of the W. E. B. Du Bois Papers, 1803-1999,
Special Collections and University Archives,
UMass Amherst Libraries*

Nina Du Bois
2302 Montebello Terrace
Baltimore, M.D.

Du Bois Cottage
2302 Montebello Terrace
Baltimore

Jan. 11 – 43

Dear Will:

I have your last letter in
which you spoke of having
ordered a fire grate to use in
the fire place . . .

Across town, on the Eastside, less than five miles north of Johns Hopkins Hospital, one will find Morgan Park, a historic African American community nestled within the wooded lots next to Morgan State University. Within this location lies the base for another neglected collection of intimate correspondence—one which has, also, only recently been transferred into accessible digital form and which has received little attention from the city and academies of Baltimore. The routes of these letters lead to an unassuming two-story house on Montebello Terrace. The house lacks public signage or extensive upkeep. It is only through a very slow speed and a focused eye that one can confirm the house number, 2302, on the corner bend of the road.

2302 Montebello Terrace does not stand out from the other houses in Morgan Park. In fact, it is almost impossible to realize the house's substantial contribution to both the city's and the country's history unless one is told by a local resident that 2302 Montebello Terrace was the home of W. E. B. Du Bois and his family for more than a decade. This neglect of recognition, of address and geographical contribution, is precisely what makes the Du Boises's personal letters, sent to and from 2302 Montebello Terrace, so pivotal in mapping Baltimore's intimate history. Contributing to the neglect is the fact that while Du Bois owned a home in Morgan Park from 1939 to 1950, he spent little time there, as he was teaching at Atlanta University and working in New York for the National Association for the Advancement of Colored People during those years.

Du Bois Cottage
2302 Montebello Terrace, Morgan Park

2302 Montebello Terrace in Morgan Park might have been W. E. B. Du Bois's residential property during the 1940's, but it actually housed other Du Bois family members: Du Bois's wife, Nina Gomer Du Bois; his daughter, Nina "Yolande" Du Bois Cullen-Williams; and his granddaughter, Yolande "Du Bois" Williams. As evidenced by the Du Boises's letters, 2302 Montebello Terrace was never actually perceived as a permanent "home" by any of its residents in the conventional sense. The property was a "home" of compromise between Du Bois and his wife, his family, and his career callings, which included "American civil rights activist, Pan-Africanist, sociologist, educator, historian, editor, poet, and scholar."

The majority of the preserved intimate letters by W. E. B. Du Bois and Nina Gomer Du Bois have only become available publicly within the last few years, through the University of Massachusetts's online archive, *Credo*, which began its development in 2009. There are over 100,000 items of correspondence by Du Bois in the *W. E. B. Du Bois Papers 1803–1999 (bulk 1877–1963)*, including both public and private correspondence. Within Du Bois's "Baltimore" correspondence are 296 pieces linked to Gomer, which include letters, pictures, receipts, programs, and schedules.

Du Bois and Gomer's intimate letters have their own interesting and compromised history. The original three-volume collection of Du Bois's correspondence, published in 1973, 1976, and 1978 by the custodian of Du Bois's correspondence, Herbert Aptheker, was intentionally edited to only include Du Bois's career letters. A review of the collection by Marion Kilson, published after the release of the second volume, states: "[I]t is especially unfortunate that Aptheker . . . decided to focus on Du Bois's public career," as Du Bois's private letters would have provided a more accurate portrayal of Du Bois.

Kilson notes that "[w]ithin the two volumes of correspondence selected by Aptheker [the third volume had not yet been published at the time of her review], there are only six letters to members of Du Bois's family" and only one to Gomer. Kilson predicts: "Had Aptheker decided to include the more revealing personal correspondence to which he had access he would have made a more distinctive contribution to our understanding of the contradictory complexity of Du Bois."

Due to Du Bois's prolific correspondence habits, all of his letters could not possibly have been included within the traditional print book format of the twentieth century; thus, massive selective editing was required at the time of their original publication. Aptheker defended his editing system in his introduction in 1973, explaining that for each topic, "a representative letter was chosen and all correspondence essentially repetitious omitted. These, and, of course, editorial judgment concerning the relative significance of the letters, were the basic principals of selection." However, as Kilson reinforces, a balance of public and private letters would have proved extremely beneficial in capturing a more accurate portrayal of Du Bois, the correspondent, in addition to his more public roles.

Aptheker admits he was aware of this void while editing the letters, stating in his introduction that "[t]he major decision to concentrate upon Du Bois's historical dimensions excluded practically all personal correspondence." Yet, it appears that Du Bois was comfortable with the fact that his intimate letters might become public after his death, as he placed his entire life correspondence (including public and personal exchanges) in Aptheker's custody in 1961. Du Bois even donated personal hate mail to Aptheker, which Du Bois kept and filed under the term "curious." Aptheker readily admits that "since neither Dr. nor Mrs. Du Bois ever suggested any form of exclusion, nor asked to examine the manuscript, the faults of this volume in selection, preparation, footnoting, and introductions belong solely to me."

Du Bois and Gomer's intimate letters help scholars, and now—through digital accessibility—the general public, to better understand why Baltimore was simultaneously "home" and not "home" for the Du Boises and why their house on Montebello Terrace has been often neglected from the city's public history. Readers can relate to the Du Boises' personal and universal familial issues, such as financial decisions/challenges, health problems and mortality fears, child/grandchildren rearing responsibilities and home maintenance, through viewing their correspondence. The letters can also help in attracting more readers to see Du Bois as a personal writer and private person, as well as a public writer and societal figure. In addition, Du Bois and Gomer's letters create a clearer understanding not only of the prominent figure of Du Bois, but also of Gomer—who, through her intimate letters, becomes much more than just "the first wife of W. E. B. Du Bois."

There are clear physical differences between Du Bois's and Gomer's intimate letters. Du Bois's letters to Gomer during their Baltimore years are typed and formal in their presentation, while Gomer's letters are hand-written, more informal, and are often penned on preprinted stationary with the letterhead: "Du Bois Cottage, 2302 Montebello Terrace, Baltimore, Maryland"—a recognition that the house was, at least temporarily, an established family residence. There are more letters from Gomer to Du Bois than there are letters from Du Bois to Gomer, and Du Bois's letters are typically longer and more developed than Gomer's.

Jeremy Smith, archivist at the Special Collections and University Archives at the University of Massachusetts, Amherst clarifies that "[m]ost of Du Bois's outgoing correspondence in the collection is not signed because [the letters] are carbon copies of the letters he actually mailed (the equivalent of a sent mail folder). Occasionally you will see one signed, which usually indicates it wasn't sent. The signed copies are theoretically with the people he sent them to." Smith speculates: "I am not sure what happened to Nina's papers after her death. My guess would be that they were destroyed or given to Yolande."

The University of Massachusetts's online archive does not provide transcriptions or annotated versions of the Du Boises' letters (only digital scans of the actual letters), so readers must decipher the words on their own (which is challenging at times—especially in the handwritten letters by Gomer). However, this process, of reading and deciphering the correspondence first-hand (without supplementary criticism or commentary), allows readers to feel the immediacy of the letters in an unfiltered setting, like they are receiving the letters, too, seventy-five years later after their mailing.

Ian Baucom suggests that "just as speech without gestures loses something, so [letters] printed rather than in the handwriting [of their authors] lose something," which is their visual and residual life force. Gomer's voice, in particular, remains tangible and alive in her handwritten letters. "Seeing" Du Bois's and Gomer's letters is a distinctly different temporal, perceptive, and sensory experience from reading transcribed versions of many other historical correspondents. In turn, the original published collection of Du Bois's letters by Aptheker might be reclassified as Du Bois's "public" letters, while the more recently digitalized collection by the University of Massachusetts presents Du Bois's "life" letters, unveiling a much broader portrait of Du Bois as a leading civil rights figure, writer, correspondent, and husband. Within this relatively new unfiltered archive, the intimate story of "The Du Bois Cottage" unfolds.

The "Du Bois Cottage" at 2302 Montebello Terrace was ready for occupancy in the spring of 1940. The house, and its location in Baltimore, was a geographical compromise between the Du Boises' earlier active, intellectual lives in New York (where the Du Boises lived while Du Bois worked for the NAACP during the years of 1909–1934) and the racial animosity that resided in Atlanta (where Du Bois lived when he was teaching at Atlanta University during the years of 1897–1910 and from 1934–1944).

Du Bois scholar David Levering Lewis points out that "[a]lthough Jim Crow reigned in law and practice in Baltimore, relations between the races were far less raw in this Upper South city than they were in Atlanta." Within this Eastside chamber, the intimacy and latter years of W. E. B. Du Bois and Nina Gomer Du Bois's marriage settled, marking the crossroads of arteries extending well beyond the state's northern and southern state boundaries.

Lewis describes this move to Baltimore as a literal and metaphorical interruption in Du Bois's life, as "Nina and Baby Du Bois flowed into the river of [Du Bois's] busy life, only to be deposited yet again on the most convenient shore." After an unsuccessful attempt to live in Atlanta with Du Bois, Gomer and baby Du Bois (Yolande's daughter, whom "had been reared in New York almost exclusively by [Gomer]") returned to New York while Du Bois commissioned a house to be built in Morgan Park in the late 1930's.

Baltimore's temporary residential docking proved to be permanent for Gomer—if not for Du Bois. While Aptheker shies away from including the familial tensions which led to the Baltimore move, Lewis is more forthcoming in his details: "Although liberated from an abusive marriage and advantaged by a secure teaching position in Baltimore, Yolande, much overweight and prone to transient maladies, remained the despair of her parents and of little consequence in the life of her bubbly daughter." Compromise was needed to help in raising the Du Boises' granddaughter. Lewis explains how "[d]espite Nina's almost visceral aversion to Atlanta and Will's decided preference for the convenience of solitary living space, both concluded that their granddaughter's welfare required them to make sacrifices." Baltimore was the geographical compromise on which this familial sacrifice settled.

Lewis references Baltimore thirteen times in his Pulitzer Prize winning biography, *W. E. B. Du Bois: A Biography*. However, the thirteen pages which mention Baltimore are completely overshadowed by the vast remaining seven-hundred-and-one pages which do not. The city is a tiny footnote in Du Bois's life. The *Baltimore Sun* depicts Du Bois's mark in Baltimore in equally brief terms: "Not much is known about [Du Bois's] life here. In those 18 years not a single interview with him appeared in this or any other daily Baltimore paper, though Du Bois's brilliant *The Souls of Black Folk* had been published 33 years before he moved to Baltimore."

The lack of media attention to Du Bois during his Baltimore years is striking, especially since Baltimore was where Du Bois "announced his second and final break with the NAACP. Here he published *Dusk at Dawn, Color and Democracy*, and *The World and Africa*. And here in the early '50's he completed his autobiography." Furthermore, in April 1949 "the president of Morgan State College informed Du Bois's office that the failure 'to condemn (Paul Robeson's) treasonable statement' (which condemned fighting against the Soviet Union) made Du Bois unfit to deliver the scheduled commencement address on June 8"—surely more than a small scar in Baltimore's history. Therefore, locating the Eastside intimacy of Du Bois and Gomer is not a task that produces neat and tidy findings. Indeed, Du Bois and Gomer's "Baltimore years" were just as much "epistolary years," based on the need for familial and geographical compromise in order to gain equal rights for African Americans, as the "Baltimore years" were a chronological timeline as city homeowners.

Du Bois first met Gomer when she was his student at Wilberforce University in Pennsylvania, the first predominantly African American private university in the country. The couple married in May 1896 and lived in Philadelphia while Du Bois completed research for the University of Pennsylvania. After Du Bois was offered a teaching position at Atlanta University in 1897, they moved to Georgia, where their first child, a son named Burghardt Gomer Du Bois who was born on October 2, 1897, died on May 24, 1899. Du Bois describes the aftermath of their son's death in "I Bury My Wife": "[H]e died. And in a sense my wife died too. Never after that was she quite the same in her attitude toward life and the world . . . Something was gone from my life which would not come back. But . . . Life was left . . . and I could plunge back into it as she could not." Du Bois notes that "[e]ven when our little girl came two years later, [Gomer] could not altogether replace the One." Gomer would forever associate Atlanta with her first child's death, living the rest of her life dedicated to her second child—Nina "Yolande" Du Bois.

Gomer persisted to chaperone Yolande well into adulthood, even after Yolande married and had her own daughter, Yolande "Du Bois" Williams. Yolande's first marriage was to the poet Countee Cullen in 1928, but the marriage quickly dissolved. Three years later, in 1931, Gomer temporarily moved in with Yolande at 1301 Madison Avenue in Baltimore, after Gomer learned that Yolande was struggling while teaching history, English, and drama in the Baltimore public school system. Lewis describes a possible source for Yolande's fatigue: her new boyfriend, Arnette Franklin, who was a Lincoln University dropout and "a bit of a rogue and the antithesis of Countee Cullen."

Not long after, "[Williams] and Yolande were married on Wednesday, September 2, 1931, in a simple ceremony in Baltimore with a philosophical Will and Nina present . . . [Du Bois] had imposed only one prenuptial condition: Williams must finish his college education. Two weeks after the wedding, the groom returned to Lincoln [University]," the same university attended by Thurgood Marshall and Clarence Mitchell, Jr..

However, within five years Yolande and Williams were divorced and Du Bois found himself writing to Williams, requesting reimbursement for the money he had given Williams for his education and starting to consider the idea of purchasing a home in Baltimore for the well-being of his immediate and extended family, in spite of Gomer's opposition to the idea.

Du Bois's February 13, 1937 letter to Gomer—sent to her at their Harlem address, highlights Baltimore as a place where his family must "settle," both geographically and emotionally. Du Bois consoles Gomer over the lack of finding a house on her first trip to Baltimore, reinforcing his perspective that Baltimore is a healthier and safer environment for their granddaughter, Du Bois Williams, than Harlem. Du Bois places Gomer's dissatisfaction in the lens of undesirable real estate, versus a heart-felt opposition to the city. His letter asserts the need to move, for the sake of their family, including the need for their daughter, Yolande, to take a larger role in raising her daughter, Du Bois Williams.

For Du Bois, who was approaching 70 years old, the exchange of intellectual, social, and creative resources in New York for the quieter and cleaner environment in Baltimore was worth the trade-off. However, Du Bois was not the one who would be primarily residing at this location. While Baltimore would provide a more accessible setting for Du Bois's granddaughter, Du Bois Williams (who was five years old at the time), and Yolande, it would deny Gomer, who was also in her late sixties at this time, her desired cultural home in New York.

A year later, on April 26, 1938, Gomer writes to Du Bois to voice her unchanged resistance to the Baltimore relocation. Even with Du Bois's and Yolande's attempts at persuading her otherwise, Gomer states, *I do not see how I can ever live in Baltimore . . . We would always be making excuses to go some where else.* Gomer is adamant in her defense against the city, emphasizing that *Baltimore hasn't the life it had twenty years ago,* and noting that even if the location provided more in its opportunities for their daughter and granddaughter, it isn't *reason for all of us being tied to Baltimore the rest of our lives.* "Being tied to Baltimore the rest of [their] lives" would, however, prove to be the case, especially for Gomer, who would pass away in the house on Montebello Terrace twelve years later.

In spite of Gomer's resistance to move to Baltimore, the Du Boises and their granddaughter moved into a brand new house in Morgan Park in 1940. Lewis describes "Du Bois Cottage": "The house was a two-story brick structure with four bedrooms under a gable roof and nicely sited on a rise in Morgan Park, a faultlessly maintained community of teachers, postal employees, and several affluent Murphies abutting Morgan State College." It was, Lewis emphasizes, "[the] six-year-old grandchild to whom *Black Folk: Then and Now* was dedicated [who] gave [Du Bois] and [Gomer] good reason to try living together again" in Baltimore. Du Bois and Gomer's granddaughter would enroll in Baltimore City Public School 103 on Division Street, the segregated school also attended by Thurgood Marshall and Clarence Mitchell, Jr.

Gomer's June 23, 1940 letter to Du Bois reveals that 2302 Montebello Terrace was technically only home to her and her granddaughter at this time, as Du Bois had returned to their former New York residence for his summer break. Gomer's reaction to her new house is telling in its disconnect from daily life: *As you see I am here in Baltimore . . . The house is very lovely but some how very strange to me for living.*

Gomer's intimate letters to Du Bois resemble those of many other wives of prominent men, regularly discussing the prominent people, issues, and institutions which were important to her husband's life and career. The letters showcase Du Bois's control of financial, career, and major residential decisions for the family, while Gomer takes charge of the home management, accounting, and domestic needs of their daughter and granddaughter. Many of Du Bois and Gomer's Baltimore letters are updates and exchanges regarding the maintenance of "Du Bois Cottage."

Intimacy and physical companionship, especially at this point in Du Bois's and Gomer's lives, are afterthoughts in their letters. Du Bois's statement at the end of his November 18, 1940 letter, that he *shall not plan to come up Thanksgiving unless something unusual happens,* suggests his absence is the norm, not the exception, at "Du Bois Cottage." Du Bois's hope for Gomer—*to enjoy Baltimore a little*—is written more as a defense of his purchase of 2302 Montebello Terrace, than as a wish for Gomer's future happiness.

Four years later, Du Bois would be forced to retire in a controversial move made by the board at Atlanta University. Afterwards, Du Bois returned "home," which was not to Baltimore, but rather to New York, and continued further employment with the NAACP. Shirley Graham, who would become Du Bois's second wife a year after Gomer's death, "secured a place for Du Bois on 'Sugar Hill' in the most prestigious apartment building in Harlem. Apartment 13-H, a one-bedroom unit atop 409 Edgecombe Avenue, awaited his signature upon arrival." The Sugar Hill District was home to many of Harlem's elite from the 1930's to the 1950's, when it housed Thurgood Marshall, Paul Robeson, Duke Ellington, Countee Cullen, Count Baisie, Joe Louis, and Bessie Buchannan, among others.

After Du Bois's permanent move to New York, Gomer writes to Du Bois at his Sugar Hill address on October 20, 1944, requesting to join him in New York, as Yolande is no longer interested in living in Baltimore. Gomer's initial assertion that Yolande is the main force behind the family's desire to leave Baltimore quickly shifts throughout the letter into a shared wish for geographical relocation, as Gomer reinforces the need to relocate their granddaughter and the economic cost of maintaining Du Bois Cottage, especially *for what we can get out of it as a home.*

Du Bois writes back to Gomer two weeks later. His November 5, 1944 letter is intense and commanding, shutting the door on Gomer's hope to sell "Du Bois Cottage": *I am not going to sell it as long as I live unless there are unforeseen changes.* He places Gomer's and Yolande's unhappiness on their shoulders, blaming their sheltered lives for contributing to their discontent: *You have never known hunger or great discomfort in any way; you have always had plenty to eat and to wear. You know that this is a world where nobody has everything.* The finality of Du Bois's decision regarding the house in Baltimore and his view of their marriage as one of permanent long-distance are clear. . . *it will not hurt either of you to live in Baltimore*. Though many would debate the legitimacy of one of Du Bois's included defenses: *I have lived in Georgia for eleven years and it has not hurt me*.

Gomer's health quickly declined during the next year, and Du Bois brought her to Montefiore Hospital in Bronx, New York, in early 1946. Du Bois writes to Gomer at Montefiore on February 8, 1946, stating that Gomer must return to Baltimore after she is released from the hospital. The letter reads like a continuation of Du Bois's November 5, 1944 letter in its justification of "Du Bois Cottage" and the compromise required for his career. Du Bois remains direct and unbending in his defense of the property, stressing that the Baltimore-based house is as adequate as any home; in fact, he asserts, its external advantages (beauty and convenience) outweigh all other disadvantages.

The letter also defines Du Bois and Gomer's marriage as a compromise, where satisfaction is gauged by public standards and convenience versus internal desires: *[n]ext May we will have been married fifty years. I have not always been able to make you happy but I have made you for the most part comfortable.* Any desire for a celebratory half-a-century union is masked through Du Bois's frustration with Gomer's resistance to return to Baltimore. He sums up his contribution to their fifty-year marriage with the statement: *I think I have done my best. For the sake, therefore, of our family and especially of Du Bois, I hope you will read this letter over several times and come to the reasonable conclusion*—to be content to live in Baltimore.

Thirteen months later, Gomer confirms Du Bois's role as a visitor at "Du Bois Cottage" in her March 29, 1947 letter: *The box of fruit came alright in good condition . . . I believe we are to look for you this weekend.* Two weeks later, on April 11, 1947, Du Bois writes a short note to Gomer, expressing his delight at her improved health after his recent visit to Baltimore. Of note in this letter is Du Bois's accepted status as a temporary visitor versus a permanent figure at "Du Bois Cottage": *I had a very interesting stay in Baltimore and lectured in Washington then returned to New York. I was especially glad to find you so cheerful and improving. I am enclosing some stamps for your use.*

The long distance marriage of Du Bois and Gomer, compromised by the compromise of "Du Bois Cottage," would endure until Gomer died in her bedroom inside the home on July 1, 1950 from complications due to suffering a stroke. Lewis notes that "'I Bury My Wife,' Will's apostrophe, was properly confessional. [Du Bois] had, he said, in effect sacrificed her happiness to his duty to the race." In the end, the compromise of having his family live in Baltimore while he taught in Atlanta, worked for the NAACP in New York, and traveled took its intimate toll. Du Bois's final "private letter" to Gomer was released as publicly as possible—in the July 15, 1950 issue of *The Chicago Globe*. Du Bois's private intimacy, in the end, belonged to the public. Du Bois freely admitted:

> *I was not, on the whole, what one would describe as a good husband. The family and its interests were never the main center of my life. I was always striving to guide the world and certainly the Negro group, so that always I was ranging away in body or in soul and leaving the home to my wife. She must often have been lonesome and wanted more regular and personal companionship than I gave. And yet on the other hand, she was as avid for the things I thought I was doing and as proud of any accomplishment as I was. One never knows under such circumstances, just what might have been changed for the better.*

Du Bois passed away thirteen years later, at age 95, in Ghana. In the decades since Du Bois sold the "Du Bois Cottage" after Gomer's death, there have only been a handful of published articles which discuss the Du Boises' connection to Baltimore. For the most part, "Du Bois Cottage" in Morgan Park, and Du Bois's years as a visiting resident, have been pushed to the background, marking another unnoticed route of intimate neglect within the Eastside.

Embracing both the public and private, and the celebrated and forgotten, the Du Boises' letters create the missing map of the Du Boises' presence in Baltimore, as well as a new understanding of the compromise attributed to that intimate distance. Viewing the Du Boises' marriage as an epistolary union during their Baltimore years helps to validate the intimate letter in its production of the ground-level communication necessary for societal advancements, especially of human rights. Du Bois and Gomer's Baltimore letters shed light on intimate decisions made in the latter years of their marriage—a marriage lived apart for public and socio-political gains—and the Eastside location of "Du Bois Cottage" involved in that compromise. The compromise of Baltimore, as well, is established as a marker within a much larger map, where intimate needs fueled and exhausted the lives needed to advance civil rights, throughout the country and its hidden history.

Conclusion

The reality of mapping the intimate heart of any city is the reality of an unfinished and incomplete map. Just as the intimate letter is perpetually in-progress as it awaits a loved one's absence, so an intimacy map remains in-waiting. As soon as chambers and routes are located and marked, new transporting methods of intimacy will inevitably surface. Baltimore's hidden heart is messy, intersectional, layered, and incomplete. Unlike revised timelines, Charm City's hidden heart continues to grow and beat, saluting the unfiltered, unedited voices of its past residents and visitors and welcoming contemporary lovers into its vulnerable and interconnected chambers.

Many other factors are involved in the process of locating and uncovering intimate letters besides the physical movement of letters from a closet or drawer to a more public and accessible venue. The following are a few of these factors, though the factors are not the only influences in public accessibility transitions, which are individual to each set of correspondents and their intimate letters. Notably, these determinants are also the same elements that this author had to negotiate in viewing Baltimore's hidden heart through a mapping of the city's intimacy history.

The first major influence which must be acknowledged in the discussion of the public accessibility of intimate letters is funding. Library of Congress Processing Technician Kristen Sosinski emphasizes that "[m]aintaining an archive is an expensive endeavor. It involves an ever growing need for space. Most public and academic libraries weed their collections—archives do not." Letters cannot be processed and published without adequate funds (public and/or private) for facility holdings and digital needs; therefore, money is needed to create and sustain online and print archives and to encourage human participation in this task. "The cost of a well-run archive seems bloated," Sosinski notes, "until you realize that the cost of preserving our cultural heritage and historical records is priceless." Douglass's, Harper's, and

Tubman's letters and artifacts (and lack of) speak volumes to this invaluable cost—of human life—in reinforcing the need for historical tribute in cultural heritage preservation.

Additionally, intimate letter discovery, processing, and publication are still labor-intensive tasks composed of physical work, time, and long-term sustainable efforts. The Du Bois papers, for example, showcase the overwhelming labor commitments required for comprehensive correspondence accessibility. "[S]pecialized [staff] are needed to acquire, organize, and provide access to collections, which are often one-of-a-kind documents not found anywhere else," Sosinski reinforces. These unique environmental and specialization requirements only enhance the complexity of the archive and its perpetually "in-progress" existence.

Legality also influences intimate letters' accessibility, especially regarding [c]opyright, ownership and privacy rights. For example, who should be the appropriate "owner" of Poe's, Emerson's, and Twain's Baltimore correspondence? Twain's current epistolary archive is stored in California, yet it is only partially accessible to its postmarked cities of origin. Furthermore, what is the appropriate length of time to wait before private papers of deceased historical figures become public? The ownership of intimate letters remains a provocative issue and one that will likely continue to be debated throughout the twenty-first century, including the implementation of legislation in determining the ownership of electronic communication.

Political and academic issues also intersect when intimate letters are discovered and/or donated to public and private institutions. Decisions about how and where intimate letters will be stored and publicly displayed are political by nature. "[A]rchiving, publishing or even simply analyzing letters is," as Magaretta Jolly reinforces in "On Burning, Saving, and Stealing Letters," "a delicate business, traversing the correspondents' relationship with other relationships between editor, publisher, archivist, and public readers." An archive's declaration of ownership of correspondents' letters and a city's declaration of ownership of its former residents' homes is poised for controversy. For example, Esther Richards's intimate letters are stored on a Mount Holyoke/Massachusetts-based online archive, while the bulk of Richards's life and letters are Baltimore-based.

Similarly, The *Mitchell Family Papers* are stored primarily at the Library of Congress, but scholars can also find further papers, including career correspondence, in the Amistad Research Center in New Orleans, Louisiana, even though the Mitchells were inarguably "of Baltimore." Such is the case for many of the correspondents included in this collection (with personal papers being housed by multiple archives in different states).

Sosinski clarifies that "[t]he degree to which politics plays a role depends on the nature of the institution and its source of funding . . . When a powerful outside figure dictates that a certain collection be given star treatment, it is easier to make a case to secure the funding and resources required to make that happen." This reality makes us question: Are the voids and holes of knowledge created by particular political preferences reinforcing the neglect and silencing of intimate letters?

Furthermore, ambiguities regarding the exclusion and/or inclusion of individual people and/or materials within prominent family archives remain a difficult decision for archivists—particularly in regard to cataloging. *The Mitchell-Jackson Family Papers* in the Amistad Research Center, for instance, provide personal papers by extended Mitchell and Jackson family members, including material about/by Lillie Carroll Jackson and her husband, Keiffer Albert Jackson. Additionally, the posthumous addition of the Eleanor Roosevelt/Lorena Hickok letters to the FDR Library is another example of epistolary extensions which do not follow traditional presidential papers protocol, in addition to papers composed before standardized archives, such as the Adamses' letters.

The time consuming nature of archives also varies by a case-by-case basis. "It is tedious and specialized work," Sosinski stresses, as "materials are [often] fragile and you have to handle them safely and carefully." Sosinski clarifies that "[u]sually, collections arrive in disarray and in desperate need of new housing." Most intimate letter collections are not as easily catalogued or dated as Haardt's and Mencken's letters or F. Scott's and Zelda Fitzgerald's correspondence. "You have to organize thousands of items physically and intellectually," Sosinski stresses, "both of which are time consuming."

Processing The *Mitchell Family Papers* at the Library of Congress has been particularly time consuming because of the amount of material in this particular donation. The Library of Congress states that the collection contains an "estimated 250,000 items. . . [including] correspondence, notebooks, legal files, NAACP records, scrapbooks, photographs, films, audio tapes, and newspapers." The March 24, 1997 press release, "Mitchell Family of Civil Rights Activists Gives Papers to Library" states that "[t]he Library plans to seek a grant to support the processing of the collection." Not surprisingly, The *Mitchell Family Papers* have not received any significant public relations follow-up since the initial 1997 donation press release.

As is the case with many archives, donations of large personal paper collections often take years, and sometimes decades, to organize, process, and publicize. "[I]f short cuts are taken in processing (e.g. minimal level descriptions) [archives]," Sosinski warns, "chances are the end user is going to struggle to comprehend the collection which will either result in the collection not being used to its fullest, or staff time devoted to working with the confused researcher."

Complications of categorizing further the challenge of creating accessible archives. Sosinski confirms that "there are many areas of overlap and areas of gray . . . Each archival collection is unique and there will always [be] something that isn't going to fit neatly into a category. Intellectually, you can describe [an artifact] to capture both the personal and the professional aspect[s]," but in the end, "[y]ou have to choose." Such is the case with many public figures' correspondence, including Thurgood Marshall's letters and the papers of other prominent government officials.

There is also a lack of a standardized template or model when categorizing archival materials. Often, archivists rely on chronological order, "or by addressee or by sender or by topic." "But other times," Sosinski emphasizes, "there is no discernable order and you have to determine the best way to organize [materials]." These categorical decisions can make the difference between a researcher gaining access to desired letters, or missing them entirely.

Yet, even amongst these complex, messy, and often contradictory conditions, we continue to write intimate letters, to read intimate letters, and to read intimate letters written to be read by others. Bland and Cross reinforce in *Gender and Politics in the Age of Letter Writing, 1750-2000* that "the letter is one of the most democratic of genres as it is accessible to the barely literate, the well educated, men and women, young and old." As such, our current world can gain much from locating and studying intimate letters, many of which were created because of societal inequities or cultural inadequacies. Without these unfiltered and intimate conversations paving the way for future actions, risky and provocative decisions may lay dormant, indefinitely.

Jolly explains how, unlike most other public forums of communication, "epistolary expression has attempted to arbitrate through love rather than judgment, through speaking about private things rather than through silencing them." A lack of attention and validity given to the intimate letter's literal and metaphorical traces and routes is surely another layer of human injustice, as it denies the role of intimacy and the human heart within larger public, geographical, and historical frameworks.

In abandoning the physical letter for a quicker and more convenient means of intimate expression, sacrifices of privacy, time, perception, and archive potential have been made. The intimate letter and the "intimacy" of the letter have been, at their hearts, compromised. Jolly reinforces the importance of having an available and private space for declaring intimacy on the page: "a letter's afterlife is as thoroughly culturally inscribed as its writing . . . [and] we need to use [intimate] writing to extend alternative visions of personal and public relationship, and to preserve the history of those who began them, if we are to have any hope of a truly just, truly protective, form of privacy."

This author hopes that readers will view the recent decline of epistolary intimacy (which coincides with the extinction of physical letters and an acceptance of a post-private world) as an opportunity to view past and present history through a newly focused, yet layered lens. Intimate letters are much more than ink and paper; they are the blood and muscle known as the human heart—our most shared and remarkable archive. To see and understand the intimacy driving the history and the future of our cities, we must validate the hidden and private communication which formed the chambers of those cities and chart the routes that grew from the hearts of the people living within them.

Notes and Sources

—Introduction—

A Birds-Eye View of the Heart of Baltimore: "A Birds-Eye View of the Heart of Baltimore," Black and White Alteration, Wikimedia Commons, last modified May 30, 2018, https://commons.wikimedia.org/wiki/File:A_birds-eye_view_of_the_heart_of_Baltimore._LOC_75694536.tif.

"civilized and gay, rotted and polite": F. Scott Fitzgerald, *A Life in Letters* (New York: Simon and Schuster, 2010), 291.

"Anyone can love a perfect place. Loving Baltimore takes some resilience": Laura Lippman, qtd. in Noah Adams, "Laura Lippman's Baltimore: Loving a Flawed Place," Crime in the City, *npr.org*, Aug. 23, 2007, https://www.npr.org/2007/08/23/13871677/laura-lippmans-baltimore-loving-a-flawed-place.

Anatomy of the arteries of the human body: "Anatomy of the arteries of the human body (1881)," Wikimedia Commons, last modified October 1, 2015, https://commons.wikimedia.org/wiki/File:Anatomy_of_the_arteries_of_the_human_body_-_descriptive_and_surgical,_with_the_descriptive_anatomy_of_the_heart_(1881)_(14764835715).jpg.

"[a] good handwritten letter is a creative act": Catherine Field, "The Fading Art of Letter Writing," *The New York Times*, Feb. 3, 2011, https://www.nytimes.com/2011/02/04/opinion/04iht-edfield04.html.

"It is too simple . . . letters merely as relics of a bygone era": Francine Prose, foreword to *Illustrated Letters: Artists and Writers Correspond,* edited by Roselyne De Ayala and Jean-Pierre Gueno (New York: Harry N. Abrams, Inc., 1998), 17.

"[l]etters have always defeated distance, but with the coming of email, time seem[s] to be vanquished as well": Thomas Mallon, *Yours Ever: People and Their Letters* (New York: Pantheon Books, 2009), 3.

"'[r]eal time' . . . isn't time at all, but rather . . . our goal in communicating . . . was the old passage of days": Ibid., 13.

"A telephone call or instant message actually conveys one *place* to another": Ibid.

"We write to taste life twice: in the moment and in retrospect": Anais Nin, "The New Woman," *In Favor of the Sensitive Man and Other Essays (*Orlando, Florida: Harcourt Brace & Co., 1994), 13.

"in retrospect . . . in the moment": Ibid.

John Willis divides epistolary study into four parts: John Willis, *More than Words: Readings in Transport, Communication and the History of Postal Communication* (Quebec: Canadian Museum of Civilization, 2007).

"[h]istorically, the post has facilitated communication": Ibid., 14.

"Communication, by post and any other media . . . is rooted in historical context": Ibid, 14.

"fascination [with intimate letters] is more complex than a simple case of voyeurism": Bill Shapiro, ed., *Other People's Love Letters: 150 Letters You Were Never Meant to See* (New York: Crown, 2007), vii.

"Many scholars contend that letters serve as the best source for researching literary history . . . since epistolary documents usually provide authentic and substantive reflections": Jeffrey Berlin, "On the nature of letters," *European Journal of English Studies 9*, no.1 (2005): 65.

"a momentary experience which incorporates but stands outside orthodox conceptions": Dorothy Lander, "Love Letters to the Dead: Resurrecting an Epistolary Art," *Omega: Journal of Death & Dying 58*, no. 4 (2008/9): 314.

"hybrid, nomadic, intricate, and oxymoronic nature": Isabel Roboredo Seara, "Epistolary: from hidden dialogue to an obsession to dialogue," *Language and Dialogue 2*, no. 3 (2012): 363.

"the distance [and] the bridge": Janet Gurkin Altman, *Epistolary: Approaches to a Form* (Columbus: Ohio State UP, 1982), 13.

"[t]he lover who takes up his pen to write his loved one": Ibid., 14.

"[b]y understanding how those who lived before us loved": Michael L. Carrafiello, "Archives of Passion: Using Love Letters to Teach the Methods of History Inquiry," *AURCO Journal 15* (2009): 160.

"The letters of Einstein and Maric, for instance, suggest strongly that passion can and does move science to greater effort": Ibid., 25.

"were not held in archives or governmental or educational-supported storage facilities": Kasper Risbjerg Eskildsen, "Inventing the Archive: Testimony and Virtue in Modern Historiography," *History of the Human Sciences 26*, no. 4 (2013): 10.

"[w]ith the disappearance of the original correspondents . . . we can be more objectively concerned with [letters'] impact as historical documents": Caroline Bland and Maire Cross, *Gender and Politics in the Age of Letter Writing, 1750–2000* (Burlington, VT: Ashgate, 2004), 4.

"[t]he archivist has been transformed . . . archival thinking has moved from evidence": Terry Cook, "Evidence, Memory, Identity, and Community: Four Shifting Archival Paradigms," *Archival Science 13,* no. 2–3 (2013): 95.

"from passive curator to active appraiser to societal mediator to community facilitator": Ibid., 95.

The Heart, Showing the Interior (1890): "Anatomy, physiology and hygiene," Wikimedia Commons, last modified September 18, 2018, https://commons.wikimedia.org/wiki/File:Anatomy,_physiology_and_hygiene_(1890)_(14762071434).jpg.

"what is written for a particular person, what is meant to be read": Emilija Dimitrijevic, "Poets' Love Letters: Private Affairs or Cultural Objects?" *Textus 18*, no. 2 (2005): 283.

"that we are dealing not only with the question of interpreting and understanding a writer": Ibid., 289.

"something that one cannot possess in the common sense of the word": Ibid., 294.

"[p]resence is a term that need not refer always to *material, corporeal* presence":

Esther Milne, *Letters, Postcards, Email: Technologies of Presence* (New York: Routledge, 2010), 2.

"the social history of private life and intimacy": Eva L. Wyss, "From the Bridal Letter to Online Flirting: Changes in Text Type from the Nineteenth Century to the Internet Era," *Journal of Historical Pragmatics 9*, no. 2 (2008): 226.

"[d]esire often presents itself first and foremost as a problem . . . [b]rute attempts to eradicate it": Eugene de De Klerk, "The Poverty of Desire: Spivak, Coetzee, Lacan, and Postcolonial Eros," *Journal of Literary Studies 26*, no. 3 (2010): 67.

In the same manner that water, when finding itself restricted, will erode resistance and establish new channels: Ibid., 67.

"assertive action in the face of uncertain assumptions": Peter Turchi, *Maps of the Imagination: The Writer as Cartographer* (San Antonio, Texas: Trinity UP, 2004), 12.

"[a]ppl[ies] knowledge, skill, and talent . . . [to] create a document meant to communicate with": Ibid.

"false starts, missteps, and surprises": Ibid.

"What elements of the literary space can be mapped and what might prove to be unmappable": Barbara Piatti and Lorenz Hurni, "Cartographies of Fictional Worlds," *The Cartographic Journal 48*, no. 4 (2009): 219.

"Envisioning maps as a compelling form of storytelling": Sebastien Caquard, "Cartography I: Mapping Narrative Cartography." *Progress in Human Geography 37*, no. 1 (2013): 136.

"dangerous elements . . . forced into the blank spaces, ocean, or the margins of the maps": Karen Piper, *Cartographic Fictions: Maps, Race, and Identity* (New Jersey: Rutgers UP, 2002), 7.

"monsters and brutes": Ibid., 6.

"the blank spaces, ocean[s], [and] the margins": Ibid., 7.

—Part One—

Baltimore, 1838: "Baltimore Street Map 1938," Wikimedia Commons, last modified June 7, 2015, https://upload.wikimedia.org/wikipedia/commons/5/5c/Baltimore_Street_Map%2C_1838.jpg.

—Chapter One—

Frederick Douglass, 1855: "Frederick Douglass as a younger man," Wikimedia Commons, last modified May 11, 2012, https://commons.wikimedia.org/wiki/File:Frederick_Douglass_as_a_younger_man.jpg.

Anna Murray Douglass, circa 1860: "Anna Murray-Douglass," Wikimedia Commons, last modified Dec. 31, 2016, https://commons.wikimedia.org/wiki/File:Anna_Murray_Douglass.jpg.

Envelope: Delivery method: unknown. Postage stamps were not introduced or utilized regularly within the United States until the early 1940's. Before that time, the recipient of the delivery was responsible for the payment of transport. Envelopes were also not traditionally used until the postage system standardized, as the envelope would add extra weight to the cost. Typically, a letter was folded and sealed, with the recipient's address listed on the outside of the letter. For more information about early postal service, see "History of Stamps," American Philatelic Society, https://stamps.org/Stamp-History.

"the most thrilling . . . [moment in the narrative] is the description Douglass gives of his feelings": William Lloyd Garrison, introduction to *Narrative of the Life of Frederick Douglass, as American Slave. Written by Himself: Electronic Edition, Documenting the American South* (University of North Carolina at Chapel Hill, 2004), ix, docsouth.unc.edu/neh/douglass/douglass.html.

"the greatest African American of the 19ᵗʰ century . . . and arguably the greatest American ever to rise from the streets of Baltimore": Tom Chalkley, "Native Son: On the Trail of Frederick Douglass in Baltimore," *Baltimore City Paper*, March 15, 2000.

Frederick Augustus Washington Bailey, who would change his name: Early childhood information about Douglass found in Frank Towers, "African-American Baltimore in the Era of Frederick Douglass," *American Transcendental Quarterly* 9, no. 3 (1995): 165–81. ESBCOhost, eds.a.ebscohost.com.goucher.idm.oclc.org/ehost/detail/detail?vid=3&sid=78df3730-6f56-430e-96c7-440f395db70f%-40sessionmgr4010&bdata=JnNpdGU9ZWhvc3QtbGl2ZSZzY29wZT1zaX-Rl#AN=9511064521&db=a9h.

It was during Douglass's pre-teen years in Baltimore that he first learned to read: Early childhood information from Douglass's narrative found in: Frederick Douglass, *My Bondage and My Freedom* (New York: Dover, 1969), 79.

"[w]ith playmates for my teachers": Ibid., 96-7.

"It is possible, and even quite probable": Frederick Douglass, *Narrative of the Life of Frederick Douglass, as American Slave. Written by Himself: Electronic Edition, Documenting the American South* (Chapel Hill: University of North Carolina at Chapel Hill, 2004), docsouth.unc.edu/neh/douglass/douglass.html, 30-1.

"a city slave is almost a free man compared with a slave on a plantation": Ibid., 45.

"I often found myself regretting my own existence": Ibid., 50.

After the death of Douglass's suspected father: Early childhood information about Douglass can also be found in: Dickson J. Preston, *Young Frederick Douglass: The Maryland Years* (Baltimore: JHU P, 1980).

"Minutes were hours, and hours were days . . . The heart of no fox or deer": Frederick Douglass, "My Escape from Slavery," *Electronic Text Center* (Charlottesville: University of Virginia Library, 1993), xroads.virginia.edu/~drbr/douglas.html.

"left with the assurance that I was all right": Ibid.

"[i]f life is more than breath and the 'quick round of blood,'": Ibid.

"Once in the hands of Mr. Ruggles": Frederick Douglass, *My Bondage and My Freedom*,

217.

"free life began on the third of September 1838": Frederick Douglass, *"My Escape from Slavery."*

"When the escaped slave and future husband of Murray": Rosetta Douglass Sprague, "Anna Murray Douglass: My Mother as I Recall Her," *Journal of Negro History 8*, no. 1 (1923): 94.

"sense of [his] newfound love's vulnerability": David Taft Terry, "Douglass, Anna Murray," *Encyclopedia of African American History*, eds. Leslie M. Alexander and Walter C. Rucker (Santa Barbara, CA: ABC-CLIO, 2010): 384.

"circle of honest and warm hearted friends": Frederick Douglass, *My Bondage and Freedom*, 210.

"The thought of such a separation": Ibid., 211.

Murray was working as a domestic worker on Caroline for a man named Wells: Information about Murray's life in Baltimore is found in Rosetta Douglass Sprague, "Anna Murray Douglass: My Mother as I Recall Her."

destroyed in the 1872 fire that burned down Douglass's house: Information about Douglass's preserved (and unpreserved manuscripts) is located in: "Frederick Douglass Papers at the Library of Congress," The Library of Congress, www.loc.gov/collections/frederick-douglass-papers/about-this-collection.

"[t]he story of Frederick Douglass' hopes and aspirations": Rosetta Douglass Sprague, "Anna Murray Douglass," 93.

Murray was born around 1813 in Caroline County, Maryland: Information about Murray's early years can be found in "Anna Murray Douglass," Archives of Maryland (Biographical Series), Maryland State Archives, Mar. 30, 2012, http://msa.maryland.gov/megafile/msa/speccol/sc5400/sc5496/051200/051245/html/051245bio.html.

Two years later, Murray went to work for a family named Wells on South Caroline Street: Rosetta Douglass Sprague, "Anna Murray Douglass," 93-4.

circles which often excluded enslaved persons: Ibid., 94.

"[Murray] had lived with the Wells family . . . so long and having been able to save the great part of her earnings": Ibid.

"as [was] the condition of most wives . . . [Murray's] identify became so merged": Ibid.

The Library of Congress currently holds the majority of the personal and public papers (including letters) of Frederick Douglass: "Frederick Douglass Papers at the Library at Congress," The Library of Congress.

***Love Across Color Lines: Ottilie Assing and Frederick Douglass* by Maria Diedrich:** Further information about Ottilie Assing and Frederick Douglass's relationship can be found in Maria Diedrich, *Love Across Color Lines: Ottilie Assing and Frederick Douglass* (New York: Hill and Wang, 2000).

***Radical Passion: Ottilie Assing's Reports from America and Letters to Frederick Douglass* by Christoph Lohman:** Further information about Ottilie Assing and Frederick Douglass's relationship can be found in Christoph Lohman, *Radical Passion: Ottilie Assing's Reports from America and Letters to Frederick Douglass* (Bern, Switzerland: Peter Lang Inc., 2000).

Lohman admits the lack of preserved letters, too, between Assing and Douglass: Christoph Lohman, *Ottilie Assing's Reports*, xvii.

"It is possible . . . that Douglass never archived her letters": Ibid., xviii.

You may perhaps want to know how I like my present condition: Frederick Douglass, "Letter to Thomas Auld (September 3, 1848)," The Gilder Lehrman Center for the Study of Slavery, Resistance, and Abolition at the MacMillan Center, Whitney and Betty MacMillan Center for International and Area Studies at Yale, http://glc.yale.edu/letter-thomas-auld-september-3-1848.

"for any man": Ibid.

Will you favor me by dropping me a line: Frederick Douglass, "'I love you but hate slavery': Frederick Douglass to his former owner, Hugh Auld, New York: 1857," The Gilder Lehrman Center for the Study of Slavery, Resistance, and the Abolition at the MacMillan Center. Whitney and Betty MacMillan Center for International and Area Studies at Yale, www.gilderlehrman.org/history-by-era/slavery-and-anti-slavery/resources/"i-love-you-hate-slavery"-frederick-douglass-his-f.

Douglass's physical return to his Baltimore "home" actually did not occur until 1864: Further information about Douglass's return to Baltimore can be found in Tom Chalkley, "Native Son."

"Maryland is now a glorious free state . . . the revolution is genuine": Ibid.

In fact, it was not until 1892 that Douglass officially left his residential mark: Information about the Douglass Place homes and recent real estate status is found in Natalie Sherman, "A piece of Frederick Douglass history is on the market," *The Baltimore Sun*, August 31, 2015, http://www.baltimoresun.com/bs-bz-douglass-row-20150831-story.html.

524 South Dallas Street: Original photograph, 2015.

"[Douglass's] words still ring, his story is still relevant": Ibid.

"letters . . . of the [societal] battlefield": John O'Connell, *For the Love of Letters: The Joy of Slow Communication* (New York: Atria, 2012), 112.

"There is in him that union of head and heart": William Lloyd Garrison, introduction to *Narrative of the Life of Frederick Douglass, as American Slave*, vi.

—Chapter Two—

Frances Ellen Watkins Harper: "File:Fewharper.jpg," Wikimedia Commons, last
modified October 2, 2008, https://commons.wikimedia.org/wiki/File:Fewharper.jpg.

Envelope: Early letter express postage systems developed in the 1840's between Baltimore,
Philadelphia, New York, and Boston. The representative envelope depicts an early
provisional stamp signed and stamped by Baltimore's postmaster in 1845, James
Buchanan. For further information about early Baltimore and U.S. postage history, see:
"Early Distribution and Usage of Postage Stamps in the United States, 1842-1904,"
Frajola, http://www.rfrajola.com/berkunEDUexhibit.pdf.

**"the best known and best loved African-American poet prior to Paul Laurence
Dunbar":** Frances Smith Foster, ed., *A Brighter Coming Day: A Frances Ellen Watkins
Harper Reader* (New York: Feminist P at City U of New York, 1990), 4.

"[f]ew sources offer additional information about Harper's life": Ibid., 39.

"devoted thirty pages of his history of the Underground Railroad'": Ibid., 5.

"[t]here is not to be found in any written work portraying the Anti-slavery struggle":
William Still, qtd. in Frances Smith Foster, 5.

"Frances Ellen Watkins Harper [was] born in 1825 in Baltimore to free blacks":
"Frances Ellen Watkins Harper," The Baltimore Literary Heritage Project, University
of Baltimore, School of Communications Design, http://baltimoreauthors.ubalt.edu/
writers/francesharper.htm.

Camden Street Station: Original photograph, 2015.

"a fervent abolitionist, a community leader, and a highly regarded teacher": Frances
Smith Foster, *A Brighter Coming Day*, 7.

**"intense commitment to abolitionist and other social welfare crusades . . . her
familiarity**
with classical and Christian mythology": Ibid.

**one who was her caregiver (her uncle) and one who was her domestic employer (a
Baltimore bookseller):** "Frances Ellen Watkins Harper (1825–1911)," Archives of
Maryland (Biographical Series), Maryland State Archives, March 16, 2012, https://
msa.maryland.gov/megafile/msa/speccol/sc3500/sc3520/012400/012499/htm-
l/12499bio.html.

**"differing sources suggest [the family who employed Harper and owned the bookstore
in which she apprenticed] may have been Quakers by the name of Armstrong":**
Ibid.

which she did not take until 1860, when she married Fenton Harper at age 35:
"Frances Ellen Watkins Harper," Poetry Foundation, 2018, https://www.poetryfounda-
tion.org/poets/frances-ellen-watkins-harper.

"directly shaped the rest of Harper's life opportunities": "Frances Ellen Watkins Harper
(1825-1911)," Maryland State Archives.

"As an insider . . . [Harper] was a black woman who felt spiritually connected": Ibid.

Ortner actually discovered the manuscript after performing a simple catalogue search: Johanna Ortner, "Lost no More: Recovering Frances Ellen Watkins Harper's *Forest Leaves*," *Common-Place: The Journal of Early American Life* 15, no. 4 (Summer 2015), http://common-place.org/book/lost-no-more-recovering-frances-ellen-watkins-harpers-forest-leaves/.

"no known copies [of Forest Leaves] exist": Foster, *A Brighter Coming Day*, 8.

Fugitive Slave Act of 1850 (a law which forbade free blacks from entering the state or otherwise face the penalty of forced slavery): "Fugitive Slave Act of 1850," Legacy of Slavery in Maryland, An Archives of Maryland Electronic Publication, http://slavery.msa.maryland.gov/html/antebellum/slavelaw1850.html.

Dissemblance must also be taken into account: Further information about dissemblance can be found in Darlene Clark Hine, *Hine Sight: Black Women and the Re-Construction of American History* (Brooklyn, New York: Carlson, 1994), 912.

"[I]t is impossible to retrieve that which has been materially discarded": Melba Joyce Boyd, *Discarded Legacy: Politics in the Life of Frances E. W. Harper, 1825–1911* (Detroit: Wayne State UP, 1994), 11.

"a contribution to the reconstruction of the fragmented and obscured legacy of Frances Harper": Ibid.

"[A Brighter Coming Day] provides Harper's full range": Ibid., 25.

"Harper's writings have now been substantially retrieved from obscurity": Ibid.

"[s]ince the writing of this book no buried diaries of Harper's have been uncovered": Ibid., 30.

a letter written by Harper to William Still: Jana Koehler, "Epistolary Politics: A Recovered Letter from F. E. W. Harper to William Still," *American Literary Realism* 49, no. 3 (Spring 2017): 283-286.

"possibly the first novel written by a black woman": Henry Gates, Jr., introduction to *The Bondswoman's Narrative* by Hannah Crafts (New York: Warner Books, 2013), xii.

An unpublished poem by Jupiter Hammon: "Jupiter Hammon and Archival Discovery," Julie McCown/Southern Utah University, September 15, 2015, https://www.juliemccown.com/single-post/2015/09/15/Jupiter-Hammon-and-Archival-Discovery.

She was, in fact, known as the "Bronze Muse": "Frances Ellen Watkins Harper," *The Baltimore Sun*, February 7, 2007, https://www.baltimoresun.com/features/bal-blackhistory-harper-story.html.

"[s]trictly speaking, Frances Ellen Watkins Harper is not one of the many writers restored": Frances Smith Foster, "Gender, Genre and Vulgar Secularism: The Case of Frances Ellen Watkins Harper and the AME Press," *Recovered Writers/Recovered Texts: Race, Class & Gender in Black Women's Literature*, 38 (1997): 46.

"long been included in the discussion of early African American literature": Ibid., 47.

"Harper was neither lost nor ignored for many reasons . . . [c]ritics and scholars embraced Harper . . . For over sixty years": Ibid., 47.

—Chapter Three—

Harriet Tubman, circa 1880: "Harriet Tubman," Wikimedia Commons, last modified March 10, 2010, https://commons.wikimedia.org/wiki/File:Harriet_Tubman.jpg.

Harriet Tubman Reward Notice 1849: "Notice published in the *Cambridge Democrat* (1849), offering a reward for the return of Harriet Tubman and her two brothers," Wikimedia Commons, last modified April 22, 2016, https://commons.wikimedia. org/wiki/File:Harriet_Tubman_Reward_Notice_1849.jpg.

Most that I have done and suffered in the service: Frederick Douglass, qtd. in Sarah Hopkins Bradford, *Scenes in the Life of Harriet Tubman* (Amazon Digital Services, 1869), 6, http://www.accessible.com.goucher.idm.oclc.org/accessible/docButton?AAWhat=builtPage&AAWhere=B00117942.PREFACE.xml&AABeanName=toc3&AANextPage=/printBrowseBuiltPage.jsp.

"the midnight sky and the silent stars": Ibid.

"[I]n a world of suspicious whites, a letter could elicit unwanted attention": Kate Clifford Larson, *Bound for the Promised Land: Harriet Tubman: Portrait of an American Hero* (New York: Random House, 2004), 65-6.

the curators at the National Museum of African American History . . . cannot determine that Tubman was the person who wrote the Xs in her hymnal: Jacquelyn Serwer, email message to the author, June 15, 2013.

Tubman, born Araminta "Minty" Ross in 1822: "Harriet Ross Tubman Davis (b. circa 1822–d. 1913)," Archives of Maryland (Biographical Series), Maryland State Archives, October 31, 2011, https://msa.maryland.gov/megafile/msa/speccol/sc5400/sc5496/013500/013562/html/013562biog.html.

"Tubman's illiteracy certainly presents a problem": Beverly Lowry, *Harriet Tubman: Imagining a Life* (New York: First Anchor Books, 2008), 7.

"what life might have been like for the American hero Harriet Tubman": Ibid., 1.

"[t]his book does not pretend to be a work of intense scholarship . . . [but] the story of a life": Ibid.

"the remembered Tubman—that is . . . the myth that draws on the factual core": Milton C. Sernett, *Harriet Tubman: Myth, Memory, and History* (Durham, N.C.: Duke UP, 2007), 3.

"Tubman may be America's most malleable icon . . . significance for . . . how we are to remember": Ibid., 3.

"By learning of Harriet Tubman . . . we learn about ourselves": Ibid.

"[b]y learning about Harriet Tubman and her place in [Baltimore] memory . . . we learn": Ibid.

"[t]he intersubjective process by which certain personalities": Ibid.

"chronicles the life history of the commemorated Tubman": Ibid., 9.

"On the cusp of adulthood, the disabled Tubman": Kate Clifford Larson, *Bound for the Promised Land*, 65.

the first of multiple successful rescues which would bring over 70 family members

and friends to freedom: "Harriet Tubman in Baltimore and Beyond," Visit Baltimore, https://baltimore.org/article/harriet-tubman-baltimore-and-beyond.

"[After the passage of the Fugitive Slave Act of 1850, Tubman's] niece": "Harriet Tubman and the Underground Railroad," Baltimore Legends and Legacies, Visit Baltimore, 2013, https://baltimore.org/article/harriet-tubman-baltimore-and-beyond.

"Tom was possibly working as a stevedore on Baltimore's docks": Kate Clifford Larson, *Bound for the Promised Land*, 89.

"made Baltimore's waterfront an ideal location from which Tubman could operate": Ibid.

"could circulate among the city's 36,000 blacks": James A. McGowan and William C. Kashatus, *Harriet Tubman: A Biography* (Santa Barbara, CA: ABC-CLIO, 2011), 28.

"were also perfectly positioned to receive news about any threats to Harriet's family": Kate Clifford Larson, *Bound for the Promised Land*, 89.

"a nest of pirates": "Baltimore and the War of 1812," Visit Baltimore, https://baltimore.org/article/baltimore-and-war-1812.

Fell's Point: Original Photograph, 2015.

"a look, a glance, a movement, a shift of the foot, or a wave of a hand": Kate Clifford Larson, *Bound for the Promised Land*, 65-6.

"[t]he midnight sky and silent stars": Frederick Douglass, qtd. in Sarah Hopkins Bradford, *Scenes in the Life of Harriet Tubman*, 6.

—Part Two—

Baltimore Circa 1846: "Baltimore circa 1846," Wikimedia Commons, last modified November 25, 2009, https://commons.wikimedia.org/wiki/File:Baltimore_ca1846_byJohnPlumbe_LOC.png.

—Chapter Four—

Eleanor Roosevelt and Lorena Hickok, March 1934: "Eleanor Roosevelt and Lorena Hickok in Puerto Rico," Wikimedia Commons, last modified October 24, 2011, https://upload.wikimedia.org/wikipedia/commons/a/a5/Eleanor_Roosevelt_and_Lorena_Hickok_in_Puerto_Rico_-_NARA_-_196171.jpg.

Envelope: The representative envelope features a stamp issued in 1934 to commemorate the 300th anniversary of the founding of Maryland. For further information about this stamp and other stamps issued in 1934 see: "US Stamps—Commemoratives of 1934-1935," https://www.stamp-collecting-world.com/usstamps_1934.html.

Letter Excerpts: Hickok's excerpt is from a letter composed on official Lord Baltimore Hotel letterhead: Lorena Hickok, qtd. in Rodger Streitmatter. *Empty Without You:*

The Intimate Letters of Eleanor Roosevelt and Lorena Hickok (Boston, Massachusetts: Da Capo Press, 2000), 139. Roosevelt's excerpt is from a letter composed on paper without letterhead: Eleanor Roosevelt, qtd. in Rodger Streitmatter, *Empty Without You*, 138.

The Lord Baltimore Hotel: Original Photograph, 2015.

"first formal interview with Eleanor Roosevelt on November 7": Michael Golay, *America 1933: The Great Depression, Lorena Hickok, Eleanor Roosevelt, and the Shaping of the New Deal* (New York: Free Press, 2013), 1.

"Eleanor had discovered [in her mid-thirties] that her husband, FDR, was having an affair": Rodger Streitmatter, *Empty Without You*, xx.

"stumbl[ing] upon a packet of lightly scented [hidden] letters": Ibid., 1.

Hickok's betrayal came from the abandonment of her live-in companion: Ibid., xix.

"found herself drawn more to the candidate's wife than to the candidate himself": Michael Golay, *America 1933*, 9.

"to offer [Hickok] a job as chief investigator for the agency": Rodger Streitmatter, *Empty Without You,* 33.

"the country to gauge the effectiveness of the nation's relief programs": Rodger Streitmatter, *Empty Without You*, 34.

"who often showed them to Franklin . . . [who often] read them out loud": Ibid.

"at the end of the day and often while lying in bed": Ibid.

"mak[ing] it possible, in eighteen months spanning 1933 and 1934: Golay, *America 1933*, 1.

"the Franklin D. Roosevelt Library opened eighteen cardboard boxes": Rodger Streitmatter, *Empty Without You*, xiv.

"3,500 letters that [ER] and 'Hick' had written during their thirty-year friendship": Ibid.

"Because of Eleanor Roosevelt's renown, their story belongs to history": Doris Faber, *The Life of Lorena Hickok: Eleanor Roosevelt's Friend* (New York: W. Morrow, 1980), 5.

"glimpses . . . of an Eleanor Roosevelt who is strikingly different": Rodger Streitmatter, *Empty Without You*, xvii.

"should not diminish [ER's] stature, but rather should serve to reassure us": Ibid.

ER's and Hickok's preserved communication begins in March 1933: Ibid., 15.

only two months before ER's death in November 1962: Ibid., 288.

In this letter, Hickok reacts to recent newspaper reports which covered ER's speech in New York City: Ibid., 138-9.

God damn it . . . none of us ought to be wearing velvet dinner gowns . . . 4,000 Baltimore children couldn't go to school: Ibid., 139.

[T]he thought of you in a blue velvet dinner gown . . . Darling--in a blue velvet dinner gown: Ibid.

"broke up a White House dinner party" by inviting ER and guests: Frederick N. Rasmussen, "Amelia and Eleanor on Night Flight to Baltimore," *The Baltimore Sun*, November 15, 2009, https://www.baltimoresun.com/news/bs-xpm-2009-11-15-0911140057-story.html.

"[m]any of [Eleanor's] sentences ramble on and on and on": Rodger Streitmatter, *Empty Without You*, xvii.

discusses wages for various local businesses: Lorena Hickok, *One Third of a Nation: Lorena Hickok Reports on the Great Depression,* eds. Richard Lowitt and Maurine Beasley (Chicago: U of Illinois P, 1981), 342.

We give free lunches to the children here . . . Never have we had enough bread . . . so that there was enough for each child: Ibid.

[L]awyers generally, he says, are advising them to ignore the NRA: Ibid.

How in God's name, he said: Lorena Hickok to Eleanor Roosevelt, 21 Nov. 1934, Correspondence of Eleanor Roosevelt and Lorena Hickok, Franklin D. Roosevelt Presidential Library and Museum National Archives, Hyde Park, New York.

the President's executive order pulling all the various representatives: Lorena Hickok to Eleanor Roosevelt, 23 Nov. 1934, Correspondence of Eleanor Roosevelt and Lorena Hickok, Franklin D. Roosevelt Presidential Library and Museum National Archives, Hyde Park, New York.

Remember how I was pleading for something of the sort a few months ago?: Ibid.

called up the Baltimore relief administration today: Ibid.

administrative bureaucracy: Ibid.

[i]n the last few months two Baltimore companies: Ibid.

[t]his morning I met the only intelligent businessman I've encountered so far in Baltimore: Ibid.

Hick my darling! That cry of 'I want something all my own' is the cry of the heart . . . for I love you: Eleanor Roosevelt, qtd. in Rodger Streitmatter, *Empty Without You,* 138.

If you can come on [untranslatable word] I can put my arms around you tonight: "Hick my darling," Letter from Eleanor Roosevelt to Lorena Hickok." *Correspondence of Eleanor Roosevelt and Lorena Hickok.* (Franklin D. Roosevelt Presidential Library and Museum National Archives. Hyde Park, New York, Fall 1934).

"began retrieving the letters she had written to Eleanor . . . she purposely destroyed hundreds of letters": Streitmatter, *Empty Without You,* xxi-ii.

"all of her letters to Eleanor written prior to November 26, 1933": Streitmatter, *Empty Without You,* 15.

"burned the most explicit of the letters": Streitmatter, *Empty Without You,* xxii.

"[w]e can only imagine what has been lost": Ibid.

—Chapter Five—

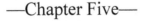

Mark Twain: "Samuel L. Clemens (Mark Twain), by Frank Millet, 1877," Wikimedia Commons, last modified April 11, 2008, https://commons.wikimedia.org/wiki/File:Samuel_L_Clemens_(Mark_Twain),_by_Frank_Millet,_1877.jpg.

Olivia Langdon/October 1869: "Olivia Langdon Clemens, 1869, (Unattributed)," Wikimedia Commons, last modified May 25, 2016, https://commons.wikimedia.org/wiki/File:Olivia_Langdon_Clemens,_1869.jpg.

Twain immediately fell in love with Langdon after viewing this picture: For further details regarding Twain and Langdon's early relationship and a visual of the ivory miniature, as well as additional descriptions and visuals of other women who influenced Mark Twain, see Alex Applebaum, "The Women Who Influenced Mark Twain," Mark Twain and His Times, University of Virginia Library, 2012, http://twain.lib.virginia.edu/projects/applebaum/olivia.html.

Envelope: To view the original envelope, addressed by Twain to Langdon, see "To Olivia L. Clemens, 26 April 1877, Baltimore, MD, (MS: CU-MARK, UCCL 01416)" Letter from Mark Twain to Olivia Langdon Clemens, Letters, Mark Twain Project, California Digital Library, UC Press, http://www.marktwainproject.org/xtf/view?docId=letters/UCCL01416.xml;query=baltimore%20olivia;sectionType1=;sectionType2=;sectionType3=;sectionType4=;sectionType5=;doc.view=facsimile;style=letter;brand=mtp#1, MS pages 33-4. The original envelope is affixed with two 3-cent Washington stamps. The 3-cent Washington stamps were printed by the National Bank Note Co. during 1870-1: "US Stamp 1870 3c Washington," Wikimedia Commons, last modified on Jan. 12, 2011, https://commons.wikimedia.org/wiki/File:US_stamp_1870_3c_Washington.jpg.

Letter: To view the original Baltimore-based letter and correspondence card, written by Twain to Langdon in 1877, see the Facsimile files of "To Olivia L. Clemens, 26 April 1877, Baltimore, MD, (MS: CU-MARK, UCCL 01416)" and "To Olivia L. Clemens, 27 April 1877, Baltimore, Md. (MS, correspondence card, in pencil: CU-MARK, UCCL 01418)," found in the digital "Letters," Mark Twain Project, California Digital Library, UC Press, http://www.marktwainproject.org/xtf/search?category=letters;rmode=landing_letters;style=mtp.

The Battle Monument Square: For more information about Monument Square and Baltimore's Washington Monument, built three years after the Battle of 1812, see "Baltimore's Washington Monument," Mount Vernon Square, Mount Vernon Place Conservancy, http://mvpconservancy.org/history/

"[n]o letters written between 20 and 26 January 1872 have been found": Lin Salamo and Harriet Elinor Smith, ed., *Mark Twain's Letters, Volume 5: 1872-1873* (Berkeley: U of California P, 1997), 31.

Twain's lecture, "Roughing It," which was held at the main hall: For further information about the history of the Maryland Institute (now the Maryland Institute College of Art), see "1847-1878 Renewal and Expansion in the Industrial Age," MICA, 2018, https://www.mica.edu/About_MICA/Facts_and_History/1847-1878_Renewal_and_Expansion_in_the_Industrial_Age.html.

"comical appearance as he entered alone": "Mark Twain in the Maryland Institute," *1871–1872 Tour Review*, Jan. 24, 1872, Twain.Lib.Virginia.Edu.

"the only public introduction that had ever delighted [Twain] was by a man": Ibid.

Five years later, Twain returned to Baltimore to view the rehearsal of a play: Dixon Wecter, ed., *The Love Letters of Mark Twain* (Westport, Connecticut: Greenwoood Publishing Group, 1976): 193-4. For further information on Ford's Theater in Baltimore see Mary Zajac's "Lord Baltimore Hotel Turns 80 Years Old," *Baltimore Style*. Baltimore Style, Jan./Feb. 2010. Mary Zajac explains that "[a]fter the federal War Department seized Ford's first theater in Washington, following the assassination of

Abraham Lincoln in 1865, Ford returned to his native Baltimore where he managed the Holliday Street Theater, became a city councilman and, for a short time, acted as mayor of the city. On Oct. 2, 1871, he opened Ford's Grand Opera House on the corner of Fayette and Eutaw streets."

There's a combat going on . . . between two men . . . [and] all the other actors and actresses: Ibid., 195.

"on the European plan, monument square, Samuel C. Little, Proprietor, Baltimore": "To Olivia L. Clemens, 26 April 1877, Baltimore, MD, (MS: CU-MARK, UCCL 01416)," Letter from Mark Twain to Olivia Langdon Clemens, Letters, Mark Twain Project, California Digital Library, UC Press, http://www.marktwainproject.org/xtf/view?docId=letters/UCCL01416.xml;query=baltimore%20olivia;sectionType1=;sectionType2=;sectionType3=;sectionType4=;sectionType5=;doc.view=facsimile;style=letter;brand=mtp#1, MS page 1.

which was formerly located at the corner of Calvert and Fayette Streets: Sadler, Drysdale and Purnell, *The State Gazette and Merchants' and Farmers' Directory for Maryland and District of Columbia* (Baltimore: Sadler, Drysdale and Purnell, Baltimore, 1871), 77.

only fourteen years earlier, housed the military provost-marshal's quarters: John Thomas Scharf, *History of Baltimore City and County, form the Earliest Period to the Present Day: Including Biographical Sketches of their Representative Men* (Philadelphia: L.H. Everts, 1881), 142.

Monument Square, Calvert and Fayette Streets: Original Photograph, 2015

Alexandroffsky," a residential property which formerly faced Hollins Street: Guy W. Hager, "Thomas de Kay Winans (1820–1878)," Friends of Orianda House, http://www.friendsoforiandahouse.com/images/ThomsWinans.pdf.

"one of America's first multi-millionaires and a pioneer of railroading": Guy W. Hager, "Ross Winans (1796–1877)," Friends of Orianda House, http://www.friendsoforianda-house.com/images/RossWinans.pdf.

"[b]y 1929, the wreckers were pulling down the great chimney": Jacques Kelly, "Mansion with a curious name kept Baltimoreans enthralled: Alexandrofsky was opulent, with fountains, chandeliers, and garden statuary," *The Baltimore Sun*, Feb. 25 2011, http://articles.baltimoresun.com/2011-02-25/news/bs-md-kelly-column-alexandroffsky-20110225_1_west-baltimore-mansion-curious-name.

The "Alexandroffsky" property is now part of the University of Maryland biotech park site: Jacques Kelly, "Path of building cranes tracks the disappearance of blue-collar Baltimore," The Baltimore Sun, July 8, 2006, http://articles.baltimoresun.com/2006-07-08/news/0607080073_1_construction-cranes-university-of-maryland-poppleton.

The estate's lion statues were moved to the Baltimore Zoo in Druid Hill Park: Jacques Kelly, "Mansion."

"Crimea" was converted into Leakin Park: Ibid.

"axels, bearings[,] trucks and carriages": Guy W. Hager, "Ross Winans."

Ross Winans's sons, Thomas and William Louis: Ibid.

The influence of spending many years in Russia was reflective in the names of Thomas Winans's homes in Baltimore: Bernice Millman, "The Dolls," Friends of Orianda

House, 2006, http://www.friendsoforiandahouse.com/Dolls.html.

Another literary representative, Jules Verne, was equally inspired by the Winans family inventions: Guy W. Hager, "Thomas de Kay Winans."

[t]he porter & his wife said Mr. Winans was out, & that all the young gentlemen were absent from the city: "To Olivia L. Clemens, 26 April 1877, Baltimore, MD, (MS: CU-MARK, UCCL 01416)" Letter from Mark Twain to Olivia Langdon Clemens, MS page 2.

it costs money to run that place & pay those 30 or 40 workmen and servants: Ibid., MS page 32.

Once inside the estate, Twain describes the entryway, party room, and saloon to Langdon: Ibid., MS pages 4-7.

Some of the early sketches in the letter include a fireplace with logs: Ibid., MS pages 7-10.

If you wish to go down cellar to see the wilderness . . . you turn a knob: Ibid., MS pages 14-5.

up a winding stairway of so slight a slant that water molasses wouldn't have flowed down it . . . had been struck by lightning . . . all manner of tools & traps: Ibid., MS pages 20-1.

Everywhere you go in this house you find mysterious knobs . . . & similar creatures fairly swarm in every nook: Ibid., MS page 23.

We entered Mr. W's (bedroom) . . . Chaos is no name for it!: Ibid.

Twain also notes Winans's unusual heating system for his bedroom . . . which read: *Asleep*: Ibid., MS pages 24-5.

a thing which you could step on, & instantly your weight was registered on a dial: Ibid., MS pages 26-7.

Final stops on Twain's physical and epistolary tour of the Winans's property include a carpenter shop, a library and music room: Ibid., MS pages 28-30.

plate-glass top—an invention of his for getting sunshine without snow: Ibid., MS pages 30-1.

You pull a string & slide a blue silk curtain along if you want to temper the sunshine: Ibid., MS page 31.

I am so given to forgetting everything that I resolved I would tell you something: Ibid., MS pages 31-2.

had a jolly adventure last night with a chap from the 'Eastern Shore': "To Olivia L. Clemens, 27 April 1877, Baltimore, Md. (MS, correspondence card, in pencil: CU-MARK, UCCL 01418)," Correspondence card from Mark Twain to Olivia Langdon Clemens, Letters, Mark Twain Project, California Digital Library, UC Press, http://www.marktwainproject.org/xtf/view?docId=letters/UCCL01418.xml;query=baltimore%20olivia;searchAll=;sectionType1=;sectionType2=;sectionType3=;sectionType4=;sectionType5=;style=letter;brand=mtp#1.

4 hours in the State Prison to-day, after rehearsal: Ibid.

it would take a book to hold all I saw & heard: Ibid.

Photograph of writers Mark Twain (left) and George Washington Cable: "ClemensCableAutographed," Wikimedia Commons, last modified January 25, 2008, https://upload.wikimedia.org/wikipedia/commons/d/d6/ClemensCableAutographed.

jpg.

"Mark Twain no sooner put his head outside the flies than the audience began to laugh as well as applaud: "Two Famous Authors: Mark Twain and George W. Cable at the Academy of Music," The (Baltimore) Morning Herald, Mark Twain in His Times, University of Virginia, Nov. 29 1884, http://twain.lib.virginia.edu/huckfinn/twntur26.html.

Nov. 28, 1884; Baltimore/ I am again in the retiring room: For further information about Cable's letters, including this one, which were scribbled notes written daily, and often, to his wife on the backs of programs from the Twain/Cable Route of 1884–1885 see "Cable's Letters Home from the Road," University of Virginia, http://twain.lib.virginia.edu/huckfinn/cablelet.html.

[W]e dine with President Gilman of Johns Hopkins University: "To Olivia Clemens, CU-MARK, UCCL 03041," Letter from Mark Twain to Olivia Langdon Clemens, Print.

Twain's November 29, 1884 letter also provides updates on the marriage statuses of the Winans and Whistler families: Ibid. For further information about the marital and career connections between the Winans and Whistlers, see "Mrs. Thomas Dekay Winans," Friends of the Orianda House, 2006, http://www.friendsoforiandahouse.com/Mrs-Thomas-Winans.html.

that dam Goddard has called with some social proposition or other: "To Olivia Clemens, CU-MARK, UCCL 03041." For more information about Henry P. Goddard, who was a soldier, writer, reporter, civil rights activist and president of Baltimore's Shakespeare Club during this time, see Calvin Goddard Zon, "Henry Perkins Goddard," http://members.tripod.com/bliss_barn/Goddard.htm.

The letter ends with Twain's expression of gratitude for family pictures: "To Olivia Clemens, CU-MARK, UCCL 03041."

I don't write every day, but often I write twice a day to make up: Ibid.

[b]ut I am blessed above my kind, with another self": "To Olivia L. Langdon, 10 January 1870 , (2nd of 2), Albany, N.Y. (MS: CU-MARK, UCCL 00407)," Letter from Mark Twain to Olivia Langdon Clemens, Mark Twain Project, California Digital Library, UC Press, http://www.marktwainproject.org/xtf/view?docId=letters/UCCL00407.xml;query=January%2010,%201870;searchAll=;sectionType1=;sectionType2=;sectionType3=;sectionType4=;sectionType5=;style=letter;brand=mtp#1.

I shall treat smoking just exactly as I would treat the forefinger of my left hand . . . to cut that finger off: "SLC to Olivia L. Langdon, 13 Jan 1870," Letter from Mark Twain to Olivia Langdon Clemens, Mark Twain Project, California Digital Library, UC Press, http://www.marktwainproject.org/xtf/view?docId=letters/UCCL00408.xml;query=January%2010,%201870;searchAll=;sectionType1=;sectionType2=;sectionType3=;sectionType4=;sectionType5=;style=letter;brand=mtp#1.

"we get a sense of [Twain and Langdon's] mutual dependence . . . until she died in 1904": Michael Frank, qtd. in Gretchen Kell, "The Olivia Myth: Letters Reveal a Truer Picture of Samuel Clemens' Wife; Her Influence on His Work," *News*, Berkeley. Edu., Nov. 29, 1995, https://www.berkeley.edu/news/berkeleyan/1995/1129/olivia.html.

Langdon has "changed from being perceived": Ibid.

"Olivia Clemens [had] developed in a legendary sort of way . . . [n]o one had the facts": Ibid. For further examples of "new" scholarly visions of Langdon, Twain, and their relationship see Laura E. Skandera-Trombley, *Mark Twain in the Company of Women* (Philadelphia, PA: U of Pennsylvania P, 1994) 131; Susan K. Harris, *The Courtship of Olivia Langdon and Mark Twain* (New York: Cambridge UP, 1996), 172-3; Ron Powers, *Mark Twain: A Life* (New York: Free Press, 2005).

Chaos is no name for it! Yet it was orderly to him: "To Olivia L. Clemens, 26 April 1877, Baltimore, MD, (MS: CU-MARK, UCCL 01416), MS page 23.

—Chapter Six—

Lydian Jackson Emerson and Edward Waldo Emerson/1840: "Lydian Jackson Emerson and Edward Waldo Emerson 1840," Wikimedia Commons, last modified June 7, 2010, https://commons.wikimedia.org/wiki/File:Daguerreotype_Lydia_Jackson_Emerson_ and_Edward_Waldo_Emerson_1840.jpeg.

Ralph Waldo Emerson/1846/Johnson: "Emerson by Johnson 1846," Wikimedia Commons, last modified October 5, 2008, https://commons.wikimedia.org/wiki/File:Emerson_by_Johnson_1846.png.

Envelopes: For further information about the first US stamps issued for carrier service in 1842, see "The Carrier Stamps," The U.S. Philatelic Classics Society, 2018, https://www.uspcs.org/stamps-covers/carriers-locals-indepent-mails/the-carrier-stamps/. The stamp pictured is "Scott 6LB3," the first stamp to have "United States City Despatch Post" featured in the design.

Letters: The letter excerpts are from correspondence sent to and from Baltimore by Emerson and Jackson, addressing Lydian's mental status in metaphorical terms.

"New England," and the "Customs, Genius, and Trade of New England": Ralph Waldo Emerson, *The Letters of Ralph Waldo Emerson*, Volume 3, ed. Ralph L. Rusk (London: Oxford UP, 1939), 117.

"a winter's health trip of several months in the *South*": George E. Bell, "Emerson and Baltimore: A Biographical Study," *Maryland Historical Magazine* 65, no. 4 (1970): 333.

"The subject was "New England": Ibid., 331.

"the country's most renowned hostelry at the time": Molly W. Berger, *Hotel Dreams; Luxury, Technology, and Urban Ambition in America, 1829–1929* (Baltimore: JHU Press, 2011), 18.

Some of Barnum's City Hotel's most renowned guests": Frederick N. Rasmussen, "New account of Booth Manhunt," *The Baltimore Sun*, May 6, 2006, http://articles.baltimoresun.com/2006-05-06/news/0605060030_1_lincoln-booth-swanson/2.

"the most comfortable of all hotels in the United States": Charles Dickens, qtd. in "Baltimore's Barnum Hotel Register," *Baltimore's Barnum Hotel Register*, http://treached.com/barnumRegister/.

Former site of Barnum's City Hotel (Equitable Building): Original Photograph, 2015.

I am very well lodged & fed in what I believe Dickens called the best hotel in America: Ralph Waldo Emerson, *The Letters*, 117.

"Charles Dickens.—This distinguished author has been in Baltimore for the last two days: "Dickens in America: Newspaper Accounts," David Perdue's Charles Dickens Home Page, https://charlesdickenspage.com/dickens_in_america_1843_newspapers. html.

"[T]he natural pitch of Baltimore, the pictorial, so to speak": Henry James, "Baltimore," *The North American Review* 183, no. 597 (1906), 261-2.

Like many other visitors, James immediately noted the contradictory nature: Ibid., 250.

"Wonderful little Baltimore, in which whether when perched": Ibid., 260.

high mass in the Cathedral here, & with great pleasure . . . It is well for my Protestantism: Ralph Waldo Emerson, *The Letters*, 117-8. For further information about Maryland's early Catholic History, see "Charles Carroll the Settler, 1660–1720," Charles Carroll House of Annapolis, 2010, www.charlescarrollhouse.org, which explores the history of Charles Carroll the Settler, who arrived in Maryland in 1689 for the sake of practicing his Catholic religion without persecution, only to be imprisoned in 1691 after he refused to renounce his faith in a public position.

Here is today the mildest climate, we left the snow half way: Ralph Waldo Emerson, *The Letters*, 118.

"Massachusetts' culture as his yardstick": George E. Bell, "Emerson and Baltimore," 332.

I cannot hear of any poets, mystics, or strong characters of any sort: Ralph Waldo Emerson, *The Letters,* 118.

[p]erhaps there is nothing very distinctive in the population: Ibid.

Have you any libraries here—"**None**": Ibid. For further information on Rev. John Nelson McJilton, Episcopal rector, poet, and Baltimore's first school superintendent (who was later removed for establishing two African American schools in the district), see Frederick N. Rasmussen, "Judge campaigns to restore reputation of city's first schools superintendent John McJilton was fired for advocating public education of African-American children," *The Baltimore Sun*, August 28, 2010, http://articles.balti-moresun.com/2010-08-28/news/bs-md-backstory-john-mcjilton-20100828_1_school-board-baltimore-city-schools-judge-campaigns.

Charles Carroll the [last surviving] Signer [of the Declaration of Independence] is dead: Ibid.

"in the evening of January 7, 1843, Emerson arrived in the Baltimore and Ohio Railroad depot: George E. Bell, "Emerson and Baltimore," 338.

"Though couched in humorous satire . . . Emerson's view of Baltimore": Ibid., 333.

[H]ow is all with you at home? . . . How fares my gracious mother?: Ralph Waldo Emerson, *The Letters*, 118.

Emerson is referring to Charles Lane, a social reformer: "Charles Lane, 1800–1870," Amos Bronson Alcott, Amos Bronson Alcott Network, http://www.alcott.net/cgi-bin/home/champions/Lane.html.

The Lyceum movement, popular in New England during the nineteenth century: "The Lyceum Circuit," The E Pluribus Unum Project, Assumption College, http://www1.

assumption.edu/ahc/Lyceum%20Site/DEFAUL~1.HTM.

Emerson's concern for home includes correspondence inquiry about his prominent New England contemporaries: Ellen Emerson, *The Life of Lidian Jackson Emerson*, ed. Delores Bird Carpenter (Boston: Twayne Publishers, 1980), xvi.

[H]ave the good angels, or that more sombre Spirit that loves you so well: Ralph Waldo Emerson, *The Letters,* 118.

"the Lord made [Jackson] curiously": Ralph Waldo Emerson, qtd. in *Selected Letters of Lidian Jackson Emerson*, ed. Delores Bird Carpenter (Columbia, MO: U of Missouri P, 1987), xv.

"was diseased from a nonhygienic life . . . [sustaining] an introverted practice": qtd. in *Selected Letters of Lidian Jackson Emerson*, ed. Delores Bird Carpenter, xv.

stones & sand & volcanic scoriae from the Antarctic Continent . . . coming from our friends the Feejees: Ibid., 123.

a homeless place a kind of hotel the whole town: Ibid., 124.

Is Ellen a good girl? Papa thinks of her in Bal-ti-more: Ibid., 124.

Therefore, it is not surprising that Jackson's January 10, 1843 letter to Emerson is addressed to another prominent man: George E. Bell, "Emerson and Baltimore," 340.

"[a]t the time of its organization in 1839, the [Mercantile Library] Association occupied rooms at the corner of Baltimore and Holliday streets": *The Notes Supplementary to the Johns Hopkins University Studies in Historical and Political Science* (Baltimore: Johns Hopkins UP, 1871–1872), 6.

My dear Husband . . . Your letter came to day and contents us well: Lidian Jackson Emerson, *Selected Letters of Lidian Jackson Emerson*, ed. Delores Bird Carpenter (Columbia, MO: U of Missouri P, 1987), 113.

[m]y turn of expression is so very happy: Ibid.

I wish I had some new stories to tell you of our beautiful poem Edith, and our excellent prose Ellen: Ibid.

"[e]xtensive cutting of household trivia has been made": Delores Bird Carpenter, ed., *Selected Letters of Lidian Jackson Emerson*, xviii.

"shed light on notable contemporaries": Ibid., xxviii.

[w]e had a meeting of the wise men and their admirers: Ibid, 114.

[T]he poor human race are to be allowed in the future . . . when we are innocent there will be no need: Ibid.

Mr Alcott was descanting on the iniquity of formal exchange: Ibid.

Mr Alcott proposes to abridge labour and live a life of ease and independence by certain ways: Ibid.

When I said with a sigh that I would rather be excused from washing those linen covers: Ibid.

I wish I had resolution to write better: Ibid.

"[b]eset by depression and morbidly obsessed with impending death and illness": Robert D. Habich, "Rev. of The Selected Letters of Lidian Jackson Emerson," ed. Delores Bird Carpenter. *The New England Quarterly* 61, no. 2 (1988): 290.

"philosophic mind and [unfiltered] deep emotions": Ibid., xviii.

"We wonder if he will ever die like other men?": Ronald A. Bosco and Joel Myerson, eds., "Emerson as Lecturer," *Emerson in His Own Time: A Chronicle of His Life, Drawn from Recollections, Interviews, and Memoirs by Family, Friends, and Associates* (Iowa City, Iowa: U of Iowa P, 2003), 34.

"He is more likely to be evaporated some sunshiny day": Ibid.

—Chapter Seven—

John Adams 1766/Benjamin Blyth: "John Adams (1766)," Wikimedia Commons, last modified on August 8, 2016, https://commons.wikimedia.org/wiki/File:John_Adams_(1766).jpg.

Abigail Adams 1766/Benjamin Blyth: "Abigail Adams," Wikimedia Commons, last modified on March 14, 2016, https://commons.wikimedia.org/wiki/File:Abigail_Adams.jpg.

Envelope addressed to Mrs. Adams: The envelope is representative of many of the envelopes, originally folded and sealed, which were forwarded to Abigail Adams by John Adams and transported via other prominent U.S. men. The envelope which inspired this representation is found in the Baltimore-based letters within the Adams Family Papers: An Electronic Archives, Massachusetts Historical Society, http://www.masshist.org/digitaladams/.

Envelope addressed to The Honorable John Adams, Esq.: The envelope is representative of many of the envelopes, originally folded and sealed, which were forwarded to John Adams by Abigail Adams and transported via other prominent U.S. men. The envelope which inspired this representation is found in the Baltimore-based letters within the *Adams Family Papers: An Electronic Archives*, Massachusetts Historical Society, http://www.masshist.org/digitaladams/.

"[t]he adoption of the Declaration of Independence was nowhere received with livelier demonstration of joy than in Baltimore": John Thomas Scharf, Thomas. *History of Baltimore City and County, form the Earliest Period to the Present Day: Including Biographical Sketches of their Representative Men* (Philadelphia: L.H. Everts, 1881), 73.

Soon after the adoption, congress aimed to strengthen its military forces: Ibid.

As tension and fighting escalated over the next few months: Ibid., 73-4.

"recover[y of] the messiness of history-as-it-happens": Joseph J. Ellis, foreword to *My Dearest Friend: Letters of Abigail and John Adams* (Cambridge, MA: Belknap Press, 2010), viii.

"a historically correct account of the American Revolution would emphasize the utter confusion": Ibid.

the preservation of their letters (about 1,160): Ibid., vii.

"[i]n part the size of the full correspondence [which] makes it the most revealing exchange": Ibid., ix.

"Martha Washington destroyed all but three of the letters she and George exchanged": Ibid., vii.

You will burn all these letters, least they should fall from your pocket and thus expose your affectionate Friend: Abigail Adams, qtd. in E. B. Gelles, "Letter Writing as a Coping Strategy: The case of Abigail Adams," *Psychohistory Review 22, no. 2* (1994): 193.

"[l]etters, then became the lifeline of her relationship with John": E. B. Gelles, *"First Thoughts": Life and Letters of Abigail Adams* (Woodbridge, CT: Twayne Publishers, 1998), 11.

as their correspondence became their main communicative network during John's chronic and lengthy absences: Ibid., 24.

Tis a great grief to me that I know not how to write nor where to send to you . . . I know not of any conveyance: Abigail Adams, My *Dearest Friend: Letters of Abigail and John Adams* (Cambridge, MA: Belknap Press, 2010), 160.

Mr. Hall, by whom this Letter will be sent, will carry several Letters to you . . . You may write to me, in Congress: John Adams, "John Adams to Abigail Adams, February 15, 1777," *Founders Online*, National Archives, NHPRC, https://founders.archives.gov/documents/Adams/04-02-02-0117.

I long to hear of your arrival and to get one Letter from B[altimor]e: Abigail Adams, *My Dearest Friend*, 161.

It is now a Month and a few days, since I left you. I have heard nothing from you: John Adams, "Letter from John Adams to Abigail Adams," 10 February 1777, [electronic edition], Adams Family Papers: An Electronic Archive, Massachusetts Historical Society, http://www.masshist.org/digitaladams/archive/doc?id=L17770210jasecond.

My Disposition was naturally gay and cheerful: John Adams, "Letter from John Adams to Abigail Adams," 17 February 1777 [electronic edition], Adams Family Papers: An Electronic Archive, Massachusetts Historical Society. http://www.masshist.org/digitaladams/.

Congress temporarily housed itself in a large building located on the southwest corner of Sharpe and Baltimore Street . . . The house was owned by Henry Fite: "Henry Fite's House, Baltimore Dec. 20, 1777-Feb. 27, 1777," Buildings of the Department of State, Office of the Historian, Bureau of Public Affairs, https://history.state.gov/departmenthistory/buildings/section4

the longest Journey, and through the worst Roads and Worst Weather: John Adams, "Letter from John Adams to Abigail Adams, 2 February 1777 [electronic edition]," Adams Family Papers: An Electronic Archive, Massachusetts Historical Society, https://www.masshist.org/digitaladams/archive/doc?id=L17770202ja.

Baltimore is a very pretty Town, situated on Petapsco River, which empties itself into the great Bay of Chesapeak: Ibid.

[t]he Streets are very dirty and miry, but every Thing else is agreeable: Ibid.

John does not hold back in his dissatisfaction with the cost of lodging . . . Yet, ironically, the same letter also emphasizes his desire to raise the interest rate: "Letter from John Adams to Abigail Adams, 7 February 1777 [electronic edition]," Adams Family Papers: An Electronic Archive, Massachusetts Historical Society, https://www.masshist.org/digitaladams/archive/doc?id=L17770207jasecond.

John's desire to understand Baltimore's unfolding religion, laws, and culture: "Letter from John Adams to Abigail Adams, 3 February 1777 [electronic edition]," Adams Family Papers: An Electronic Archive, Massachusetts Historical Society, http://www.

masshist.org/digitaladams/archive/doc?id=L17770203ja.

a Place called Fells Point, a remarkable Piece of Ground: John Adams, "Letter from John Adams to Abigail Adams, 10 February 1777 [electronic edition]," Adams Family Papers: An Electronic Archive.

a Bason before the Town . . . a Fortification erected, on this Point: Ibid.

"**dearest friend**": a purposeful reference to the greeting often used by John and Abigail Adams in their letters.

I am sure no separation was ever so painfull to me as the last . . . Many circumstances concur to make it so: Abigail Adams,"Letter from Abigail Adams to John Adams, 26 January 1777 [electronic edition]," Adams Family Papers: An Electronic Archive, Massachusetts Historical Society, http://www.masshist.org/digitaladams/archive/doc?id=L17770126aa.

"**[i]n keeping with eighteenth-century norms that disapproved of explicit mentions of pregnancy in letters'**": Margaret A. Hogan and C. James Taylor, eds., *My Dearest Friend: Letters of Abigail and John Adams* (Cambridge, MA: Belknap Press, 2010), 159.

I am anxious to hear how you do . . . You know what it is: John Adams, "Letter from John Adams to Abigail Adams, 10 February 1777 [electronic edition]," Adams Family Papers: An Electronic Archive.

"**[t]he epistolary tone [of the eighteenth century] established varying degrees of intimacy**": E. B. Gelles, "First Thoughts," 6.

"**Religion, for instance, was so acceptable a topic . . . [f]eelings on the other hand**": Ibid., 7.

I wish my Lads were old enough: John Adams, "Letter from John Adams to Abigail Adams, 21 February 1777 [electronic edition]," Adams Family Papers: An Electronic Archive, Massachusetts Historical Society, https://www.masshist.org/digitaladams/archive/doc?id=L17770221ja.

The soldiers are good men and true. But the officers? The commanders!: John Quincy Adams, *Memoirs of John Quincy Adams, comprising portions of his diary from 1795 to 1848* (Philadelphia: J. B. Lippincott & Co., 1874-1877), 319.

"**(i)n most histories these personal factors are airbrushed out**": Joseph J. Ellis, foreword to *My Dearest Friend*, ix.

"**John's [and Abigail's] letters provide the clearest window that we have**": Ibid.

—Part Three—

Johns Hopkins Hospital, 1903: "Johns Hopkins Hospital, Baltimore, Md. LCCN96507075.jpg," Wikimedia Commons, last modified July 4, 2018, https://commons.wikimedia.org/wiki/File:Johns_Hopkins_Hospital,_Baltimore,_Md._LCCN96507075.jpg.

—Chapter Eight—

H. L. Mencken, Ben Pinchot, photographer: "H-L-Mencken-1928," Wikimedia Commons, last modified Sept.30, 2016, https://commons.wikimedia.org/wiki/File:H-L-Mencken-1928.jpg.

Sara Haardt, 1920-1929: "Sara Haardt," Wikimedia Commons, last modified March 10, 2018, https://commons.wikimedia.org/wiki/File:Sara_Haardt.jpg.

Envelopes/stamps: The representative envelopes showcase the three main medical institutions/residential address exchanges between Mencken and Haardt. The stamps shown are representative of the years of the correspondence between Maple Heights Sanitarium, Union Memorial Hospital, and Johns Hopkins Hospital: 1924: "Hugo-monument 5c 1924 U.S. stamp.1.jpg," Wikimedia Commons, last modified April 5, 2014, Hugo-monument 5c 1924 U.S. stamp.1.jpg; 1931: "General Pulaski 1931 Issue-2c," Wikimedia Commons, last modified Feb. 22, 2010, https://commons.wikimedia.org/wiki/File:General_Pulaski_1931_Issue-2c.jpg; 1935: "Connecticut tercentenary 1935 U.S. stamp.1.jpg," Wikimedia Commons, last modified March 23, 2014, https://commons.wikimedia.org/wiki/File:Connecticut_tercentenary_1935_U.S._stamp.1.jpg.

1524 Hollins Street: Original Photograph, 2015.

"I have lived in one house in Baltimore for nearly 45 years . . . It is as much a part of me as my two hands": Charles Fecher, *Mencken: A Study of His Thought* (New York: Alfred A. Knopf, 1978), 47.

"was deprived of his ability to read and write [after his stroke] was a grotesque irony that wasn't lost on Mencken himself . . . Mencken thought for a moment and finally said, 'Ah, yes, he died the same year I did'": Jon Winokur, *The Portable Curmudgeon* (New York: Plume, 1992), 25.

"the delusion that one woman differs from another": H. L. Mencken, *A Mencken Chrestomathy* (New York: Alfred A. Knopf, 1949), 619.

"the great secret of happiness in love is to be glad that the other fellow married her": Ibid., 621.

I worship you, H. M. / Guess who?: "H. L. and Sara Haardt Mencken Collection," Manuscript and Rare Book Collections, Special Collections, Goucher College Library, Goucher College, Baltimore, Maryland, Courtesy of the Enoch Pratt Free Library.

Darling/ I have gone out for a while. / I will be back in time to fix your supper: Ibid. The bulk of H. L. Mencken's and Sara Haardt's correspondence, housed at Goucher College, is published in Marion Elizabeth Rodgers, *Mencken and Sara: A Life in Letters: The Correspondence of H. L. Mencken and Sara Haardt* (New York: Double Day, 1987).

"personalities, so to speak, are not revealed brilliantly or in the altogether": H. L. Mencken, qtd. in Marion Elizabeth Rodgers, *Mencken and Sara*, 65.

In fact, it was an evening with Mencken that inspired Anita Loos to write *Gentlemen Prefer Blondes*: Marion Elizabeth Rodgers, *Mencken the American*, 245.

"by the late 1920's it [was] clear that America's most notorious bachelor [was]

smitten": Fred Hobson, review of *Mencken and Sara, A Life in Letters: The Private Correspondence of H. L. Mencken and Sara Haardt*, ed. Marion Elizabeth Rodgers, *South Atlantic Review* 53, no. 2 (1988): 128.

"with mock seriousness: 'I formerly was not as wise as I am now . . . the wise man frequently revises his opinions. The fool, never'": H. L. Mencken, qtd. in Marion Elizabeth Rodgers, *Mencken the American*, 347.

Mencken met Haardt in 1923 after giving a lecture at Goucher College: Marion Elizabeth Rodgers, *Mencken and Sara*, 5.

Mencken, a fifteen-year old 1896 valedictorian . . . "missed few opportunities to disparage the higher education that he had spurned": Vincent Fitzpatrick, *H. L. Mencken* (Macon, Georgia: 2004), 4.

Haardt was an unlikely match for Mencken in many ways: Marion Elizabeth Rodgers, *Mencken the American*, 251–2.

Mencken had debilitating bouts with hay fever, and Haardt was often admitted to Baltimore hospitals for months because of various illnesses: Marion Elizabeth Rodgers documents Haardt's life-long health struggles: Haardt was born a "blue baby" and also contracted smallpox and typhoid as a child. "For the rest of her life [Haardt] would battle against illness: from tuberculosis, from a lesion in her left eye, from appendicitis, and from the removal of a tubercular kidney": Marion Elizabeth Rodgers, *Mencken and Sara*, 20.

Mencken and Haardt's early letters document Prohibition-era drinks and meals: Marion Elizabeth Rodgers, *Mencken & Sara*, 91. For further information about Mencken's role as a one of history's strongest supporters of Baltimore's reputation as a "wet city" and the failure of Prohibition in the state of Maryland, see *Michael T. Walsh*, "The Rise and Fall of Prohibition in Baltimore, Maryland 1918–1933," *Baltimore or Less*, May 6, 2012, http://www.baltimoreorless.com/2012/05/the-rise-and-fall-of-prohibition-in-baltimore-maryland-1918-1933/.

Their lunch and dinner dates quickly blossom into a "slow and uneven" courtship: Marion Elizabeth Rodgers, *Mencken and Sara*, 103.

"was partly due to the 40-something Mencken living with his mother": Jill Rosen, "Poetic Passions, Tragic Partings Among Baltimore's Greatest Romances," *The Baltimore Sun*, Feb. 8, 2013, http://www.baltimoresun.com/entertainment/sun-maga-zine/bs-sm-baltimore-love-20130117-story.html.

"The carapace of H. L. Mencken, the hardboiled critic we soon discovered, had been developed as a defensive mechanism": Sara Mayfield, *The Constant Circle: H. L. Mencken and His Friends*, (New York: Delacorte Press, 1968), 115.

"[i]t is a literal fact that I still think of Sara every day of my life, and almost every hour of the day": H. L. Mencken, "May 31, 1940," *The Diary of H. L. Mencken*, ed. Charles A. Fecher (New York: Alfred A. Knopf, 1989), 139-40.

Before I get stuck in Alabama for the rest of the summer I want you to get me straight on this short-story business . . . How does one do it? I mean, see you: Sara Haardt, "Sara Haardt, Goucher College, May the twentieth, 1923," qtd. in Marion Elizabeth Rodgers, *Mencken and Sara*, 77. Goucher College was originally located at St. Paul and 23rd Street, which is now known as the Charles Village area.

to write something and I am wondering if anything could come out of a Baltimore second-story back: Ibid.

Goucher College, St. Paul Street, 1920: "Goucher College, (between classes) Baltimore, Md.," Wikimedia Commons, last modified September 15, 2016, https://commons.wikimedia.org/wiki/File:Goucher_College,_(between_classes)_Baltimore,_Md.jpg.

"Soulful Highbrow": Ann Henley, "Sara Haardt and 'The Sweet, Flowering South'." *Menckeniana: A Quarterly Review* 129 (1994): 4.

Domeniques: "Domenique's" was located at 702 Cathedral Street, two doors down from the house that would become Mencken and Haardt's marriage home seven years later. Maison Domenique's restaurant was named after "Arrobbia Domenique, a proprietor of Marconi's restaurant": Marion Elizabeth Rodgers, *Mencken and Sara*, 78.

These have been dog days at college and I am looking forward to the meeting as the only inspiring thing that could happen: Sara Haardt, "Sara Haardt, Goucher College, May the twenty-sixth, 1923," qtd. in Marion Elizabeth Rodgers, *Mencken and Sara*, 78.

"favorite doctrines that 'the whole world would be better if the human race was kept gently stewed'": H. L. Mencken, qtd. in Marion Elizabeth Rodgers, *Mencken the American*, 221.

Mencken's early letters to Haardt follow her from Goucher College on St. Paul Street to Maple Heights Sanitarium in Sparks, Maryland, where she was hospitalized for acute bronchitis and tuberculosis in 1924: Marion Elizabeth Rodgers, *Mencken and Sara*, 114.

Former Maple Heights Sanitarium, Sparks, Maryland: Original Photograph, 2019

Has the janitor yet tried to kiss you? It is coming! Also, you say nothing about the nurses getting drunk: H. L. Mencken, "H. L. Mencken, 1524 Hollins St., Baltimore, May 12th, 1924," qtd. in Marion Elizabeth Rodgers, *Mencken and Sara*, 138–9.

[D]on't let a small flare-up alarm you . . . I suspect that my own temperature ranges between 85 and 108: H. L. Mencken, "H. L. Mencken, 1524 Hollins St., Baltimore, February 6th, 1925," qtd. in Marion Elizabeth Rodgers, *Mencken and Sara*, 193.

"[m]arriage is a wonderful institution, but who would want to live in an institution?": Discrepancy remains about the originator of this quote. Other possible Vaudeville-era originators include Groucho Marx, Mae West, and W. C. Fields.

Mencken and Haardt continued to date from 1927-1930, writing regularly: Marion Elizabeth Rodgers, *Mencken and Sara*, 274-461.

The Union Memorial Hospital: "MedStar Union Memorial Hospital (1923) on E. 33rd Street, 201 E. University Parkway, Baltimore, MD 21218," Photograph by Eli Pousoon, January 3, 2019, Baltimore Heritage, Flickr, https://www.flickr.com/photos/baltimoreheritage/46608318081/in/photolist-fab65j-9zBenS-6DcPYM-7kFx2U-oE-r6oY-2e1BPa4-bsXFeN-5rGZxM-57Dufb-6qdhZy-auCadk-4Rrggd-fab5Nf-hFpZZ-8ne55N-7x5Z1j-aEWFzj-5XNvgu-apu6i7-4RcqcP-LvXZ3S/.

By the end of 1929, Haardt's "health was on the decline, [and] so too was Mencken's popularity": Marion Elizabeth Rodgers, *Mencken and Sara*, 404.

as happy as the boy who killed his father: H. L. Mencken, "H. L. Mencken, 1524 Hollins St., Baltimore, April 25th, 1930," qtd. in Marion Elizabeth Rodgers, *Mencken and Sara*, 443.

I bust with love!: Ibid.

"The worst of the marriage is that it makes a woman believe that all other men are just as easy to fool": H. L. Mencken, *A Mencken Chrestomathy*, 621.

It is all very thrilling . . . and I think the place is going to be sweet: Sara Haardt, "Sara Haardt, June the tenth, 1930," qtd. in Marion Elizabeth Rodgers, *Mencken and Sara*, 461.

704 Cathedral Street: Original Photograph, 2015.

Last night my temperature was normal for the first time (it was your kiss): Sara Haardt, "The Union Memorial Hospital, Baltimore, MD., March the tenth [1931]," qtd. in Marion Elizabeth Rodgers, *Sara and Mencken*, 463.

[i]t has rained, a fine drizzle, since early morning, and the house is as quiet as a tomb: Sara Haardt, "The American Mercury, 730 Fifth Avenue, New York, June the twelfth, 1932," qtd. in Marion Elizabeth Rodgers, *Mencken and Sara*, 471.

If I weren't patriotic, and a born Democrat, I'd be weeping: Sara Haardt, "June the twenty-first, 1932," qtd. in Marion Elizabeth Rodgers, *Mencken and Sara*, 478.

I Love You/Love You horizontally and vertically on the page, ending her letter with three rows of X's and the number: *1,000,000,000,000,000,000,000,000*: Ibid.

If there is no letter tomorrow morning I'll begin to pitch and heave: H. L. Mencken, "H. L. Mencken, 704 Cathedral St., Baltimore, Wednesday, September 6, 1934," qtd. in Marion Elizabeth Rodgers, *Mencken and Sara*, 501.

Tonight I am going down to Highlandtown with Buchholz to try Hausner's beer: Ibid. Haausner's, located at 3244 Eastern Avenue, served the Baltimore community from 1926–1999.

I hate to think of coming home to the empty house: Ibid.

Mencken was also being worn down at this point in his life by his opposition to FDR: For additional information about the Gridiron Club Dinner on December 8, 1934 see "H. L. Mencken and President Franklin Delano Roosevelt at the Gridiron Club, 1934," Remembering Baltimore, October 15, 2017, http://www.rememberingbaltimore.net/2017/10/h-l-mencken-and-president-franklin.html.

Johns Hopkins Hospital: "Johns Hopkins Hospital, early photo," Wikimedia Commons, last modified August 16, 2014, https://commons.wikimedia.org/wiki/File:Johns_Hopkins_Hospital,_early_photo.jpg.

Haardt writes to Mencken from Johns Hopkins Hospital on March 31, 1935, updating him on her temperature (*normal*): Sara Haardt, "Mrs. H. L. Mencken, 704 Cathedral Street, Baltimore, Maryland, Sunday, March the thirty-first, 1935," qtd. in Marion Elizabeth Rodgers, *Mencken and* Sara, 513.

The next day, Mencken updates Haardt on his blood pressure (*very good for an old boozer*) . . . and his displeasure that *[t]he house is horribly lonely and gloomy*: H. L. Mencken, "H. L. Mencken, 704 Cathedral St., Baltimore, April 1ˢᵗ, 1935," qtd. in Marion Elizabeth Rodgers, *Mencken and Sara*, 513.

"attitude toward doctors and medicine would be roughly parallel to a Catholic's attitude toward priests . . . He thought they could do miracles . . . as a matter of fact, sometimes they do, but not as often as he thought": August Mencken, qtd. in Marion Elizabeth Rodgers, *Mencken: The American Iconoclast, The Life and Times of the*

Bad Boy of Baltimore (Oxford UP: New York, 2005), 531.

yet she composes a telegram on April 30, 1935, relating time-sensitive information: Sara Haardt, "[Telegram], Western Union, Baltimore MD, H L Mencken, APR 30 1935 6:51 PM," Marion Elizabeth Rodgers, *Mencken and Sara*, 514.

Mencken merely provides instructions for the connection of a record player, with the declaration that, after successful installation, *[y]ou will then bathe in* art: H. L. Mencken, "H. L. Mencken, 704 Cathedral St., Baltimore, April [?], 1935," qtd. in Marion Elizabeth Rodgers, *Mencken and Sara*, 515.

The house is a desert./ H: Ibid.

"I was fifty-five years old before I envied anyone, and then it was not so much for what others had as for what I had lost": H. L. Mencken, qtd. in Marion Elizabeth Rodgers, *Mencken the American*, 421.

"If I ever marry, it will be on a sudden impulse—as a man shoots himself": H. L. Mencken, qtd. in Jon Winokur, *The Portable Curmudgeon*, 23.

—Chapter Nine—

F. Scott Fitzgerald/1921, Gordon Bryant: "F. Scott Fitzgerald, 1921," Wikimedia Commons, last modified Feb. 18, 2008, https://commons.wikimedia.org/wiki/File:F._Scott_Fitzgerald,_1921.png.

Zelda Fitzgerald/1922, Metropolitan Magazine: "Zelda Fitzgerald, 1922," Wikimedia Commons, last modified Feb. 18, 2008, https://commons.wikimedia.org/wiki/File:Zelda_Fitzgerald,_1922.png.

Envelopes/stamps: The representative envelopes depict the primary sender/recipient locations of F. Scott Fitzgerald and Zelda Fitzgerald's correspondence while Zelda was hospitalized in Baltimore. There are additional hotels in which Scott and Zelda stayed, such as the Rennert and Stafford, which are not pictured here or within the chapter. The first envelope contains the nicknames that Zelda used for herself and Scott during her Phipps correspondence: The stamps shown are representative of the years of correspondence: 1932: "Stamp US 1932 2c Washington," Wikimedia Commons, last modified April 21, 2008, https://commons.wikimedia.org/wiki/File:Stamp_US_1932_2c_Washington.jpg; 1935: "Connecticut tercentenary 1935 U.S. stamp.1.jpg," Wikimedia Commons, last modified March 23, 2014, https://commons.wikimedia.org/wiki/File:Connecticut_tercentenary_1935_U.S._stamp.1.jpg.

"early morning visits of F. Scott Fitzgerald [to 704 Cathedral Street], demanding [Mencken and Haardt] listen to portions of his new novel: Marion Elizabeth Rodgers, *Mencken and Sara: A Life in Letters: The Correspondence of H. L. Mencken and Sara Haardt* (Double Day: New York, 1987), 56.

"Often this would occur just when Sara had drifted off to sleep . . . and then Fitzgerald would write an apologetic note: Ibid.

Scott and Zelda first met in July 1918 in Montgomery, Alabama, where Zelda grew up with Sara Haardt: Kendall Taylor, *Sometimes Madness is Wisdom: Zelda and Scott*

Fitzgerald, A Marriage (New York: Random House, 2003), 50.

Zelda had recently graduated from high school and Scott, almost 22 years old, was stationed at Camp Sheridan, Alabama as a lieutenant in the infantry: Ibid., 1.

The two were quickly engaged . . . and married in April of 1920: Jackson R. Bryer and Cathy W. Barks, eds., *Dear Scott, Dearest Zelda: The Love Letters of F. Scott & Zelda Fitzgerald* (London: Bloomsbury, 2002), 5.

The popular couple relocated constantly within the United States during this time . . . Soon after, Zelda entered the Prangins Clinic in Nyon, Switzerland, where she stayed until September 1931: Ibid. Jackson R. Bryer and Cathy W. Barks's collection, *Dear Scott, Dearest Zelda*, provides a comprehensive summary of the Fitzgeralds' lives, in addition to transcriptions of their letters.

After a short return to Montgomery, Alabama, the Fitzgeralds relocated to Baltimore in January 1932, where H. L. Mencken referred Scott to Adolf Meyer: Greg Rienzi, "Great Scott: Fitzgerald's Baltimore," *The JHU Gazette*, The Johns Hopkins University, Sept. 28, 2009, http://gazette.jhu.edu/2009/09/28/ scholars-fans-of-author%E2%80%99s-work-gather-in-the-city-he-once-called-home/.

"[c]o-creators of their own legend in which fantasy and fact often blurred": Kendall Taylor, *Sometimes Madness is Wisdom*, xiv.

During Zelda's first stay in Baltimore at Johns Hopkins Hospital, in the winter of 1932, Scott returned to their rented home in Montgomery, Alabama: Jackson R. Bryer and Cathy W. Barks, eds., *Dear Scott, Dearest Zelda*, 145.

Scott "usually stayed at the Rennert Hotel, only a short walk from Mencken and Haardt's house on Cathedral [Street]": Kendall Taylor, *Sometimes Madness is Wisdom*, 255. "When the Rennert Hotel opened its doors at the corner of Saratoga and Liberty streets in 1885, it was described in newspaper accounts as being the 'highest type of American hostelry.' It was the creation of Robert Rennert, the son of German immigrant parents, who started in the hotel business as a young man working at the famed Guy's Monument House in Monument Square": Fred Rasmussen, *The Baltimore Sun*, Jan. 19, 1997, http://articles.baltimoresun.com/1997-01-19/features/1997019222_1_ rennert-oysters-hotel-business. Today, a parking lot claims the Rennert Hotel's space.

"What is extraordinary is that the years of Zelda's greatest discipline as a writer . . . coincided exactly with those years when she was first hospitalized: Sally Cline, *Zelda Fitzgerald: Her Voice in Paradise* (New York: Arcade Publishing, 2004), 5.

The row of brick houses from the window at night present a friendly conspiracy to convince us of the warmth and pleasantness of life: Zelda Fitzgerald, "114. To Scott, February 1932," qtd. in Jackson R. Bryer and Cathy W. Barks, eds., *Dear Scott, Dearest Zelda*, 147.

perfect for the house that we'll never have: Ibid., 148.

a place, Zelda explains, caught between dreams and reality: Ibid.

"When we remember we are all mad, the mysteries disappear and life stands explained": Mark Twain, *The Wit and Wisdom of Mark Twain: A Book of Quotations* (Dover: Dover Thrift Editions, 1999), 1.

One of her February 1932 letters is particularly acute in its capture of her mental and physical status and her surprise at finding her own face reflected in the mirror: Zelda Fitzgerald, "116. To Scott, February 1932," qtd. in Jackson R. Bryer and Cathy

W. Barks, eds., *Dear Scott, Dearest Zelda*, 150.

Whistlerian: Ibid.

I wish we had a house, dear: Ibid., "117. To Scott, February/March 1932," 151.

A February/March 1932 letter to Scott admits Zelda's fancy for the city and its potential as a future entertainment outlet: Ibid., 151.

a marvelous place, a prosperous, middle-age distinguished lawyer with many artistic hobbies: Ibid., "118. To Scott, February/March 1932," 153.

"life stands explained": Mark Twain, *The Wit and Wisdom*, 1.

it was during Zelda's initial stay in Baltimore that she shifted from offering herself in "tender disguises" in her letters to Scott to "identifying 'her plight' with that of the 'crazy people' she saw in Phipps": Scott Donaldson, *Fool for Love: F. Scott Fitzgerald* (New York: Congdon and Weed, 1983), 95.

a vast black shadow . . . swallow: Zelda Fitzgerald, "119. To Scott, Early March 1932," qtd. in Jackson R. Bryer and Cathy W. Barks, eds., *Dear Scott, Dearest Zelda*, 154.

[s]ometimes I feel like a titan and sometimes like a three-months abortion: Zelda Fitzgerald, "120. To Scott, Early March 1932," qtd. in Jackson R. Bryer and Cathy W. Barks, eds., *Dear Scott, Dearest Zelda*, 156.

my spiritual carcass is being gnawed by superior vultures to myself: Zelda Fitzgerald, "122. To Scott, March 9, 1932," qtd. in Jackson R. Bryer and Cathy W. Barks, eds., *Dear Scott, Dearest Zelda*, 159.

"[W]hile [Zelda] complained about the hospital's environment . . . inwardly she was grateful for the clinic's protection [from herself]": Kendall Taylor, *Sometimes Madness is Wisdom*, 258.

there's a nurse who sticks her head in the door to see that I don't strangle myself on the shadows every five minutes: Zelda Fitzgerald, "124. To Scott, Late March 1932," qtd. in Jackson R. Bryer and Cathy W. Barks, eds., *Dear Scott, Dearest Zelda*, 161.

While Zelda resided at the Phipps Clinic during 1932, Scott rented a fifteen-room Victorian house in Towson, Maryland named La Paix: Jackson R. Bryer and Cathy W. Barks, *Dear Scott, Dearest Zelda*, 169.

"It had gables and porches, fifteen or sixteen rooms, and it was full of night sounds": Nancy Milford, *Zelda: A Biography* (New York: Harper & Row, 1970), 257.

"clear the land for St. Joseph Hospital": Gwinn Owens, "The embers of La Paix," *The Baltimore Sun*, Sept. 24, 1996, http://articles.baltimoresun.com/1996-09-24/news/1996268139_1_fitzgerald-zelda-personified.

Fitzgerald actually found the property with the help of Edgar Allan Poe, Jr.: Kendall Taylor, *Sometimes Madness is Wisdom: Zelda and Scott Fitzgerald, A Marriage* (New York: Random House, 2003), 265.

La Paix Cottage, Towson, Maryland: Courtesy of the Maryland Historical Society, Image ID# PP105.07, Getz, Ca. 1910, La Paix Photograph Collection, Special Collections Department, Maryland Historical Society.

La Paix provided a transitional half-way existence for Zelda: Jackson R. Bryer and Cathy W. Barks, eds., *Dear Scott, Dearest Zelda*, 169.

Complications and tragedies mounted at La Paix: Jackson R. Bryer and Cathy W. Barks, eds., *Dear Scott, Dearest Zelda*, 170. Zelda's profits from *Save Me the Waltz* were a mere $120.73: Ibid.

"there was a fire at La Paix [in 1933], which apparently started when Zelda burned some old clothes in a neglected upstairs fireplace . . . the house badly damaged": Jackson R. Bryer and Cathy W. Barks, *Dear Scott, Dearest Zelda*, 171.

Zelda's brother committed suicide in August of 1933, and a month later Scott and Zelda's friend Ring Lardner died: Ibid.

becoming the dark tragic destiny of being an instrument of something uncomprehended, incomprehensible, unknown . . . succeeded merely in crashing [her]self, almost me + Scotty: F. Scott Fitzgerald, "128. To Zelda, 1932," qtd. in Jackson R. Bryer and Cathy W. Barks, eds., *Dear Scott, Dearest Zelda*, 172.

"dominated by Scott's increasing alcoholism and [Zelda's] own mental suffering": Sally Cline, *Zelda Fitzgerald*, 4.

shut[ting] yourself away: F. Scott Fitzgerald, "130. To Zelda, Summer 1933?," qtd. in Jackson R. Bryer and Cathy W. Barks, eds., *Dear Scott, Dearest Zelda*, 176.

The schedule: Ibid., 177.

the best protection is the schedule and then the schedule and again the schedule: Ibid.

In December of 1933 Scott and Zelda moved from La Paix to a smaller rented house in Baltimore at 1307 Park Avenue: Ibid., 171.

She remained at the Phipps Clinic until March of 1934, after which she was transferred to Craig House: Ibid., 177.

In May of 1934, Zelda returned to Baltimore, to reside at Sheppard and Enoch Pratt Hospital in Towson for the next two years: Jackson R. Bryer and Cathy W. Barks, eds., *Dear Scott, Dearest Zelda*, 197.

1307 Park Avenue: Original Photograph, 2015.

Zelda's mental state fluctuated from 1934–1936, from productive mania to depressive silence: Jackson R. Bryer and Cathy W. Barks, eds., *Dear Scott, Dearest Zelda*, 198.

Sheppard Pratt Psychiatric Hospital: Original Photograph, 2015.

Scott freely admits his anxieties caused by Zelda's institutionalization and their separated relationship . . . yet feels relieved to know Zelda is *within hearing distance again*: F. Scott Fitzgerald, "147. To Zelda," qtd. in Jackson R. Bryer and Cathy W. Barks, eds., *Dear Scott, Dearest Zelda*, 198.

The artistic process . . . is one not of selfish intention, but of shared human honesty: Zelda Fitzgerald, "152. To Scott, After June 14, 1934," qtd. in Jackson R. Bryer and Cathy W. Barks, eds., *Dear Scott, Dearest Zelda*, 205.

"self and world come close together, and *touch each other* and then go beyond even that, and become *part of each other*": John Wylie, "Landscape, absence, and the geographies of love," *Transactions of the Institute of British Geographers* 34, no. 3 (2009): 278.

1.) I am lonesome. 2.) I have no relatives or friends and would like to make acquaintance with a Malayian warrior. 3.) I do not cook or sew or commit nuisances about the house: Zelda Fitzgerald, "156. To Scott, October 1934," qtd. in Jackson R. Bryer and Cathy W. Barks, eds., *Dear Scott, Dearest Zelda*, 210.

The Sheppard Pratt hospital is located somewhere in the hinter-lands of the human consciousness and I can be located there any time: Ibid.

Life is difficult. There are so many problems. 1) The problem of how to stay here and 2) The problem of how to get out: Ibid.

"[t]hroughout June, July, and August she persisted in whatever ways were open to her to try to harm herself": Nancy Milford, *Zelda, A Biography*, 304.

by admitting her inadequacy in sending anything from *an empty world*, especially in the fall season, a time of year which exemplifies the reality that *all times are sad from their transience*: Zelda Fitzgerald, "162. To Scott, Fall 1935," qtd. in Jackson R. Bryer and Cathy W. Barks, eds., *Dear Scott, Dearest Zelda*, 216.

Zelda was transferred to Highland Hospital in Asheville, North Carolina in April of 1936: Jackson R. Bryer and Cathy W. Barks, eds., *Dear Scott, Dearest Zelda*, 217.

A sense of the Baltimore streets in summers of elms and of the dappled shade over the brick: Zelda Fitzgerald, "171. To Scott, August 1936," qtd. in Jackson R. Bryer and Cathy W. Barks, eds., *Dear Scott, Dearest Zelda*, 228.

She, in return, will look for a small natural wonder for Scott: Ibid.

"coinciding of [human and] landscape, of unifying the visible and the invisible, seer and seen": John Wylie, "Landscape, absence, and the geographies of love," 287.

Scott's friends and family speculated that this was the point when Scott realized that he and Zelda would likely never live together again, prompting a deep depression: Jackson R. Bryer and Cathy W. Barks, eds., *Dear Scott, Dearest Zelda*, 218.

In 1939, Zelda was stable enough to take an extended leave from the hospital. She and Scott traveled a bit during this year, including a trip to Cuba: Ibid., 269.

After the Cuba trip, in April of 1939, Zelda wrote to Scott in New York City (where he was staying with his sister and brother-in-law) from the Hotel Stafford in Mount Vernon: Zelda Fitzgerald, "220. To Scott, April 1939," qtd. in Jackson R. Bryer and Cathy W. Barks, eds., *Dear Scott, Dearest Zelda*, 282. F. Scott had briefly lived at the Hotel Stafford before moving to Hollywood in 1936. For further information about the Hotel Stafford see: Frederick N. Rasmussen, "The Stafford: a grand ole dame falls on hard times," *The Baltimore Sun*, Sept. 30, 2000, http://articles.baltimoresun.com/2000-09-30/features/0009300035_1_new-hotel-stafford-baltimore.

The short note is typical Zelda, expressing extreme apology, intense gratitude, and exaggerated optimism: Ibid.

Less than two years later, Scott was dead. Eight years after Scott's death, Zelda perished in a fire in Highland Hospital at age 48: Jackson R. Bryer and Cathy W. Barks, eds., *Dear Scott, Dearest Zelda*, 386.

"[p]art of our strangeness of being human is our need of boundaries, parameters, definitions, explanations . . . the need for them to be overturned": Jeanette Winterson, "Written on the Body," Jeanette Winterson, 2013, http://www.jeanettewinterson.com/.

—Chapter Ten—

Esther L. Richards: "Esther L. Richards/ by unidentified photographer, black and white photograph," The Esther L. Richards Collection, Courtesy of The Alan Mason Chesney Medical Archives of The Johns Hopkins Medical Institutions, https://medicalarchives.jhmi.edu:8443/papers/richards_el.html

Abby Howe Turner: "Abby Howe Turner (1875-1957), Wikimedia Commons, last modified on Oct. 15, 2015, https://commons.wikimedia.org/wiki/File:Abby_Howe_Turner_(1875_-_1957).jpg

Envelope: The representative envelope is based on one of Esther Richards's envelopes addressed to Abby Howe Turner, located in the digital archives of Mount Holyoke College: Esther Richards, "The Esther Richards Letters, 1915-1920," The American History and Genealogy Project, Mount Holyoke College History, Aug. 8, 2013, https://www.mtholyoke.edu/~dalbino/letters/erichards1.html. Richards's envelopes are pre-addressed with the Johns Hopkins Hospital return address and many contain the George Washington 1908 issue 2 cents stamp: "George Washington 1908-Issue-Two-Cents," Wikimedia Commons, last modified on Jan. 5, 2011, https://commons.wikimedia.org/wiki/File:George_Washington_1908_Issue-Two-Cents.jpg.

Abby Howe Turner graduated from Mount Holyoke College in 1896 and served on its faculty from 1896–1901 and from 1904–1940: "Turner Papers, ca 1896–1960," Five College Archives and Manuscript Collections, Mount Holyoke College Archives and Special Collections, April 2008, http://asteria.fivecolleges.edu/findaids/mountholyoke/mshm147_main.html/.

Richards graduated in 1910 from Mount Holyoke College: "The Esther L. Richards Collection," The Alan Mason Chesney Medical Archives of The Johns Hopkins Medical Institutions, The Johns Hopkins Health System and The Johns Hopkins University, 1999, http://www.medicalarchives.jhmi.edu/papers/richards_el.html/.

the same institution that Emily Dickinson attended for one year: "Emily Dickinson's Schooling: Mount Holyoke Female Seminary," Emily Dickinson Museum, Trustees of Amherst College, 2009, https://www.emilydickinsonmuseum.org/mount_holyoke/.

even though Dickinson did not graduate, she "drew on [Mt. Holyoke's] knowledge of the natural world to create [her] artistic works": Miriam R. Levin, *Defining Women's Scientific Enterprise: Mount Holyoke Faculty and the Rise of American Science* (Lebanon, NH: U P of New England, 2005), 2.

Esther L. Richards was born in Hollison, Massachusetts in 1885 to David Richards and Esther Loring . . . where she was psychiatrist-in-charge of the outpatient department of the Phipps Clinic: "David Richards Family Papers, 1855–1927." Massachusetts Historical Society, 2014, http://www.masshist.org/collection-guides/view/fa0344/.

"[i]n addition to her medical and academic responsibilities, Richards was very active on the lecture circuit": "The Esther L. Richards Collection," The Alan Mason Chesney Medical Archives.

Henry Phipps Building, Johns Hopkins Hospital: Original Photograph, 2015.

Abby Howe Turner—was born in 1875 in Nashua, New Hampshire, to George Turner and Emeline Cogswell Turner: "Abby Howe Turner (1875–1957) Genealogy," Geni, last modified January 13, 2015, https://www.geni.com/people/Abby-Howe-Turner/6000000017543178508/.

After receiving her undergraduate degree from Mount Holyoke in 1896, Turner studied at a variety of top tier institutions: "Turner Papers, ca 1896–1960," Five College Archives and Manuscript Collections.

She became a full professor of physiology and zoology at Mount Holyoke College in 1913, where she founded the department of physiology: "Abby Howe Turner 1896," The American History and Genealogy Project, Mount Holyoke College History, August 8, 2013, https://www.mtholyoke.edu/~dalbino/women19/abby.html/.

Donna Albino notes that Turner "liked to write to her friends when she was away from campus": "Letters to Abby Howe Turner," The American History and Genealogy Project, Mount Holyoke College History, August 8, 2013, https://www.mtholyoke.edu/~dalbino/letters/turner.html/.

"Women's letters rarely just exchange information . . . [i]nstead, they tell stories; they tell secrets . . . And, along the way, they usually without meaning to—write history": Lisa Grunwald and Stephen J. Adler, *Women's Letters: America from the Revolutionary War to the Present* (New York: Dial Press, 2005), 1.

"some of [Turner's] correspondents returned her letters to them at some point (or their next of kin did) . . . [However, there are not any preserved copies of] the letters that [Turner] wrote to [Richards]": Donna Albino, email message to author, July 16, 2014.

"could not locate any letters . . . [in their] correspondence materials in the files for both Esther Richards '10 and Abby Turner '98": Caroline Palmer, e-mail message to author, 21 July 2014.

"a colony of talented women scientists, employed and unemployed, formed around Johns Hopkins University in the 1920's and 1930's": Margaret W. Rossiter, *Women Scientists in America: Struggles and Strategies to 1940* (Baltimore: JHU Press, 1984), 207.

"an unusually rich group": Ibid., 208.

"[e]ven the limited success that women scientists had attained by 1940 had required the best effort of a host of talented women": Ibid., xviii.

"notable female scientists at seven major women's colleges": Margaret W. Rossiter, *Women Scientists in America*, 19.

The Rev. said 'If Onesimus had lived in Balt. today people would have considered him the product of his heredity & environment, & sent him to the Phipps Clinic: Esther Richards, Letter from Esther Richards to Abby Howe Turner, February 27, 1916, "The Esther Richards Letters, 1915-1920," The American History and Genealogy Project, Mount Holyoke College History, last updated January 6, 2017, https://www.mtholyoke.edu/~dalbino/letters/text/richards48.html.

It has been warm here . . . but the patients have not minded it much. You see they are southerners:: Esther Richards, Letter from Esther Richards to Abby Howe Turner, August 7, 1917, "The Esther Richards Letters, 1915-1920," The American History and Genealogy Project, Mount Holyoke College History, last updated January 6, 2017, https://www.mtholyoke.edu/~dalbino/letters/text/richards12.html.

[t]he heat is so hard on your spirit, I know from past summers: Ibid.

where the children have suffered fearfully, & their lives are snuffed out easily: Ibid.

cry[ing] at night, and in the daytime when they trudge by the clinic over the hot & dusty walk: Ibid.

told [Richards] [h]ow many maids she carried abroad with her when she first went after marriage: Esther Richards, Letter from Esther Richards to Abby Howe Turner, March 10, 1915, "The Esther Richards Letters, 1915-1920," The American History and Genealogy Project, Mount Holyoke College History, last updated January 6, 2017, https://www.mtholyoke.edu/~dalbino/letters/text/richards29.html.

She was interested to know how I survived such close & continuous contact with the "masses": Ibid.

[t]he battle with me is pretty much alone: : Esther Richards, Letter from Esther Richards to Abby Howe Turner, September 4, 1920, "The Esther Richards Letters, 1915-1920," The American History and Genealogy Project, Mount Holyoke College History, last updated January 6, 2017, https://www.mtholyoke.edu/~dalbino/letters/text/richards24.html.

Please write me often. I need your letters: Ibid.

How slip-shod they do things at the Harvard Medical & that nice discrimination against our sex!: Esther Richards, Letter from Esther Richards to Abby Howe Turner, September 29, 1924, "The Esther Richards Letters, 1921-1932," The American History and Genealogy Project, Mount Holyoke College History, last updated January 6, 2017, https://www.mtholyoke.edu/~dalbino/letters/text/richards43.html.

"less conservative & aristocratic": Ibid.

[Mount Holyoke] seemed ideal when I left 7 yrs ago, and now it might suffocate me if I stayed there long enough: Esther Richards, Letter from Esther Richards to Abby Howe Turner, February 22, 1917, "The Esther Richards Letters, 1915-1920," The American History and Genealogy Project, Mount Holyoke College History, last updated January 6, 2017, https://www.mtholyoke.edu/~dalbino/letters/text/richards66.html.

Education does not educate emotions of selfishness, & greed & Ego striving. Only the Grace of God does that: Esther Richards, Letter from Esther Richards to Abby Howe Turner, February 13, 1932, "The Esther Richards Letters, 1921-1932," The American History and Genealogy Project, Mount Holyoke College History, last updated January 6, 2017, https://www.mtholyoke.edu/~dalbino/letters/text/richards89.html.

in conjunction with Smith, Goucher, Mt. H. Bryn Mawr for endowment campaign interest: Esther Richards, Letter from Esther Richards to Abby Howe Turner, February 17, 1920, "The Esther Richards Letters, 1915-1920," The American History and Genealogy Project, Mount Holyoke College History, last updated January 6, 2017, https://www.mtholyoke.edu/~dalbino/letters/text/richards64.html.

—Part Four—

Map showing the plan of Baltimore, 1878: "EB9_Baltimore.jpg," Wikimedia Commons, last modified June 5, 2014, https://commons.wikimedia.org/wiki/File:EB9_Baltimore.jpg.

—Chapter Eleven—

"The Sleeper": "Illustration to a poem published by poe 1900," "Edgar Allan Poe-Poem-The Sleeper1-Noel ArM.jpg," Wikimedia Commons, last modified on July 25, 2008, https://commons.wikimedia.org/wiki/File:Edgar_Allan_Poe-Poem-The_Sleeper1-Noel_ArM.jpg.

Edgar Allan Poe: "Edgar Allan Poe Portrait," Wikimedia Commons, last modified March 9, 2007, https://commons.wikimedia.org/wiki/File:Edgar_Allan_Poe_portrait.jpg.

Signature of Edgar Allan Poe: "Firma Poe," Wikimedia Commons, last modified October 15, 2008, https://commons.wikimedia.org/wiki/File:Firma_Poe.png

Virginia Poe: "Virginia Poe," Wikimedia Commons, last modified March 4, 2008, https://commons.wikimedia.org/wiki/File:VirginiaPoe.jpg.

Envelope: The envelope representation is modeled after Poe's letter to Sara Whitman, housed in the digital archives in the American Antiquarian Society: "Edgar Allan Poe [graphic]," American Antiquarian Society, 2017, https://catalog.mwa.org/vwebv/holdingsInfo?searchId=3929&recPointer=0&recCount=10. Prior to utilizing postage stamps and customized ink stamps, postmasters hand signed postage receipts directly onto letters and envelopes. The represented envelope includes a signed postage receipt written in the early 1830's.

Letter: The excerpt is from Poe's August 29, 1835 letter to Maria (and Virginia) Clemm: Edgar Allan Poe, "Edgar Allan Poe to Mrs. Maria Clemm and Miss Virginia Clemm — August 29, 1835 (LTR-048)," Edgar Allan Poe Society of Baltimore, last modified May 10, 2009, https://www.eapoe.org/works/letters/p3508290.htm.

"It was my luck to fall in love only with women from whom age, death, and marriage to others separated me": Edgar Allan Poe, paraphrased by ed. Thomas Ollive Mabbott, noted in *Edgar Allan Poe: Complete Poems* (Chicago: U of Illinois P, 1969): 158.

"to make them strong and healthy. . . to put them to sleep when restless": qtd. in Jeffrey Meyers, *Edgar Allan Poe: His Life and Legacy* (New York: Cooper Square Press, 1992), 5.

By the time Poe was three years old, his father had abandoned the family and died and his mother had passed away from tuberculosis: Richard P. Benton, "Friends and Enemies," 1.

"closely associated with some woman who could play the role of mother to him": Ibid.

The interception of early letters that Poe wrote from the University of Virginia to his fifteen-year-old girlfriend/fiancée in Richmond, Sarah Elmira Royster: Jeffrey Meyers, *Edgar Allan Poe*, 29.

After Poe was discharged from the U.S. Army in 1829, he applied to West Point and boarded near his Baltimore relatives: "The John Allan Period," The Edgar Allan Poe Society of Baltimore, (Baltimore, 1997): https://www.eapoe.org/works/ostlttrs/pl661c01.htm.

until his appointment came through in March 1830: Richard P. Benton, "Friends and Enemies," 2.

Records also show that Poe was in Baltimore on December 10, 1829, when he sold a slave belonging to Maria Clemm: Ibid.

"dilemma of bondage, with both slavery and the constructed ideal": Joan Dayan, "Amorous Bondage: Poe, Ladies, and Slaves," *American Literature* 66, no. 2 (1994): 240.

"ladies . . . who turn into revenants and lovers who turn into slaves": Ibid., 267.

Poe was living in Baltimore when his second volume of poetry, Al Aaraaf, Tamerlane, and Minor Poems was published: Richard P. Benton, "Friends and Enemies," 2.

Poe's return to Baltimore in March 1831, after being expelled from West Point: Jeffrey Meyers, *Edgar Allan Poe*, 50.

was welcomed by Maria Clemm and her family, who now offered him a home at their small quarters at 3 Amity Street: Ibid., 56.

3 Amity Street: "PoeHouse-Baltimore," Wikimedia Commons, last modified on October 9, 2007, https://commons.wikimedia.org/wiki/File:PoeHouse-Baltimore.jpg.

"the least documented and most obscure period of his life": Jeffrey Meyers, *Edgar Allan Poe*, 59.

"(i)n 1832 half the prisoners in the Baltimore City Jail were insolvent debtors": Ibid., 63.

"lived in humble and desperate circumstances": Ibid., 59.

"intense emotional attachments to both Maria and Virginia Clemm": Ibid., 60.

After he left the city to work as an assistant editor of the *Southern Literary Messenger*: Richard P. Benton, "Friends and Enemies," 7.

"had offered to take [Maria] and Virginia into his home, support them, and, in addition, provide for Virginia's education": Ibid., 3.

I am blinded with tears while writing this letter . . . My bitterest enemy would pity me: Edgar Allan Poe, "Edgar Allan Poe to Mrs. Maria Clemm and Miss Virginia Clemm — August 29, 1835 (LTR-048)," Edgar Allan Poe Society of Baltimore, https://www.eapoe.org/works/letters/p3508290.htm.

[you] have both tender hearts—and you will always have the reflection that my agony is more than I can bear: Ibid.

not one soul to love me: Ibid.

I am afraid to trust it to the mail, as the letters are continually robbed: Ibid.

I cannot advise you. . . Ask Virginia. Leave it to her: Ibid.

My love, my own sweetest Sissy, my darling little wifey: Ibid.

just received another letter from [Maria] announcing the rect. of mine: Ibid.

My heart bleeds for you: Ibid.

"Mrs. Clemm rejected Neilson Poe's offer . . . [and] she and Virginia joined Edgar . . . Edgar and Virginia were married there on 26 May 1836": Richard P. Benton, "Friends and Enemies," 3.

"proved too small to accommodate them": Ibid. 3.

that the owner of the *Southern Literary Messenger* grew unhappy with Poe due to his conflicting ideas and his periodic drinking: Ibid. 3.

"Maria Clemm herself . . . was perhaps altogether the most important woman": Ibid., 3.

"Mrs. Clemm did her best to care for her 'Eddie' and to help him": Ibid., 4.

Fanny Osgood and Elizabeth Ellet, two women on the literary circuit in New York, were extremely jealous: Jeffrey Meyers, *Edgar Allan Poe*, 192.

Sarah Helen Whitman and the widowed Sara Elmira Royster Shelton also played large roles in Poe's epistolary body after Virginia's death: In *The Book of Love: Writers and their Love Letters*, Cathy Davidson describes how "Poe blamed himself for [Virginia's] death from tuberculosis during the winter of 1847. An alcoholic who was prone to profound depressions, Poe sought solace from his guilt over his wife's death in the company of two women." Sarah Helen Whitman was a widowed poet Poe "had met on one of his lecture tours." Nancy "Annie" Richmond, to whom Poe was "desperately attracted to . . . already had a husband and was unwilling to leave him in order to marry Poe.": Cathy Davidson, *The Book of Love: Writers and their Love Letters* (New York: Plume, 1996), 89.

"My poor Virginia was continually tortured (although not deceived) by [Ellet's] anonymous letters": Edgar Allan Poe, qtd. in Jeffrey Meyers, *Edgar Allan Poe*, 192.

the tattling of many tongues . . . [l]ove alone shall guide us. . . [and] heal my weakened lungs: Virginia Clemm Poe, "[Valentine to Edgar Allan Poe]," manuscript, February 14, 1846," Edgar Allan Poe Society of Baltimore, last modified Aug. 3, 2011, https://www.eapoe.org/geninfo/vcpvalp.htm

[o]ur Mother will explain to you why I stay away from you this night. I trust the interview I am promised, will result in some substantial good: Edgar Allan Poe, "Edgar Allan Poe to Mrs. Virginia Poe — June 12, 1846 (LTR-232)," Edgar Allan Poe Society of Baltimore, last modified May 10, 2009, https://www.eapoe.org/works/letters/p4606120.htm

soul-life: "Edgar Allan Poe (ed. Killis Campbell), 'To my Mother,' The Poems of Edgar Allan Poe, Ginn and Company, 1917, p. 133," Edgar Allan Poe Society of Baltimore, last modified August 25, 2017, https://www.eapoe.org/works/campbell/kcp1755.htm.

I was never really insane, except on occasions where my heart was touched: Edgar Allan Poe, "Edgar Allan Poe to Mrs. Maria Clemm — July 7, 1849 (LTR-323)," Edgar Allan Poe Society of Baltimore, last modified on May 10, 2009, https://www.eapoe.org/works/letters/p4907070.htm.

"Poe liked to worship women from afar, in letters and in verse": Jeffrey Meyers, *Edgar Allan Poe*, 221.

"ill-health, nervous temperament, difference in age, financial considerations, family responsibilities": Ibid.

"Poe constantly recycled the feelings . . . if not the actual words of his love letters": Ibid., 122.

"delirium tremens . . . a lethal amount of alcohol . . . congestion of the brain . . . cerebral inflammation . . . encephalitis": Kenneth Silverman, *Edgar A. Poe: Mournful and Never-Ending Remembrance* (New York: Harper Perennial, 1991), 435-6.

"trunk Poe brought from Richmond. . . containing. . . a packet of letters form Elmira Shelton": Ibid., 436.

Pray for me, Helen; pray for me: Ibid., 444.

"Indeed she said that after his death she destroyed hundreds of letters written to him": Ibid., 443.

"had countless requests for samples of [Poe's] writing": Ibid., 447.

Maria passed away on February 16, 1871 at Church Home in Baltimore: Earl Arnett, Robert J. Brugger and Edward C. Papenfuse, *Maryland: A New Guide to the Old Line State* (Baltimore: JHU Press, 1999), 322.

a charity home for the elderly which had once been called Washington Medical College: Kenneth Silverman, *Edgar A. Poe*, 446.

—Chapter Twelve—

Thurgood Marshall, between 1930-1945: "Thurgood-Marshall," Wikimedia Commons, last modified Sept. 10, 2018, https://commons.wikimedia.org/wiki/File:Thurgood-Marshall.jpg.

Photograph of Vivian Burey Marshall: "Vivian 'Buster' Burey Marshall," WikiTree, 2018, https://www.wikitree.com/wiki/Burey-2.

Envelope: The representative envelope and affixed stamps are modeled after a pre-addressed envelope Marshall used to mail a letter to Charles Houston on September 23, 1935: "Civil Rights Movement: Origins," Smithsonian National Postal Museum, https://postalmuseum.si.edu/freedom/p10.html. Stamps: Washington Three Cent Stamp, "720.jpg," Wikimedia Commons, last modified May 4, 2011, https://commons.wikimedia.org/wiki/File:720.jpg; Washington Two Cent Stamp, "2-cent Washington stamp, 1912," Wikimedia Commons, last modified May 3, 2011, https://commons.wikimedia.org/wiki/File:2-cent_Washington_stamp,_1912.jpg.

Letters: The letters image symbolizes the correspondence between Thurgood Marshall and Vivian Burey Marshall which remains in existence, though inaccessible through traditional preserved and/or published venues. Image: https://free-images.com/display/grey_antique_letter_texture.html.

"he left Baltimore in the 1930s and was 'glad to be rid of it forever'": Thurgood Marshall, qtd. by Ronald Collins, "Book Preview: Another Thurgood Marshall biography coming this winter," review of Young Thurgood: The Making of a Supreme Court Justice by Larry S. Gibson, SCOTUSblog, Aug. 24, 2012, http://www.scotusblog.com/2012/08/book-preview-another-thurgood-marshall-biography-coming-this-winter/.

first wife, Vivian Burey Marshall, with whom he lived in Baltimore from 1930 to 1938: Ron Cassie, "Justice for All: Fifty Years After

Thurgood Marshall's Supreme Court Confirmation, Baltimore's great dismantler of Jim Crow remains a colossus of U.S. History," *Baltimore Magazine*, Aug. 7, 2017, https://www.baltimoremagazine.com/2017/8/7/justice-for-all-50-years-after-thurgood-marshall-supreme-court-confirmation.

"tendency to gloss over important within-group differences": Walter R. Allen, "African American Family Life in Societal Context: Crisis and Hope," *Sociological Forum* 10, no. 4 (1995): 569.

"the [LOC online] collection contains little material from [Marshall's] pre-judicial career.": Patrick Kerwin, email message to the author. Aug. 4, 2014.

Walter White, who was executive secretary of the NAACP from 1931 to 1955: "Nation's Premier Civil Rights Organization," NAACP, 2018, https://www.naacp.org/nations-premier-civil-rights-organization/.

"handwritten news of the trip": Michael G. Long, *Marshalling Justice: The Early Civil Rights Letters of Thurgood Marshall* (New York: HarperCollins, 2011), 68.

"is one of the few extant letters to [Marshall's] first wife": Ibid.

"[t]he letters to Vivian seem few and far between . . . found nothing more substantive . . . [and] suspect[s] [Burey's] family . . . would be one of the best finds in research about Marshall": Michael G. Long, email message to the author, Aug. 5, 2014.

"[Marshall's letter's] tenderness is rarer still": Michael G. Long, *Marshalling Justice*, 68.

Dearest Shooksie:/ This is really beautiful country down here: Thurgood Marshall, qtd. in Michael G. Long, *Marshalling Justice*, 68.

be good: Ibid.

I have been eating so much that I am sure I have gained more weight: Ibid.

"sleuthing has led him to courthouses and clerk's office records": Thurgood Marshall, Jr., qtd. by Larry S. Gibson, foreword to *Young Thurgood: The Making of a Supreme Court Justice* (Amherst, New York: Prometheus Books, 2012), 9.

"popular belief [that] Marshall hated Baltimore": Larry S. Gibson, *Young Thurgood*, 11.

"while Marshall did have some bad memories of Baltimore's stifling racial segregation": Ibid., 12.

"[t]his early period of Marshall's life had shaped his personality, attitudes, priorities, and work habits": Ibid., 14.

Thurgood Marshall was born "Thoroughgood Marshall" on July 2, 1908 . . . William Marshall, temporarily relocated the family to Harlem while he worked on the New York Central Railroad: Ibid., 36-41.

"the family returned to Baltimore and moved in with [Marshall's mother's] brother Fearless Williams": Ibid., 42.

For the next two decades, Marshall's father worked various waiter jobs: Ibid., 42.

"went to the courthouse in Baltimore and watched civil and criminal trials": Ibid., 44.

"at the same time ornery and affable, stern and softhearted": Ibid.

"by teaching me to argue . . . [h]e never told me to be a lawyer": Ibid.

"Marshall, unlike his more outgoing classmate, the future entertainer Cab Calloway": Ibid., 74.

"[t]here was never a time while growing up when Thurgood Marshall felt disconnected from his family": Ibid., 50.

After attending Henry Highland Garnett School (Public School 103), Marshall

attended the **Colored High School:** Ibid., 62. Public School 103 was also previously known as the Division Street School, located at 1315 Division Street. Today, the school—now named Thurgood Marshall Elementary School—stands in ruins, paused in renovation efforts and damage from a 2016 fire.

Marshall's class was the last class to use the building, as a new Junior/Senior High School (named Frederick Douglass High School) was built for African American students in 1925: Ibid., 78.

located at the Calhoun, Baker, and Carey Streets: Ibid., 65.

"sending him to the basement and requiring that he memorize portions of the Constitution": Edward Gunts, "Lessons in city's civil rights heritage at P.S. 103," *The Baltimore Sun*, Oct. 31, 2005, http://articles.baltimoresun.com/2005-10-31/features/0510310202_1_baltimore-committee-cultural-heritage-baltimore-city.

"Before I left that school, I knew the whole [Constitution] by heart": Thurgood Marshall, qtd. by Juan Williams, *Thurgood Marshall*, 35.

"maintaining his reputation as a cutup and prankster": Juan Williams, *Thurgood Marshall: American Revolutionary* (New York: Crown Books, 1998), 34.

"remembered Thurgood acting up one day when the teacher left the classroom": Ibid., 35.

"Thurgood was full of the devil. He threw a piece of chalk and hit me in the eye": Charlotte Shervington, qtd. in Juan Williams, *Thurgood Marshall*, 35.

"First we decided to get married five years after I graduated, then three, then one": Vivian Burey Marshall, qtd. in Larry S. Gibson, *Young Thurgood*, 101.

After graduation, newlyweds Thurgood and Burey moved into Thurgood's parents' house: Ibid., 105.

which was already housing Marshall's parents, Marshall's brother and his brother's wife and son: Ibid., 116.

Former site of 1838 Druid Hill Avenue: Original Photograph, 2015.

Marshall commuted from Baltimore to Washington, D.C. for the next three years: Ibid., 107.

"to document and photograph the stark differences between black and white schools": Ibid., 124.

Marshall would take two additional road trips with Houston in the 1920's: Ibid., 121.

"a group of educated young women that sought to assist its members": Ibid., 156.

Burey's decision not to tell Marshall about her terminal lung cancer diagnosis: "Vivian 'Buster' Burey dies at 44," American Radio Works, American Public Media, http://americanradioworks.publicradio.org/features/marshall/busterdies.html.

"would forward . . . not only to law enforcement officials but also to the national media": Michael G. Long, *Marshalling Justice*, 70.

"In an angry letter on behalf of a majority of the Supreme Court, Chief Justice William H. Rehnquist": Neil A. Lewis, "Chief Justice Assails Library on Release of Marshall Papers," Archives, *The New York Times*, May 26, 1993, https://www.nytimes.com/1993/05/26/us/chief-justice-assails-library-on-release-of-marshall-papers.html.

"[a] public figure may be accountable in one sense and to one degree to the general public": Anita L. Allen, "Privacy Isn't Everything: Accountability as a Personal and Social Good," *Alabama Law Review* 54 (2003): 1383.

"[t]he late Supreme Court Justice Thurgood Marshall was accountable for his personal life": Ibid.

Family members often feel a violation of intimacy will take place by the public exposure of personal letters: Dena Goodman, "Old Media: Lessons from Letters," *French Historical Studies* 36, no. 1 (2013): 6.

"Justice Rehnquist's letter said the library misinterpreted the agreement Justice Marshall signed . . . it would have understood the need to keep the materials private for a longer time": Neil A. Lewis, "Chief Justice Assails."

"that is what historians do; at the very heart of our work is reading other people's mail": Dena Goodman, "Old Media," 6.

"letters show us that our intimate ties are what make it possible to face the dangers": Emily Bernard, "Love Letters, Straight from the Heart," review of *A Love No Less: More than Two Centuries of African American Love Letters* by Pamela Newkirk, *Black Issues* 5, no. 3 (2003): 51.

"[w]e [the Manuscript Division at the Library of Congress] initially asked for his papers around 1965": Debra Newman Ham, qtd. in Lucy D. Suddreth, "Thurgood Marshall: His Papers at LC Document a Career in Civil Rights," *Library of Congress Information Bulletin* 52, no. 4, Library of Congress, Feb. 22, 1993, http://www.loc.gov/loc/lcib/93/9304/marshall.html.

"we began to hear rumors that Justice Marshall was planning to destroy his papers": Ibid.

It was not until after Marshall's retirement in 1991, with a third request from the Library of Congress: Ibid.

which is why, even with an ambiguous mapping, his part in the formation of the intimate chamber of Westside Baltimore is so important: For an intriguing and parallel metaphorical mapping of race and economics in post-Emancipation Baltimore, see Sherry H. Olson's "Baltimore Imitates the Spider," *Annals of the Association of American Geographers* 69, no. 4 (1979): 574, in which Olson explains that "the movements of people and the transportation of commodities on which urban geographers have tended to fixate, are the basics for the less visible circulation of money and capital which we have often neglected or taken for granted. In the production of urban form as in the morphogenesis of animals, plants, or natural landscapes, dominant periodicities form and point to the forces at work." Olson quotes D'Arcy W. Thompson, who theorized "[f]orm is a diagram of forces," in applying Baltimore's geographical and architectural elements as active forces in the city's history: "Baltimore's brick rows, marble steps, and tarred roofs are a diagram of social forces."

"fought for racial justice without becoming a racist . . . simultaneously idealistic and pragmatic . . . a passionate advocate": Larry S. Gibson, qtd. in Ronald Collins, "Book Preview: Another Thurgood Marshall biography coming this winter," review of *Young Thurgood: The Making of a Supreme Court Justice* by Larry S. Gibson. *SCOTUSblog*, Aug. 24, 2012, http://www.scotusblog.com/2012/08/book-preview-another-thurgood-marshall-biography-coming-this-winter/.

"the figure . . . The combination of [Marshall's] reclusiveness and his standing": Juan Williams, *Thurgood Marshall*, xviii.

"that Marshall laid the foundation for today's racial landscape": Ibid.

"[d]uring his last news conference in June 1991, after announcing his retirement, Justice Marshall said that he wished to be remembered with 10 words'": Lucy D. Suddreth, "Thurgood Marshall."

"That he did what he could with what he had": Thurgood Marshall, qtd. in Lucy D. Suddreth, "Thurgood Marshall: His Papers at LC Document a Career in Civil Rights," *Library of Congress Information Bulletin* 52, no. 4, Library of Congress, Feb. 22, 1993, http://www.loc.gov/loc/lcib/93/9304/marshall.html.

—Chapter Thirteen—

Mitchell Family: Juanita Jackson Mitchell, Clarence Mitchell III (standing), Clarence Mitchell, Jr., and Kieffer Mitchell: "Mitchell Family. Juanita Jackson Mitchell, Clarence Mitchell III (standing), Clarence Mitchell, Jr., and Keiffer Mitchell. Paul Henderson, undated. Maryland Historical Society, HEN.00.B1-041," Maryland's Civil Rights Era in Photographs, ca. 1935-1965, Paul Henderson Photographs and Blog, https://hendersonphotos.wordpress.com/baltimores-black-history/people/henderson-collection-reference-photograph-box-00-b1-111/.

Letters/Envelopes: This image represents the private collections and archives of intimate letters and envelopes, such as those of Clarence Mitchell, Jr. and Juanita Jackson (Mitchell), only accessible through private and/or familial permission.

"from the personal collection—love letters written by Clarence—that are in the private collection controlled by Michael Mitchell": Denton Watson, email message to the author, Aug. 21, 2014.

"to be the most important unprocessed archive on the modern civil rights era": James H. Billington, "Mitchell Family of Civil Rights Activists Gives Papers to Library," *Library of Congress Information Bulletin* 56, no. 6, March 24, 1997, https://www.loc.gov/loc/lcib/970324/mitchell.html.

it was Watson's exposure to Mitchell and Jackson's intimate letters that dramatically shaped the biographical portrait he paints: Denton L. Watson, *Lion in the Lobby: Clarence Mitchell, Jr.'s Struggle for the Passage of the Civil Rights Laws*. New York: Morrow, 1990), xiii.

1216 Druid Hill Avenue: Original Photograph, 2015.

"the matriarch of one of Baltimore's oldest civil rights families": "Juanita Jackson Mitchell (1913–1992)," Maryland Women's Hall of Fame, Maryland State Archives, 2001, https://msa.maryland.gov/msa/educ/exhibits/womenshall/html/mitchell.html.

"the school desegregation suits championed by [Jackson] made Maryland the first Southern state to integrate its school system": "Juanita Jackson Mitchell (1913-1992)," Maryland Women's Hall of Fame.

Mitchell spent the first few years of his life in a small house on Stockton Street near Pressman Street: Denton L. Watson, *Lion in the Lobby*, 35.

Thurgood Marshall Elementary School: Original Photograph, 2015.

Part of the reason that Mitchell and Marshall did not know each other during their childhood years was their three-year age difference: Denton L. Watson, *Lion in the Lobby*, 37.

"A more important reason, though . . . was the difference in their social status: Ibid.

"home was on prized Druid Hill Avenue . . . [t]hey thought that the black residents there were having such a difficult time:" Ibid., 38.

The young men would eventually meet at Douglass High School, and then again at Lincoln University: "Clarence M. Mitchell, Jr.," *The Baltimore Sun*, Feb. 9, 2007, http://www.baltimoresun.com/features/bal-blackhistory-mitchell-story.html.

Douglass High School was also the site of another vital connection: Denton L. Watson, *Lion in the Lobby*, 53.

"showing religious and educational motion pictures in churches and schools from town to town": Ibid., 51.

"pioneering endeavor provided blacks with a welcome alternative to the generally demeaning depictions": Ibid.

Lillie Carroll Jackson was also considered a mother of the civil rights movement: Sierra Hallmen, "Lillie Carroll Jackson Museum," Baltimore Heritage, https://explore.baltimoreheritage.org/items/show/518.

After traveling on the road as a family for eight years, the Jacksons moved to 1326 McCulloch Street: Denton L. Watson, *Lion in the Lobby*, 53.

"her girls maintain a very high standard of decorum . . . made it clear that the girls could not dare look at boys": Ibid.

"Boys and books don't go together": Lillie Carroll Jackson, qtd. in Denton L. Watson, *Lion in the Lobby*, 53.

"Juanita's parents had an iron-clad prohibition against her socializing with boys.": Clarence Mitchell, Jr., qtd. in Denton L. Watson, *Lion in the Lobby*, 53.

In 1927, Lillie Carroll Jackson withdrew Juanita from Morgan State College during her sophomore year . . . Carroll the challenged the Dean: Denton L. Watson, *Lion in the Lobby*, 55.

"Mitchell swept her off her feet with his 'silver-tongued oratory . . . not only a smooth talker in private . . . [and] knew how to hold an intelligent woman's attention": Juanita Jackson Mitchell, qtd. in Denton L. Watson, *Lion in the Lobby*, 63–4.

Watson describes the Baltimore that Mitchell and Jackson returned to after college as the same "mean" and contradictory city: Denton L. Watson, *Lion in the Lobby*, 57.

"up-South Baltimore": Thurgood Marshall, qtd. in Denton L. Watson, *Lion in the Lobby*, 57.

"[t]he *Afro-American* found . . . that Black-owned clothing stores in the community were outnumbered by white-owned stores seven to one": Andor Skotnes, "'Buy Where You Can Work': Boycotting for Jobs in African-American Baltimore, 1933–34," *Journal of Social History* 27, no. 4 (1994): 740.

"[t]he segregationism under which African Americans in Baltimore lived . . . [there were] nominally integrated public places in the city": Andor Skotnes, *A New Deal for All? Race and Class Struggles in Depression-Era Baltimore* (Durham: Duke UP, 2012), 30.

Watson notes Jackson "believed in him . . . [and] he found himself 'thinking and doing things [he] would never otherwise dream of doing'": Clarence Mitchell, Jr., qtd. in Denton L. Watson, *Lion in the Lobby*, 85.

whatever else there is before me now is your dream not mine: Clarence Mitchell, Jr., qtd. in Denton L. Watson, *Lion in the Lobby*, 85.

"[l]etter writing, while a sign of civilization, is also a high-risk occupation": Roger Rosenblatt, "Don't Write Any Letters," *Time* 117, no. 25 (1981), http://content.time.com/time/magazine/article/0,9171,950570,00.html.

"[l]etters conceal almost nothing, which accounts for their power . . . [as] one looks for things to be said in letters that are not said elsewhere": Ibid.

intoleran[ce] of cowardice in others: Clarence Mitchell, Jr., qtd. in Denton L. Watson, *Lion in the Lobby*, 86.

he expresses his dismay at the media's silence regarding a recent unjust sentencing in Atlanta of a fourteen-year-old boy: Denton L. Watson, *Lion in the Lobby*, 84.

Mitchell criticizes Atlanta's media accounts of the sentencing: Denton L. Watson, *Lion in the Lobby*, 86.

In the letter, Mitchell utilizes the metaphor of a rose: Ibid., 93-4.

A rare fragrance: Clarence Mitchell, Jr., qtd. in Denton Watson, Lion in the Lobby, 94.

"were Baltimore's dream couple . . . [they] represented a generation of their race": Denton L. Watson, *Lion in the Lobby*, 97.

"[t]he older generation supported [Mitchell and Jackson] as they developed a new blueprint for freedom": Ibid.

"Let me shorthand it this way . . . [i]f Netflix were to green-light a *House of Cards* prequel set in that era, Mitchell would be a star character at every stage of the legislative process": Henry Louis Gates, Jr., "Who Was the Unsung Hero of the 1964 Civil Rights Act?" *The Root*. The Root, June 30, 2014, https://www.theroot.com/who-was-the-unsung-hero-of-the-1964-civil-rights-act-1790876217.

"at night": Ibid.

"give the Mitchell family and Baltimore a more prominent place in civil-rights history": Juan Williams, qtd. by Marilyn MacCraven, "The Mitchell Papers: New Revelations," *The Baltimore Sun*, Apr. 15, 1995, http://articles.baltimoresun.com/1995-04-15/news/1995105027_1_clarence-mitchell-mitchell-papers-juanita.

"Williams was able to make only limited use of the papers in his research": Ibid.

—Chapter Fourteen—

W. E. B. Du Bois in front of Baltimore home, ca 1945: "W. E. B. Du Bois in front of Baltimore home, ca. 1945," W. E. B. Du Bois Papers (MS 312), Special Collections and University Archives, University of Massachusetts Amherst Libraries, http://credo.library.umass.edu/view/zoom/mums312-i0467.

W. E. B. Du Bois and his wife, Nina Du Bois, ca. 1945: "W. E. B. Du Bois and his wife, Nina Du Bois, ca. 1945," W. E. B. Du Bois Papers (MS 312), Special Collections and University Archives, University of Massachusetts Amherst Libraries, http://credo.library.umass.edu/view/full/mums312-i0469.

Envelope: The representative envelope, with affixed stamp, is modeled after the only envelope categorized under Nina Gomer Du Bois in the Credo/UMassAmherst archive— Nina's death announcement: http://credo.library.umass.edu/view/full/mums312-b273-i067. Stamp: "Thomas Jefferson US Postage Stamp," Dreamstime.com, LLC, 2018, https://www.dreamstime.com/editorial-stock-image-thomas-jefferson-us-postage-stamp-united-states-circa-united-states-depicting-image-rd-president-united-states-image85363474.

Du Bois Stationary/Letter to W. E. B. Du Bois from Nina Gomer Du Bois: The representative stationary and letter excerpt are modeled after a letter written by Gomer to Du Bois on January 11, 1943. The actual letter is digitally archived in the Credo/UMassAmherst Special Collections and Archives: Du Bois, Nina. "Letter from Nina Du Bois to W. E. B. Du Bois, January 11, 1943," W. E. B. Du Bois Papers (MS 312), Special Collections and University Archives, University of Massachusetts Amherst Libraries, http://credo.library.umass.edu/view/full/mums312-b160-i411.

Du Bois owned a home in Morgan Park from 1939 to 1950: "W. E. B. Du Bois," The Baltimore Literary Heritage Project, University of Baltimore, School of Communications Design, http://baltimoreauthors.ubalt.edu/writers/webdubois.htm.

Du Bois Cottage: Original Photograph, 2015.

but it actually housed other Du Bois family members: "W. E. B. Du Bois, Nina, and Yolande in Morgan Park (Baltimore)," ChickenBones: A Journal for Literary & Artistic African American Themes, April 30, 2011, http://www.nathanielturner.com/dubois-toyolande1958.htm.

"American civil rights activist, Pan-Africanist, sociologist, educator, historian, editor, poet, and scholar": "National Association for the Advancement of Colored People History: W.E.B. Du Bois," NAACP, 2014, https://www.naacp.org/naacp-history-w-e-b-dubois/.

"[I]t is especially unfortunate that Aptheker . . . decided to focus on Du Bois's public career": Marion Kilson, "Veiling Words: The Correspondence of W. E. B. Du Bois," *Reviews in American History* 4, no. 4 (1976): 580.

"[w]ithin the two volumes of correspondence selected by Aptheker [the third volume had not yet been published at the time of her review]: Ibid.

"Had Aptheker decided to include the more revealing personal correspondence": Ibid., 581.

"a representative letter was chosen and all correspondence essentially repetitious omitted": Herbert Aptheker, *The Correspondence of W.E.B. Du Bois, Volume I, 1877–1934* (Amherst, MA: U of Mass P, 1973), xxiv.

"[t]he major decision to concentrate upon Du Bois's historical dimensions excluded practically all personal correspondence": Ibid.

Du Bois even donated personal hate mail to Aptheker, which Du Bois kept and filed under the term "curious": Ibid.

"since neither Dr. nor Mrs. Du Bois ever suggested any form of exclusion": Ibid.

"[m]ost of Du Bois's outgoing correspondence in the collection is not signed": Jeremy Smith, email message to the author, Feb. 18, 2015.

"I am not sure what happened to Nina's papers after her death": Ibid.

"just as speech without gestures loses something": Ian Baucom, "Afterword: States of Time," *Contemporary Literature* 49, no. 4 (2008): 21.

The "Du Bois Cottage" at 2302 Montebello Terrace was ready for occupancy in the spring of 1940: David Levering Lewis, *W. E. B Du Bois: A Biography*, (New York: Henry Holt, 2009), 636.

where the Du Boises lived while Du Bois worked for the NAACP during the years of 1909-1934 and from 1944-1948 . . . where Du Bois lived when he was teaching at Atlanta University during the years of 1897-1910 and 1934-1944: For further information on Du Bois's role in the NAACP and Atlanta University see: "History of the NAACP," Nation's Premier Civil Rights Organization, 2018, https://www.naacp.org/nations-premier-civil-rights-organization/ and Derrick P. Alridge, "W. E. B. Du Bois in Georgia," University of Georgia, May 14, 2003, New Georgia Encyclopedia, https://www.georgiaencyclopedia.org/articles/history-archaeology/w-e-b-du-bois-georgia

"[a]lthough Jim Crow reigned in law and practice in Baltimore": David Levering Lewis, *W. E. B. Du Bois: A Biography*, 636.

"Nina and Baby Du Bois flowed into the river of [Du Bois's] busy life": David Levering Lewis, *W. E. B. Du Bois: A Biography*, 630.

"had been reared in New York almost exclusively by [Gomer]": Ibid., 628.

"Although liberated from an abusive marriage and advantaged by a secure position": Ibid.

"[d]espite Nina's almost visceral aversion to Atlanta and Will's decided preference for the convenience of solitary living space": Ibid.

"Not much is known about [Du Bois's] life here": Gilbert Sandler, "Du Bois and the city," *The Baltimore Sun*, Jan. 4, 1994, http://articles.baltimoresun.com/1994-01-04/news/1994004143_1_dubois-arnette-baltimore.

"announced his second and final break with the NAACP": Ibid.

"the president of Morgan State College informed Du Bois's office that the failure 'to condemn (Paul Robeson's) treasonable statement' made Du Bois unfit": David Levering Lewis, *W. E. B. Du Bois: A Biography*, 687.

Wilberforce University in Pennsylvania, the first predominantly African-American private university in the country: "About WU," Wilberforce University, http://www.wilberforce.edu/about-wilberforce/.

After Du Bois was offered a teaching position at Atlanta University in 1897, they moved to Georgia, where their first child, a son named Burghardt Gomer Du Bois born on October 2, 1897, died: "Du Bois, Burghardt," DuBoisopedia, Special Collections and University Archives at U Mass-Amherst, http://scua.library.umass.edu/duboisopedia/doku.php?id=about:du_bois_burghardt.

"[H]e died. And in a sense my wife died too . . . Something was gone from my life which would not come back . . . Life was left . . . and I could plunge back": W. E. B. Du Bois, "I Bury My Wife," *W. E. B. Du Bois: A Reader*, ed. David Levering Lewis (New York: Henry Holt, 1995), 143.

Du Bois notes that "[e]ven when our little girl came two years later, [Gomer] could not altogether replace the One": Ibid.

Yolande's first marriage was to Countee Cullen, the poet, in 1928, but the marriage

quickly dissolved: Scott Christianson, "Du Bois comes home from the grave," The Berkshire Edge, May 20, 2014, https://theberkshireedge.com/du-bois-comes-home-grave/. Cullen's birthplace is unclear. Some accounts list Cullen's birth as Baltimore, while others list New York or Kentucky: Gerald Early and Clifton H. Johnson, "About Countee Cullen's Life and Career," Modern American Poetry, U of Illinois at Urbana-Champaign, 1999–2014, http://www.english.illinois.edu/maps/poets/a_f/cullen/life. htm. The Baltimore connection which Cullen is famous for is not his birth, however, but the poem, "Incident," which addresses Baltimore's racism in the early twentieth century.

Three years later, in 1931, Gomer temporarily moved in with Yolande at 1301 Madison Avenue in Baltimore: David Levering Lewis, *A Biography* 537; "W. E. B. Du Bois, Nina and Yolande in Morgan Park (Baltimore)," Chicken Bones: A Journal for Literary and Artistic African-American Themes, Chicken Bones, http://www.nathanielturner.com/duboistoyolande1958.htm.

a possible source for Yolande's fatigue: her new boyfriend, Arnette Franklin, who was a Lincoln University dropout and "a bit of a rogue and the antithesis of Countee Cullen": David Levering Lewis, *W. E. B. Du Bois: A Biography,* 537.

"[Williams] and Yolande were married on Wednesday, September 2, 1931 . . . [Du Bois] had imposed only one prenuptial condition": Ibid.

Du Bois found himself writing to Williams, requesting reimbursement for the money Du Bois had given him for his education: Du Bois, W. E. B. Du Bois, Letter from W. E. B. Du Bois to Arnett F. Williams, 1936, W. E. B. Du Bois Papers (MS 312), Special Collections and University Archives, University of Massachusetts Amherst Librarieshttp://credo.library.umass.edu/view/full/mums312-b080-i460.

Du Bois consoles Gomer over the lack of finding house . . . including the need for their daughter, Yolande, to take a larger role in raising her daughter: W. E. B. Du Bois, Letter from W. E. B. Du Bois to Nina Du Bois, February 13, 1937, W. E. B. Du Bois Papers (MS 312), Special Collections and University Archives, University of Massachusetts Amherst Libraries, http://credo.library.umass.edu/view/full/mums312-b082-i009.

I do not see how I can ever live in Baltimore . . . We would always be making excuses to go some where else: Nina Gomer Du Bois, Letter from Nina Du Bois to W. E. B. Du Bois, April 26, 1938, W. E. B. Du Bois Papers (MS 312), Special Collections and University Archives, University of Massachusetts Amherst Librarieshttp://credo.library. umass.edu/view/full/mums312-b160-i260.

Baltimore hasn't the life it had twenty years ago . . . reason for all of us being tied to Baltimore the rest of our lives: Ibid.

"The house was a two-story brick structure with four bedrooms under a gable roof": David Levering Lewis, *W. E. B. Du Bois: A Biography*, 636.

"[the] six-year-old grandchild to whom *Black Folk: Then and Now* was dedicated": Ibid., 628.

Du Bois and Gomer's granddaughter would enroll in Baltimore City Public School 103 on Division Street: Ibid., 636.

the segregated school also attended by Thurgood Marshall: Edward Gunts, "Lessons in city's civil rights heritage at P.S. 103," The Baltimore Sun,

Oct. 31, 2005, http://articles.baltimoresun.com/2005-10-31/
features/0510310202_1_baltimore-committee-cultural-heritage-baltimore-city.

As you see I am here in Baltimore . . . The house is very lovely but some how very strange to me for living: Nina Gomer Du Bois, Letter from Nina Du Bois to W. E. B. Du Bois, June 23, 1940, W. E. B. Du Bois Papers (MS 312), Special Collections and University Archives, University of Massachusetts Amherst Libraries, http://credo.library.umass.edu/view/full/mums312-b160-i325.

shall not plan to come up Thanksgiving unless something unusual happens: W. E. B. Du Bois, Letter from Nina Du Bois to W. E. B. Du Bois, November 18, 1940, W. E. B. Du Bois Papers (MS 312), Special Collections and University Archives, University of Massachusetts Amherst Libraries, http://credo.library.umass.edu/view/full/mums312-b091-i254.

to enjoy Baltimore a little: Ibid.

"secured a place for Du Bois on 'Sugar Hill' in the most prestigious apartment building in Harlem": David Levering Lewis, *W. E. B. Du Bois: A Biography*, 648.

The Sugar Hill District was home to many of Harlem's elite from the 1930's to the 1950's: "Literary Harlem," The Writer's Spot, Feb. 3, 2016, http://thewriterspot. weebly.com/literary-locations/literary-harlem.

As Yolande is no longer interested in living in Baltimore . . . and the economic weight of maintaining Du Bois Cottage: Nina Gomer Du Bois, Letter from Nina Du Bois to W. E. B. Du Bois, October 20, 1944, W. E. B. Du Bois Papers (MS 312), Special Collections and University Archives, University of Massachusetts Amherst Libraries, http://credo.library.umass.edu/view/full/mums312-b102-i341.

for what we can get out of it as a home: Ibid.

I am not going to sell it as long as I live unless there are unforeseen changes: W. E. B. Du Bois, Letter from W. E. B. Du Bois to Nina Du Bois, November 5, 1944, W. E. B. Du Bois Papers (MS 312), Special Collections and University Archives, University of Massachusetts Amherst Libraries, http://credo.library.umass.edu/view/full/ mums312-b102-i345.

You have never known hunger or great discomfort in any way: Ibid.

it will not hurt either of you to live in Baltimore: Ibid.

I have lived in Georgia for eleven years and it has not hurt me: Ibid.

stating that Gomer must return to Baltimore after she is released from the hospital: W. E. B. Du Bois, Letter from W E. B. Du Bois to Nina Du Bois, February 8, 1946, W. E. B. Du Bois Papers (MS 312), Special Collections and University Archives, University of Massachusetts Amherst Libraries, http://credo.library.umass.edu/view/ full/mums312-b110-i063.

Du Bois remains direct and unbending in his defense of the property: Ibid.

[n]ext May we will have been married fifty years. I have not always been able to make you happy: Ibid.

I think I have done my best. For the sake, therefore, of our family and especially of Du Bois: Ibid.

The box of fruit came alright in good condition . . . I believe we are to look for you this weekend: Nina Gomer Du Bois, Letter from Nina Du Bois to W. E. B. Du Bois, March 29, 1947, W. E. B. Du Bois Papers (MS 312), Special Collections and

University Archives, University of Massachusetts Amherst Libraries, http://credo. library.umass.edu/view/full/mums312-b160-i433.

I had a very interesting stay in Baltimoreand lectured in Washington: W. E. B. Du Bois, Letter from W. E. B. Du Bois to Nina Du Bois, April 11, 1947, W. E. B. Du Bois Papers (MS 312), Special Collections and University Archives, University of Massachusetts Amherst Libraries http://credo.library.umass.edu/view/full/ mums312-b113-i345.

Gomer died in her bedroom inside the home on July 1, 1950 from complications due to suffering a stroke: Herbert Aptheker, *The Correspondence of W.E.B. Du Bois, Volume II, 1934–1944* (Amherst, MA: U of Mass P, 1976), 218.

"'I Bury My Wife,' Will's apostrophe, was properly confessional. [Du Bois] had, he said, in effect sacrificed her happiness": David Levering Lewis, *W. E. B. Du Bois: A Biography*, 688.

I was not, on the whole, what one would describe as a good husband: W. E. B. Du Bois, "I Bury My Wife," *W. E. B. Du Bois: A Reader*, ed. David Levering Lewis (New York: Henry Holt, 1995), 142–3.

Du Bois passed away thirteen years later, at age 95, in Ghana: The year after Gomer's death, Du Bois married Shirley Graham, denounced the United States, and moved to Ghana, where Du Bois would receive his citizenship in 1963 at the age of 95: "W. E. B. Du Bois Dies is Ghana; Negro Leader and Author, 95," *The New York Times on the Web*, Aug. 28, 1963, https://archive.nytimes.com/www.nytimes.com/learning/ general/onthisday/bday/0223.html. Researching Du Bois and Gomer's intimate Baltimore letters quickly uncovers other personal letters between Du Bois and Shirley Graham. Du Bois and Graham's letters, while mailed outside of the Baltimore land- scape, crossed through two decades of the fifty-plus years of Du Bois and Gomer's marriage. The letters between Du Bois and Graham start in 1932 when Graham was a young graduate student at Oberlin College and wrote to Du Bois for academic advice and continue throughout Du Bois and Gomer's marriage. While this author feels it is necessary to acknowledge the overlapping intimate letters between Du Bois and Gomer, and Du Bois and Graham, for the sake of the constructed map of Du Bois's intimacy, the focus of this project is on Baltimore-based letters, and as such, only the letters between Du Bois and Gomer during their "Baltimore years" are explored.

In the decades since Du Bois sold the "Du Bois Cottage" after Gomer's death, there have only been a handful of published articles which discuss the Du Boises's connection to Baltimore: A February 24, 1997 *Baltimore Sun* article about "Baby Du Bois" introduces "Dr. Du Bois Williams" to late twentieth century Baltimore: "W. E. B. Du Bois relative is taking on his mission but granddaughter's style will be different, she says" describes the late-in-life quest of Dr. Williams to "tackle modern issues that face some in the African-American community: teen-age pregnancy, low self-esteem, grief and lax parental involvement with children": Melody Simmons, "W. E. B. Du Bois relative is taking on his mission but granddaughter's style will be different, she says," *The Baltimore Sun*, Feb. 24, 1997, http://articles.baltimoresun.com/1997-02- 24/news/1997055013_1_du-bois-niagara-movement-bois-centre. A January 4, 1994 *Baltimore Sun* article presents Arnette Williams, Yolande's second ex-husband (Du Bois's son-in-law and the father of Du Bois Williams) to the public. Williams, who was retired from the State Department and living in Cross Keys at the time of the article's publication, remembered his father-in-law, Du Bois, "was always prompt. Whenever he had a speaking engagement, and I remember that he spoke occasionally at the Bethel church on Druid Hill Avenue, he'd always arrive early. But he'd leave early, too. He did not like to stand around and make small talk": Gilbert Sandler, "Du Bois and the city," *The Baltimore Sun*, Jan. 4, 1994, http://articles.baltimoresun.com/1994-01-04/news/1994004143_1_dubois-arnette-baltimore. In the interview, Williams confirms Du Bois's reputation "as an angry radical—an elite, arrogant and brilliant man who did not suffer fools gladly," yet Williams also adds that "what most people don't know about him is that he had a terrific sense of humor. I mean he was funny . . . And more than that, he loved to read the comics. Believe it or not, the irascible and notoriously serious-minded W. E. B. Du Bois, first black ever to receive a doctorate from Harvard, loved to read the funnies": Gilbert Sandler, "Du Bois and the city."

—Conclusion—

"[m]aintaining an archive is an expensive endeavor": Kristen Sosinski, Library of Congress Library Technician, email message to the author, Feb. 12, 2015.

"The cost of a well-run archive seems bloated . . . until you realize that the cost of preserving our cultural heritage": Ibid.

Legality also influences intimate letters' accessibility, especially regarding [c]opyright, ownership and privacy rights: Ibid.

"[A]rchiving, publishing, or even simply analyzing letters is . . . a delicate business, traversing the correspondents' relationship": Margaretta Jolly, "On Burning, Saving, and Stealing Letters," *New Formations* 67 (2009): 25.

"[t]he degree to which politics plays a role depends . . . When a powerful outside figure": Kristen Sosinski, email message tot the author.

"It is tedious and specialized work . . . materials are [often] fragile": Ibid.

"[u]sually, collections arrive in disarray and in desperate need of new housing": Ibid.

"You have to organize thousands of items physically and intellectually . . . both of which are time consuming": Ibid.

"estimated 250,000 items. . . [including] correspondence, notebooks, legal files": "Mitchell Family of Civil Rights Activists Gives Papers to Library," *Library of Congress Information Bulletin* 56, no. 6, The Library of Congress, Mar. 24, 1997, https://www.loc.gov/loc/lcib/970324/mitchell.html

"[t]he Library plans to seek a grant to support the processing of the collection": Ibid.

"[I]f short cuts are taken in processing . . . chances are the end user is going to struggle": Kristen Sosinski, email message to the author.

"there are many areas of overlap and areas of gray . . . Each archival collection is unique . . . [y]ou have to choose": Ibid.

"or by addressee or by sender or by topic": Ibid.

"But other times . . . there is no discernable order": Ibid.

"the letter is one of the most democratic of genres": Caroline Bland and Maire Cross, *Gender and Politics in the Age of Letter Writing, 1750–2000* (Burlington, VT: Ashgate, 2004), 6.

"epistolary expression has attempted to arbitrate through love rather than judgment": Margaretta Jolly, "On Burning, Saving, and Stealing Letters." *New Formations* 67 (2009): 34.

"a letter's afterlife is as thoroughly culturally inscribed as its writing": Ibid., 27.

"[and] we need to use [intimate] writing to extend alternative visions": Ibid., 34.

Special Permissions provided by the Maryland Historical Society; The Alan Mason Chesney Medical Archives of The Johns Hopkins Medical Institutions; the W. E. B. Du Bois Papers, 1803-1999 (*bulk* 1877-1963), UMass Amherst; and the Enoch Pratt Free Library, H. L. Mencken Room Collection and Resources.

Acknowledgments

Versions of the included chapters have been previously released in the following publications: "Literary and Physical Sanctuary: Letters by H. L. Mencken and Sara Haardt": *Menckeniana* (Enoch Pratt Free Library, 2019); "Anatomical Reading of Correspondence: A Case Study of Epistolary Analysis Networks": *Viral Networks: Connecting Digital Humanities and Medical History* (Virginia Tech Publishing, 2018); "Hidden Correspondence by Frederick Douglass to Anna Murray (Douglass)": *Critical Insights: Social Justice and American Literature* (Salem Press, 2017); "(Un)written Words by Harriet Tubman, and Eleanor Roosevelt and her Journalist, Lorena Hickok": *Popular Culture Review* (Westphalia Press, 2017). Additional chapters have been presented at the following national and international academic conferences: Dublin Writers' Conference: "Creative Nonfiction," Dublin, Ireland (2017); IJAS Conference: "A City's Hidden Desires: Mapping Intimacy through Letters," Munich, Germany (2016); CEA Conference, Women/Women Connections: Creating Identities: "Mapping a City's Desires from the Outside-In: Intimate Baltimore Correspondence Between Eleanor Roosevelt and her Journalist, Lorena Hickok," Denver, CO (2016); MAPACA Conference, American Studies: "'Orderly Chaos': Mark Twain's Baltimore Letters to Olivia Langdon Clemens," Philadelphia, PA (2015); PCA/ACA National Conference, Libraries, Archives, Museums, and Popular Research: "Love in the Time of Archives: Identifying, Retrieving, and Connecting Intimate Correspondence through American Archives," New Orleans, LA (2015); CEA Conference, American Studies: "Contradiction in the Love Letters of H.L. Mencken and Sara Haardt," Baltimore, MD (2014); MAPACA Conference, Disability Studies: "Writing within Walls, F. Scott and Zelda's Fitzgerald's Correspondence in Baltimore," Atlantic City, NJ (2013).

This project would not have been possible without the guidance and editorial expertise of Dr. Julie Cary Conger, who believed in this vision from the very beginning and spent an enormous amount of time reading and critiquing its various versions. I would also like to thank Dr. Joy Myree-Mainor and Dr. Frank Casale for their positive support and vital feedback. Dr. Monifa Love Asante deserves much credit for offering early inspiration and mapping potential, even before the heart was fully formed. Additional thanks are due to the English Department at Morgan State University, including the direct and indirect contributions of Dr. Milford Jeremiah, Dr. Meena Khorana, Clay Goss, and Dr. Dolan Hubbard. My cousin, Kimberly Caulder, was extremely helpful in connecting me to other Library of Congress staff members, especially in regard to national archive practices. Tom Ewing, Director of the Viral Networks Workshop and Associate Dean of Graduate Studies and Research at Virginia Tech, and Nathaniel Porter, Social Science Data Consultant and Data Education Coordinator at Virginia Tech, also deserve acknowledgement in providing extensive networking, data analytics, and humanities consulting, courtesy of a National Endowment of the Humanities grant and a collaborative partnership with the National Institutes of Health/National Library of Medicine.

About the Author

Katherine Cottle is the author of *I Remain Yours: Secret Mission Love Letters of My Mormon Great-Grandparents, 1900-1903* (Creative Nonfiction, 2014), *Halfway: A Journal through Pregnancy* (Memoir, 2010), and *My Father's Speech* (Poetry, 2008), all published by Apprentice House/Loyola University Maryland. Cottle received her Ph.D. in English/Professional Writing from Morgan State University in 2015 and currently teaches writing at Goucher College in Towson, Maryland.

Apprentice
House Press
Loyola University Maryland

Apprentice House is the country's only campus-based, student-staffed book publishing company. Directed by professors and industry professionals, it is a nonprofit activity of the Communication Department at Loyola University Maryland.

Using state-of-the-art technology and an experiential learning model of education, Apprentice House publishes books in untraditional ways. This dual responsibility as publishers and educators creates an unprecedented collaborative environment among faculty and students, while teaching tomorrow's editors, designers, and marketers.

Outside of class, progress on book projects is carried forth by the AH Book Publishing Club, a co-curricular campus organization supported by Loyola University Maryland's Office of Student Activities.

Eclectic and provocative, Apprentice House titles intend to entertain as well as spark dialogue on a variety of topics. Financial contributions to sustain our work are welcomed. Contributions are tax deductible to the fullest extent allowed by the IRS.

To learn more about Apprentice House books or to obtain submission guidelines, please visit www.apprenticehouse.com.

Apprentice House
Communication Department
Loyola University Maryland
4501 N. Charles Street
Baltimore, MD 21210
Ph: 410-617-5265 • Fax: 410-617-2198
info@apprenticehouse.com • www.apprenticehouse.com